State and Class

A Study in Capitalist Development

◆

ÇAĞLAR KEYDER

VERSO
London · New York

First published by Verso 1987
© 1987 Çağlar Keyder

Verso
UK: 6 Meard Street, London W1V 3HR
USA: 29 West 35th Street, New York, NY 10001 2291

Verso is the imprint of New Left Books

British Library Cataloguing in Publication Data

Keyder, Çağlar
  State and class in Turkey: a study in
  capitalist development.
  1. Turkey — Economic conditions
  I. Title
  330.9561   HC492

US Library of Congress Cataloging in Publication Data

Keyder, Çağlar.
  State and class in Turkey.
  Includes index
  1. Turkey—Economic conditions. 2. Capitalism—
Turkey—History—19th century. 3.Capitalism—Turkey—
History—20th century. I. Title.
HC492.K497 1987   338.9561   87–14992

ISBN 0–86091–165–9
ISBN 0–86091–877–7 (pbk.)

Typeset by Pentacor Limited, High Wycombe, Bucks.
Printed in Great Britain by Biddles Ltd, Guildford.

Contents

Acknowledgements

This book grew out of a feeling that Turkish studies were excessively insular and that students of social, political and economic change in the Third World could benefit from a knowledge of the Turkish example. Accordingly I have tried to draw the historical picture in broad outline, while concentrating at greater length on the theoretical interpretation that might provide the reader with the necessary port of entry to what I assume is foreign territory.

The manuscript was completed over several years and I have incurred several debts over that period. Immanuel Wallerstein offered me various kinds of support without which I could not have thought of undertaking this project. The Maison des Sciences de l'Homme provided a welcome fellowship during the tenure of which I started writing. Perry Anderson's editorial comments were a pleasure to read and contemplate. Faruk Birtek and Şevket Pamuk were, as usual, generous with their time, ideas and disagreements. Reşat Kasaba, Faruk Tabak, Zafer Toprak, Susan Boyd and Neil Sargent all read and commented on the manuscript. V.M.B-K made it all possible. With this note of thanks goes the usual disclaimer: I am solely responsible for the contents of the book.

Introduction

This is an interpretive history that seeks to illuminate some macro-sociological concerns through the analysis of a particular social formation. The history of Turkey is fertile ground for such an endeavour; as the following outline suggests, it provides substance to many of the theoretical issues in development literature.

The Ottoman Empire was transformed under capitalist incorporation and was dismantled through the success of various nationalist separatisms. At the level of social relations, capitalist incorporation led to the rise of a bourgeois class and its coexistence/conflict with the traditional bureaucracy. It was this bureaucracy which, in the course of the dissolution of the Empire, constructed a new nation-state and attempted to effect its transition to modernity. While the new nation-state remained dominated by the bureaucratic class, a growing bourgeoisie increasingly challenged the authoritarian regime. In terms of economic policy, the bureaucracy was identified with the statism of the inter-war period. The post-war era witnessed both a liberalism under US hegemony, and the coming to power of the bourgeoisie's own party. The import-substituting industrialisation that followed during the 1960s and 1970s led to the gradual ascendance of capitalist relations, to increasing domination by the bourgeoisie and to the emergence of a capitalist state.

This broad outline suggests that most of the theoretical questions relating to peripheral development can be raised fruitfully within the context of Turkish history. I have undertaken this book partly in order to analyse this history within the framework of the literature on peripheral development, and also as an attempt to discuss the theoretical concerns that I mentioned above in the historical context I know best.

Within the general endeavour, I have specified two particular developments in Turkish history which account for an important part of the social origins of Turkish politics. These specificities are the absence of large-scale land ownership in the agrarian structure, and the expulsion of a majority of the Christian bourgeoisie during and after World War I. The nature of the agrarian structure implied that a bureaucracy deriving its power solely from its position in the state structure was unchallenged by a landed class with an autonomous social base. Concomitantly, there was no possibility of oligarchic rule in conjunction with foreign capital. Instead, the bureaucracy reacted against incorporation into the capitalist system, and a class struggle ensued between it and the burgeoning bourgeoisie. When the economic conjuncture promised immediate returns to petty producers in the market, the dispersion of ownership in agriculture prepared the background for a populist reaction against the bureaucracy. The success of the post-1950 accumulation model was due in part to the implications of an agrarian transformation with large numbers of petty producing peasantry.

The second theme, that of an ethnically differentiated bourgeoisie who exit from the stage, provides a key to understanding the nature of the class struggle in the dissolution of the Empire, and an explanation for the particular unfolding of the political transformation during the Republic. Had the Greek and Armenian bourgeoisie pursued their political aims within the Ottoman framework, the Young Turk experiment of 1908–18 might have resulted in the constitution of a capitalist state under bourgeois domination rather than bureaucratic reformism. Ethnic differentiation and imperialist intervention dislocated the social struggle and diverted the momentum of capitalist transformation. The economic, political and ideological gains of the Ottoman bourgeoisie were reversed after the large-scale departure and expulsion of Greeks and Armenians during the 1914–24 period. With a fledgeling Moslem bourgeoisie, the bureaucratic party retained political rule, while at the same time it attempted to control and direct a state-centred socio-economic transformation.

The debate around 'dependency' has fuelled an extensive methodological discussion in development literature. I might as well declare that the point of departure of the account presented in the following chapters is a reconstituted 'world-systems' perspective suggesting that global capitalism provides the context within which class struggle determines local developments. The processes of the capitalist system are such that boom and crisis periods are reproduced in national arenas, although the political and ideological accommodations of these are naturally specific. Turning points of the world economy are crucial, because at such junctures particular local social groups and their political projects gain greater importance and help to determine the subsequent balance of forces. Thus, the great depression of the nineteenth century (1873–1896) ushered in ideological conservatism and the parallel eclipse of the Westernising party in the Empire. The mid-century boom had consolidated the recentralisation of the state under the rule of a modernising bureaucracy. Similarly, during the 1896–1914 period, an activist current gained ascendancy, spurred on by a rapidly developing economy, and attempted to strengthen the state against imperialist dissolution. The correspondences during the Republican period were even more direct: it was due to the 1930s' depression that economic reconstruction and the momentum of the merchant bourgeoisie were arrested, allowing bureaucratic control to achieve centrality. Again, because of the dismantling of the world order in the inter-war period, the bureaucracy could opt for a politically directed national economy, following the experience of Italy and Germany. At the end of World War II, Turkey, along with other countries of the 'free world', was under considerable pressure to adopt parliamentary forms. This conjuncture and the booming world economy permitted the bourgeoisie to constitute its own political rule, and to reconstruct the administrative apparatus of the state accordingly. Development of capitalism gradually made way for an industrialisation strategy similar to the post-1945 experiences of other middle-income peripheral countries under the hegemony of the manufacturing bourgeoisie.

In addition to the long waves of alternate boom and crisis periods in the world economy the pattern described by the successive phases of British hegemony, hegemonic rivalry and the rise of Germany prior to World War I, the breakdown of the international order in the inter-war period and the establishment of US hegemony following World War II provided an important dimension to the global context. The prevailing ideologies associated with these patterns of domination in international politics, such as the drive for the formation of nation-states before and after World War I, the statism of the German model and the preference for formal democracy during the Cold War, were particularly resonant in Turkey. All this should not be taken as professing a preference for dependency and externalism. To reiterate my methodological bias: the world system provides a context and a set of constraints within which class struggle at the national level determines specific outcomes. Radical shifts in the political balance of forces coincide with turning points in the world economic and political order, when a new set of constraints come into play and a local accommodation of these external developments is on the agenda.

The adoption of the historical approach is as much a declaration of faith in favour of a particular causality as it is a result of the belief that the writing of history is itself a political act. The nature of this exercise dictated that only the Ottoman/Turkish trajectory be analysed at any length, and received wisdom was deemed sufficient in reference to the evolution of the world system. I am aware that the impression conveyed by this approach might be one of an artificial isolation and reification of national history. Within the same framework, my approach has been retrospective: no effort is made to deal with the totality of the Ottoman Empire, and only that geographical area which eventually became the Turkish state has been included in the analysis. The rest of the Empire is classified along with 'the world'.

The narrative also focuses on the relations among dominant classes and fractions, and their attempts to attain, maintain, and employ state power. The peasantry and the working class enter the picture only indirectly and in subordinate fashion. This is because neither of the two producing classes was sufficiently strong or organised directly to influence the outcome of the political struggle; it was either the bureaucracy or groups within the bourgeoisie who, through their conflict, defined the parameters of state policies, administrative forms and the political regime. The options available to subordinate classes were more often determined by the outcome of the struggle for supremacy than by their own political activity. This consideration underlies the absence of an account of socialist politics in the following chapters.

A final note: it will be obvious to the reader that I would like to situate this work of synthesis in the growing literature that combines history, political economy and sociology. Within that broad spectrum, studies of incorporation into the world economy, historical dependency and articulation of modes of production (despite the seemingly irreconcilable differences in conceptualisation) have informed the second, third and fourth chapters. The literature on bourgeois revolutions and on the Marxist theory of the state is a constant reference, particularly for the Republican period. The Latin American literature attempting to periodise phases of 'dependent development' and to formulate the relation between the external context and internal social movements (I am thinking primarily of Cardoso's work) was especially important in understanding the post-1950 period in Turkey. Traces of the theoretical framework of the 'regulation' school will be discernible in chapters dealing with the post-1960 industrialisation model. I have liberally borrowed from debates on Latin American populism and on European fascism in the discussion of ideology in the final chapter. Despite this theoretical indebtedness I have chosen not to burden the reader with references at each instance of conceptual allusion and have confined the use of footnotes to important material on Ottoman/Turkish history.

I

Before Capitalist Incorporation

The Ottoman Empire was not feudal: the nature of the state, its role in the determination of the class structure, in social reproduction and in that class structure itself was fundamentally different from the pre-capitalist order we have come to know as European feudalism. Historically, the Ottoman order was constructed upon the Byzantine and the Eastern Roman precedent. In contrast to Western Europe, in the eastern half of the Roman Empire the small peasantry had remained intact and had not been replaced by a rival labour system such as slavery or serfdom. During the medieval period, trade had not been eclipsed to the same degree as in Europe. Besides being on long-distance caravan routes, Anatolia, the core of the Empire, was also the scene of mercantile settlements on the coast, inherited from early antiquity. The emergence of the Byzantine Empire as a viable military presence allowed for a renewed consolidation of those distinctive factors that made up the economic life of Anatolia.

As an imperial presence grafted onto an economic order temporarily disrupted during Hellenistic decline, Byzantine rulers discovered the obvious mode of establishing the palace's dominance over the society. The peasantry, remaining independent, was expected to pay an annual and proportional tax, collected directly by the political authority through its delegated functionaries. Trade, on the other hand, would be under central control, both as a means of efficient taxation and in order to secure the closure of the realm against an overly free commercialism. Insofar as this prescription succeeded in allowing the palace to effectively extract a good portion of the economic surplus, the political authority could continue to exercise its power.[1] Any challenge to the established relationship between the rural producers and the central authority threatened not only the physical reproduction of the peasantry but also the social position of the bureaucracy. For this reason attempts to transform the agrarian economy or the mode of surplus extraction were resisted not only by the peasantry (as in the Western European case) but also by the central bureaucracy, as threats to the reproduction of the exisiting social system.

Local potentates at times constituted a challenge to the central bureaucracy by attaining independent economic power in the sense of being able to circumvent the central bureaucracy, simply by withholding – in personal appropriation – the surplus extracted from the peasantry. In other words, local lords could declare a degree of autonomy which would translate into a challenge to the central authority in that the central authority would no longer be receiving its designated share in the extracted agrarian surplus. Such was the practice of powerful Anatolian dynasties who, during the tenth century, undertook to collect taxes in their own name.[2] This deviation from the norm implied simultaneously the further enrichment of the local potentates, the relative decline of the central bureaucracy, and, possibly, a higher degree of exploitation of the peasantry. Nonetheless, these shifts did not constitute a transformation of the agrarian structure and its implied class structure, because conditions under which local powers could establish themselves as progenitors of a rival social system were absent. Consequently, local lords did not come to regard the peasantry as serfs whose independent status could be reduced. The peasantry carried out production with essentially the same organisation of labour, scale, and distribution of land. The tax (or rent) was collected in the same manner and by the same functionaries who formerly served the central authority. The only change – that of the destination of the tax – could not be immediately grasped by the producer as constituting a fundamental transformation. The lack of an alternative social design implied by greater local autonomy meant that, rather than social change, centralisation and decentralisation would merely alternate as forms of organisation for utilising the surplus. When the centre was strong the surplus was funnelled efficiently to the imperial bureaucracy; when the centre was weak, local

potentates retained most of it. Only the imposition on this
dialectic of an external incentive might have provoked the
instigation of radically different relations between the producers and the collectors of surplus. Local lords might then
have attempted to organise production under a labour system
more appropriate to the extraction of greater surplus of a
commercial kind. During the period of dissolution of the
Byzantine Empire, such external incentives were not paramount. The weakening of the central bureaucracy had been
initiated principally through military reversals, and continued
with the strengthening of provincial potentates. Provincial
families became stronger and acceded to the imperial seat as
new dynasties. They made attempts to fortify the centre, but
could not reverse the decline to imitate the cyclical pattern of
the Chinese. Eventually the Empire lost the critical size it
required in order to preserve a sufficient tax base. Latins from
the west and Turks from the east battered the gates until
Byzantium was reduced to a small principality during the
fourteenth century and finally conquered by the Ottomans in
the fifteenth.

There has been much ideological debate concerning the
continuity between Byzantine and Ottoman Empires.[3] At one
extreme there are proponents of an interpretation which posits
a complete historical break. Nationalist versions of Turkish
history would like to trace the basic organisational tenets and
the institutional structure of the Ottoman Empire to distant
Turkic (or Islamic, depending on the version) forms, positing
successive incarnations of a fundamental essence in the format
of various Turkish/Islamic states. In this view, there is no room
for a Byzantine heritage; the Ottoman Empire simply happens
to occupy a geographical territory similar to the Eastern Roman
Empire without, however, taking over any of the pre-existing
structures. A similar view is advanced by certain Western
historians who refuse to identify a difference between medieval
Europe and the Byzantine Empire. To put it crudely, they see
the East as having an equally feudal social formation which was
ready to evolve into the modern age on the eve of its
dismantling. In this view, Turkish invasions of Anatolia and the
Balkans emerge as the historical factor that prevented the
autonomous evolution which would have catapulted the Byzantine Empire into the cultural and economic revival of the
fifteenth and sixteenth centuries. The Ottomans, who were the

carriers of Islamic ideals and forms of organisation, are said to
have established an order fundamentally different from the
Christian one, which is supposed to explain the historical
divergence of European and Oriental trajectories.[4]

In certain fields of analysis, especially at the level of culture
and everyday life, a view emphasising the synthesis and
articulation of elements indigenous to the two traditions is
prevalent.[5] This approach would see the manifestation of a
post-Byzantine Helleno-Turkic entity in Ottoman Anatolia
embracing a Near Eastern civilisation. Thus various similarities
which can be discovered in cultural elements such as music,
festivities, daily life, and even folk religion, would prove that at
least until the nineteenth century, the Ottoman Empire
provided an adequate shell for the reproduction of a unitary
Anatolian culture. It was more surprising that at the more basic
level of the agrarian structure and class formation implied by
this structure, all the essential elements were also reproduced.
Like the Byzantine central authority, the Ottoman palace was
instituted on the basis of its privileged relation with an
independent peasantry. A strongly centralised bureaucratic
structure was supposed to establish and secure the conditions
for the healthy reproduction of a peasant society, whose
surpluses would be extracted in the form of taxes. Once again
the main threat originated in the local potentates who could
interfere in this happy equation to deprive the centre of its
revenue sources, while at the same time reducing the independence of the peasantry.

During the Ottoman conquest of Anatolia, the social
structure of the invaders inclined toward the formation of
decentralised vassal principalities under the domination of
powerful military families. In fact, these families demonstrated
concretely the dimensions of a synthesis with the sedentary
population, through intermarrying with their counterparts in
Byzantine provinces. By the middle of the fifteenth century, the
Islamisation of Anatolia seemed to proceed more along the
lines of 'mergers' at each social stratum than through military
conquest. It was not until the capture of the seat of power itself
that the ruling Ottoman dynasty became powerful enough to
confront the new Byzantine-Turkic magnates. During the last
two centuries of its formal existence, the Byzantine palace had
helplessly witnessed a growing fragmentation of power in the
countryside. Rich magnates, small landlords, monasteries and
towns had increasingly escaped the control and legislation of

the centre, while the peasantry gradually became more dependent on local overlords. The peasantry's degree of independence was still substantially greater than in the case of a feudal serf, but the trend was toward feudalisation. It was the centralisation of power by the Ottoman dynasty which brought this development to an end, and concomitantly 'arrested' the evolution of an aristocracy in the Western sense.

In order to find the model for Ottoman land legislation, it is necessary to go further back in Byzantine history to the celebrated Land Code, which probably dates from the post-Heraclian era. Following upon the increase in the numbers of independent cultivators under Heraclius, the Land Code had been legislated in recognition that this stratum constituted the foundation of the social structure.[6] It sought to protect the peasants' landed and other property and also established the village as a communal unit with fiscal responsibility, thus underlining the relationship between payment of taxes and possession of land. In later periods of Byzantine history, the Land Code remained an ideal model, with the actual agrarian structure increasingly diverging from it. During the tenth century, attempts were made – without success – to reverse the decline of the independent peasantry by strengthening the sanctions relating to the Land Code. After the eleventh century the fragmentation of authority and the subjugation of the peasantry to dependent status advanced conjointly to destroy the social basis of the Empire. It was Ottoman centralisation some three centuries later which succeeded in restoring the basic contours of the classical Byzantine agrarian structure, thus bringing it closer to the ideal picture of the Land Code.

Ottoman legislation concerning the agrarian structure clearly demonstrated that the new dynasty's immediate concern was the restoration of the economic base of an independent peasantry. All land was reconverted into state property, which did not cause any juridical problems, since land in the Byzantine Empire had also been formally in the ownership of the state. All labour services were abolished, and a single tax replaced previous dues and obligations. At the same time a unit of land based on the ploughing capacity of a pair of oxen was established, which would be in the inalienable possession of a peasant family.[7] Since all land was juridically under state proprietorship, the central authority could, in principle, ensure the perpetuation of a land regime based precisely on such holdings possessed by independent peasant families.

The classical institutional structure of the Ottoman Empire stipulated a large number of independent peasants, each in possession of more or less similar amounts of land, who paid a proportional tax to centre-appointed functionaries. These functionaries, in turn, either transferred the tax or delivered a service – usually of a military but sometimes of a civic nature – to the centre. Their crucial characteristic was that they derived their status not from inheritance or local influence but from having been appointed by the central authority. Similarly, their privilege could easily be revoked, reducing them to subject status. In theory, after the fifteenth century, only the dynastic family enjoyed the distinctive position of a self-evident status which allowed the Sultan to create or to destroy the fortunes of powerful servants. The exercise of such absolute power evidently required an effective mechanism to stifle the germination of peripheral nodes of strength. The perpetuation of the classical model could not be ensured without the elimination of would-be magnates; from the point of view of the palace, subjects had to be reduced to controllable status unless they were elevated by decree.

This mechanism of control, which found its most telling expression in the legislation concerning the agrarian structure, also extended to the urban economy, in the form of strict institutionalisation of manufactures and trade. It can be argued that the controls on trade and manufacturing, together with the stipulations aimed at linking the urban and the rural economic networks (stipulations on provisioning of cities and on the location of rural manufacturers, for example), amounted to a rudimentary effort to create a centrally designated division of labour.[8] Since external economic ties were supposed to be even more severely restricted and subject to permission, the internal division of labour could be more effectively regulated and perpetuated. In fact, control over external trade was necessary in order to ensure the stability of the structure within which political control over the economy could be exercised.

As long as a division of labour was maintained and the economic actors performed the tasks expected of them, the political ideal of reproducing the social hierarchy without challenge from the ranks could be entertained. It could be expected, however, that the exercise of authority by the centre required not only the propagation of an ideology to legitimate the desired order, but also the coercive apparatus able to deliver the required sanctions. It was in the latter sphere that Ottoman system integration was eventually threatened. As before in the case of the Byzantine Empire, ideological challenges to Ottoman rule did not derive from the alternative hegemonic project of a contesting group from within the social system. They arose in tandem with the capitalist integration of the Empire, and in response to the mediated needs of a new economic order. Long before such needs arose, however, the coercive monopoly of the central authority had been challenged, and nodes of peripheral power rivalling the central authority came into existence. Once again, the key to understanding the challenge to the paramount status of the central authority lies in the transformation threatening the agrarian structure.

As mentioned above, the Ottoman centralisation efforts succeeded, after the conquest of Istanbul, in eliminating the vestiges of traditional power retained by families which had participated in the invasion of Anatolia. The social order dependent upon a strong central authority was disturbed, however, before a century had elapsed. The establishment of political order, and the economic stability implied therein, had contributed to a rapid population increase in the sixteenth century. After the 1550s grain prices began to increase in response to Malthusian pressure, which reduced the fixed-money taxes levied by state functionaries. These functionaries, who were obliged to deliver military service in exchange for the taxes they collected, could not operate under growing fiscal pressure. As they abandoned their patrimonies, land was seized by local military functionaries and influential individuals in provincial administration. The peasantry was thus pressured from both sides: from former functionaries who now put their military experience to private use in brigandage, and the newly powerful landlords whose demands far exceeded the single tax instituted by the strong centre. When the European price revolution hit the Ottoman Empire with a consequent foreign demand for grain and sheep, the newcomers in agriculture attempted even more forcefully to benefit from trading opportunities by increasing their share out of agricultural production. Only in a minority of cases, however, could landlords force the peasantry to remain in their original homesteads and work for them through some form of tenancy arrangement. For the most part, peasants migrated to settle in new villages where they opened up land to which they could acquire possessionary rights through payment of taxes.[9]

The emergence of a stratum of influential landlords could only be tolerated by a weakened central authority. In fact developments during the same period contributed to a growing fiscal crisis within the Ottoman state, which rendered the central authority more impotent when confronted with challenges from the provinces. Although tax or surplus extracted from the peasantry was the primary revenue of the state, especially during the sixteenth century, other sources of revenue also became (quantitatively) significant. These derived from the geographical location (overland trade routes) and the military prowess (continuous territorial expansion) of the Empire. As trade routes began to shift, however, and territorial expansion came to a halt, so did the contributions of these two factors to the fisc. In addition, the fiscal structure based in part on the delivery of military service by the smallest tax collectors, had outlived its purpose together with the decline in the importance of the cavalry. The palace thus found itself witnessing an erosion of the non-agrarian revenue base, while the revenue it could collect was in an increasingly non-functional form, and while its expenditures in money terms were increasing (partly due to inflation). The growing fiscal crisis ensured that the centre could not mobilise the coercive apparatus required for reversing the emerging trend in the countryside. Attempts at raising state revenues exacerbated the situation by introducing yet more disruptive elements into the agrarian structure.[10]

Without strong control from the centre, local functionaries increased their economic and political stature in direct ratio to the proportion of the revenue they retained as their own. During the seventeenth century, the Ottoman centre attempted to reassert its supremacy by preventing such an increase in the power of the local functionaries, especially that of the provincial governors. However, the new tax collection scheme, designed to increase revenue, militated against this attempt: after the demise of the classical system of military service in lieu of taxes, revenue was increasingly collected through tax-farming. Tax-farmers functioned in the same manner as their French counterparts: the right to collect taxes would go to the highest bidder, who would pay the sum to the state in advance. Tax-farmers, through their right to collect taxes, established semi-official standing, the exercise of which was itself a source of increased status. In being forced to rely increasingly on tax-farmers, the palace created the conditions for an explosive marriage of political power and legitimate position through which agricultural surplus could be extracted. In the eighteenth century, in fact, Ottoman lands did come under the increasing domination of local notables who controlled the tax-farming hierarchy. These local notables lived in the provincial centres, content to extract the agricultural surplus from the independent peasantry. Under the collective name of *ayans* they extended their influence beyond the countryside as they attempted to regulate the urban economy as well. During the latter half of the eighteenth century *ayan* councils in provincial capitals began to function as urban patriciates, deciding not only on internal trade and guild permits regulating the economy, but also on urban revenues and expenditures.[11] The central government, which had also increasingly submitted to the influence of the *ayan*, was forced to recognise their ascendancy and to ratify the existing organisation of provincial urban centres. During the eighteenth century *ayans* could even secure the appointment of their own servants to the higher posts of the central administration.

The beginning of the end of the *ayans* arrived in the form of a document in which the Sultan formally recognised that he was sharing his no-longer-absolute power with potentates whose power derived from local sources. Within four decades of the signing of this Bill of Union (1807), however, the central authority secured the defeat at the political and, to a great extent, at the economic level of the local magnates. It may be argued that the crucial factor in this reversal was the Mohammad Ali incident, which crystallised the attitude of the Great Powers toward the internal evolution of the Ottoman Empire. When Mohammad Ali, a former *ayan* of Rumelia, became the governor of Egypt and started to administer the province through old Ottoman codes now directed to mercantilist ends, he provided to the Great Powers a concrete illustration of the dangers of local autonomy. In the conflict between the Sultan and his governor, Britain took the side of the centre. In exchange for concessions from the Porte, Britain supported the Sultan in the military conflict with Mohammad Ali, and ensured his defeat, together with his precocious experiment in national development.[12]

After the defeat of the Egyptian *ayan*, the Sultan mobilised his new model army against other *ayans* in the realm. During the 1840s they were also disciplined, settled outside the areas they dominated, or brought to Istanbul in servile bureaucratic capacity; and in most cases suffered a disbanding of their retinues.[13] The Porte had succeeded in centralising the fiscal function by eliminating the local intermediaries. Once again tax-farming reverted to the centre's control to be allocated on pecuniary guidelines instead of being considered as the hereditary right of *ayans*. *Ayans* who remained strong in their realms, despite the campaign to expropriate their holdings, continued to exploit their domain farms, but were no longer rulers in the image of the Sultan.

At the height of their power the *ayans* remained local replicas of the central authority. Their principal revenue derived from assuming the tasks of the state in collecting various dues and taxes. They often controlled a domain farm which was cultivated through a sharecropping arrangement, while the large majority of the peasantry continued as independent producers whose only obligations were the annual tithe. The exaction of labour services, even on the domain farm, was infrequent. Thus it was not from the control of the land or, more directly, of the peasantry, that the *ayans* derived their power: it was a dependent power, based on the parameters and the assumptions of the social system whose dissolution had occasioned their emergence. As they were unable to fashion an alternative system of labour use during the short period of their ascendancy, they could change the agrarian structure only temporarily, and then not in essence. The summary reversal of the evolution ushered in by the *ayans* underlines the temporary nature of this change: when the dust settled the peasantry emerged again as independent family farmers, and there were no landless peons. This was partly due to the Porte's effort to dismantle *ayans'* holdings, but also to the fact that no legal and political institutions existed through which the permanent bondage of the peasantry could result. In fact one important *ayan* in the beginning of the nineteenth century had been forced to import sharecroppers from Morea to work on his lands in Western Anatolia. We may say that *ayans* had been successful in replacing the authority of the centre, but they remained unable to alter the basic assumptions of that rule.[14]

It is also possible to see the *ayans* as representing a failed attempt towards the formation of a feudal-aristocratic class. Not only did they fulfil the material requirements to emerge as a class, but they also seemed to have had the subjective intention of sharing in political power. Like the Byzantine aristocracy some centuries earlier, they were the product of centrifugal developments in a patrimonial empire and, like them, their power was based on devolution of authority. Nor were they willing to bargain solely for a share in the surplus: they represented a local challenge to the ubiquitous command structure of the centre. In putting themselves forward as a *de facto* urban government, and in their attempt at a 'magna carta' with the Sultan, they championed a political project as well. From this point of view it may be more fair to ascribe their inability to substantially alter the agrarian structure to the resistance of the centre. Had they had the time to carry out the logical extension of their political project, we might have witnessed the transformation of tax collecting rights into something akin to feudal property rights, with the historically given independence of the peasantry also threatened. It seems, however, that the entrenched traditions of material existence and political rule successfully resisted this threat. When the centre regained the ability to exercise its rule, its principal concern was precisely to establish the conditions for the independence of the peasantry. The latter half of the nineteenth century was a period of restoration of the agrarian structure.[15]

While such a restitution was especially relevant in the case of Anatolia, in the outlying regions of the Empire the political impact of the *ayans* served to accelerate nationalist and secessionist movements. As in the case of Mohammad Ali, *ayans* mobilised local interests against the centre, and provided expression to the demands of newly emerging urban classes. Within the multi-ethnic imperial dynamic, the periphery experienced *ayan* influence in the form of an impetus to state-forming and nationalist tendencies, while for the core areas, where the 'political' impact was not articulated into separatism, the *ayan* period assumed importance because of the evolution of the relationship between the peasants and the central authority. In this perspective the eighteenth century emerges as one of failed feudalisation, and the *ayan* incident as one of arrested development of an aristocracy.

We will have occasion in a later chapter to discuss the material conditions that allowed the peasantry to maintain its independent status despite a cyclical evolution in the strength of the centre. Here we shall discuss the implications of an agrarian structure dominantly characterised by small ownership for the transformation of the class structure following the Empire's incorporation into world markets. The failure of the *ayan* momentum meant that as contact with external markets increased rapidly during the nineteenth century, the transformation instigated through trade would act upon a society which, in its basic structure, was closer to its classical period than to the previous century. There were most probably a greater number of large farms than in the sixteenth century, but they were dwarfed by the literally millions of small holdings. More importantly, the failure to enclose and monopolise land implied that dispossessed peasantry, who would accept wage employment or subsistence level remuneration in a different labour-use arrangement, did not exist. Consequently, capitalist or plantation farming could not be readily engaged in. Sharecropping on larger farms also depended on the difficulty of reproducing the conditions of independent production, not because of an inability to gain access to land, but because of the peasants' losing the title to draught animals or tools. As long as the peasantry was not dispossessed of its land, there would be a shortage of both wage workers and sharecroppers; and large-scale production in agriculture would be undermined.[17] At various times during the nineteenth century in fact, starting with the importation of Morean peasants for sharecropping, the material conditions demonstrated the difficulty of carrying out large-scale production. An attempt by would-be colonialists to establish export-oriented capitalist farms in Western Anatolia demonstrates this point. They had no difficulty in securing land; the labourers they could find, however, demanded high wages, did not commit themselves on a long-term basis, and were generally undependable.[18] For most of the nineteenth century and until World War I, available data suggest that rural and urban wage rates in Anatolia were about half or a little less than half of British levels, despite a much greater discrepancy in per capita incomes.[19]

The difficulty in establishing large-scale commercial agriculture implied the non-development of landed oligarchy in the Latin American mode. From the point of view of actual developments, there was an even more important implication of the absence of a well-defined commercial landlord class. This consequence gained so much importance within the world ideological atmosphere of the nineteenth century that it can be argued to have been the proximate cause of Turkish national movements in the particular form they took. In contrast to the case of a small number of large and commercialised landlords who might concentrate the surplus and its means of exchange in their own hands, the dispersion of the marketed surplus in the hands of small producers required a parallel dispersion of mercantile activity in the Empire. Thus a numerically large class of intermediaries, dealing with the circulation of world-market oriented commodities, was implied by the existing structure. Merchants of varying sizes proliferated, ranging from village level to the great ports of trade and engaged in buying and selling the peasant surplus. The fact that there were no large landlords with sufficient surplus to control the market attached a qualitative importance to merchant capital as well. In its extent and through the fact that it was articulated into peasant production rather than large holdings, merchant capital quickly became dominant in those areas where agriculture was integrated into world markets.

It must be mentioned that merchants' activity did not consist entirely of buying and selling existing surpluses. Peasant producers had to be attracted, cajoled, or forced to produce the desired goods. In colonies where merchants acted in the name of political authority, such a result could be achieved through various impositions in the form of labour conscription or a new tax. In the Ottoman Empire, as we shall presently discuss, the state class found itself in conflict with the merchants, and were loath to see the peasantry slipping into the realm of the market. The actual degree of commercialisation of the producers was attained in spite of the political authority rather than because of it. Merchant capital was strongly allied with interest-bearing capital in this quest. Often large traders advanced money loans to smaller merchants who in turn contracted peasant producers to deliver a certain output when the harvest was in or when production was completed. In such cases merchants doubled as moneylenders, with all the well-known implications of such activity in peasant societies. Indebtedness led to high interest rates and dependence and further need for the intervention of the moneylender.

It was not always the case that merchant capital and interest-bearing capital, trade and moneylending, were embodied in the same person. Especially since the *ayan* domination of tax collection was reversed, tax-farming had become a widespread mode of earning interest on money advanced to the authorities. Tax-farming usually functioned through a succession of moneylenders, with a large banker in Istanbul obtaining the right to collect a particular tax in a particular area which he would subsequently sub-contract.[20] Sub-contracting might eventually involve a small town moneylender who would actually collect the designated taxes. It is easy to see that this particular series of exchanges also involved a large number of persons who might or might not be simultaneously integrated into the circuits of trade. Once again it was the maintenance of the small peasant structure against the attempted domination of a landlord class, together with the right of the central authority to collect taxes, which allowed for the existence of a large number of money capitalists located in the tax-farming structure.

Popular wisdom in the nineteenth century identified petty traders and moneylenders with the non-Moslem subjects of the Empire. In fact there was supposed to be a division of labour whereby Greeks were involved in commerce, and Armenians in moneylending.[21] While no fine statistical analysis is available to support this belief we may think of historical reasons to argue its overall validity. During the eighteenth century some fundamental institutional innovations had structured the unequal relation between the Empire and European powers. The long-standing capitulatory regime, which had initially served the purposes of the Ottoman centre in enabling the Palace to exercise strict control over external economic relations, had remained, until the eighteenth century, an instrument of absolute power; through it Sultans could unilaterally distribute privilege to foreign states, but this generosity was repealable and needed to be renegotiated upon the ruler's death. With the gradual insertion of the Empire into the European inter-state system, the Ottoman Sultans had been led to accept bilateral agreements which did not require renegotiation at the death of the signatory ruler. Bilateral agreements also implied reciprocity, stipulating that Ottoman subjects could engage in business in Europe in exchange for the same right granted to Westerners in the Empire.[22] With the same set of agreements the right of foreign ambassadors to administer commercial affairs and adjudicate legal problems within their subject communities was extended to extraterritoriality. In effect, a system was created through which envoys of European states enjoyed sovereign rights and could grant protection to their passport holders. This was a potentially explosive situation, destroying the legitimacy of the local state and creating groups of true or assumed national identity, outside the reach of the political authority.

Inasmuch as these groups enjoyed privileges and immunities that the local population could not aspire to attain, extraterritoriality created a social chasm of unbridgeable dimension.[23]

With the gradual weakening of the Ottoman state, and especially since European public opinion began to see the Sultan and his law as the embodiment of absolutist evil, ambassadors became less scrupulous in their granting of protected status to Christian subjects of the Empire. As early as the eighteenth century the Austrians were supposed to have distributed a quarter of a million of such privileging documents in territories later lost to the Empire. In the core areas as well, ambassadors were willing to distribute or sell 'hundreds of thousands of passports' to Greeks and Armenians, who were thus liberated from Ottoman citizenship.[24] During the nineteenth century the numbers of passport holders who had originally been Ottoman subjects increased, at the same time as immigrants from all over the Mediterranean began to arrive in commercially prominent port cities, attracted to the atmosphere of unbridled profit-seeking and lawless capitalism. Especially after the Crimean War in mid-century, the immigrant lumpen population of such cities grew, the protection and immunity to which they were subject rendering ineffective all attempts at urban reform and control of corruption.[25]

What is popularly known as the Levantine population were that part of the privileged passport holders who came to be involved in European business dealings in the Ottoman Empire. When the level of trade with the West began to increase, Europeans attempted to secure the institutional conditions for orderly conduct in business matters. A fundamental requirement in their eyes was the establishment of the primacy of a legal structure within which contracts could be enforced. This required either that the society be governed in two separate realms, with one immune from Ottoman intervention – this was the reasoning behind the extraterritorial system of granting privileges – or that reforms be carried out to change the overall legal-institutional structure. The latter proposition was also actively pursued and culminated in the reform movement around the middle of the century: in 1839, 1856 and 1867 the Palace was pressured to declare its willingness to recognise certain rights of citizenship, freedom of religious practice, a degree of sanctity of private property, and the right of foreign nationals to own property.[26] Nevertheless, with the expansion of trade, it was the Levantine population which formed the principal link between European markets and local producers. Representative agencies of merchant houses were established in port cities which in turn engaged non-Moslem Ottomans (some of whom obtained foreign passports in this way) to serve as intermediaries. This pattern quickly drove Moslem merchants out of the field. Not only did European traders prefer to work with Christians, but institutionally as well, they felt that Christians with foreign passports could be brought to court under the consular legal system. A similar selection process was at work in moneylending. In the circuit of tax-farming, large loans usually originated directly in foreign-controlled banks or via rich moneychangers of Istanbul, collectively known as Galata bankers. Once again, both subjective feelings and objective conditions pushed for the employment of non-Moslems to constitute the links between the source of capital and the actual producers whose surpluses were converted into interest payments.

It is no wonder that nineteenth century travellers to the Ottoman Empire expressed their impression that Moslems had no business sense and were fit only to till the soil, while Greeks and Armenians were industrious and forward-looking. By the mid-nineteenth century a good proportion of the non-Moslem population of the Empire had developed as a class of compradors, mediating between peasant producers and foreign capital. What might have evolved into a landholding oligarchy had been largely eliminated; the palace bureaucracy, however, was present, transformed but more effective compared to the period prior to the restoration of central authority. In a sense, then, the nineteenth century class structure could be considered to have resulted from the integration into the world economy of a classical agrarian Empire, consisting of independent peasant producers and a bureaucratic class. The mechanisms through which economic integration proceeded were carried mostly by the non-Moslem population of the Empire, thereby introducing an ethnic and religious element to overlay the emerging class differentiation. The process of class formation was thus a complex affair with political and ideological determinations cutting through the economic ground. Within this process, the class map of the final years of the Empire was drawn through the interplay of peasants, bureaucrats and compradors – and especially the latter two, since peasants were generally quiet. In order to investigate this interplay in its historical development, we must first identify the mechanisms integrating the Ottoman Empire into the world system. Following that account we will return to the formation of classes through the unfolding of their struggle.

II

The Process of Peripheralisation

The centralisation of the Empire during the nineteenth century reasserted the absolute rule of the Sultan and his servants against authority deriving from local power. The new model was based on the ideal version of the classical pattern which envisaged a large number of small producers, none of whom had the ability to accumulate wealth in order to change their status, and a class of functionaries totally and hierarchically subordinate to the Palace. The absolute ruler had the ability to advance or to revoke privileges at will; therefore status associated with being in the functionary class derived entirely from bureaucratic position held, rather than from wealth or family heritage. In this system the basic relation of surplus extraction was that which obtained between the peasant producers and the bureaucratic class. The peasants' surplus was extracted in the form of taxes, and redistributed within the bureaucracy. Certainly, a small part of the surplus thus extracted was spent on establishing the conditions for economic reproduction: maintenance of a road network, hydraulic projects, and the like. The larger part of the surplus, however, went towards the state functionaries' consumption and luxury expenditure. Their ranks provided personnel for the administrative, military, judiciary and religious institutions which served the political and ideological reproduction of the social system.[1] What constituted the common characteristic of the lowest tax-collecting functionary and the vizier on one hand, and the kadi and the janissary on the other hand, was the fact that they were found on the same side of the surplus extracting

25

relationship, differing only as to their location in the hierarchy and their varying functions. It is true that there were frequent conflicts among these fractional positions and, as discussed above, among levels of tax-collecting functionaries. These conflicts should be interpreted as intra-class problems either relating to the distribution of the surplus or deriving from competing projects concerning system regulation – akin, in fact, to conflicts among bourgeois fractions in capitalism. We would argue then, that functionaries constitute a state-class due to their structural location within a mode of production based on the extraction of surplus (in the form of taxes) from an independent peasantry. Furthermore, they share a common ideological perspective and a political attitude, especially when their relationship with the actual producers is considered.

Although such a system provides for potentially less antagonistic social relations than, say, feudalism, the ideology propogated by the state-class still plays a major role. Of the institutions that serve to legitimate the state-class, the judiciary and the clerical are of paramount importance. Their doctrine emphasises the symbiotic relationship between the peasantry and the rulers, and the beneficent nature of this rule. The famous 'circle of justice' that epitomises the presumed relationship suggests that economic reproduction, i.e. the production of surplus, depends on ideological reproduction, i.e. the judicious dispensation of justice and political order by the authorities.[2] The very nature of this legitimation, where the ruler is cast as the omniscient power who secures the global conditions in the realm for smooth functioning of the system, gives to the state-class a self-conception of paternalist wisdom. This is why diagnoses of system-disintegration by political homoeopaths conclude that the cure should be found in wiser rulers. It is also the reason why the perspective of reform is limited to musings over the bureaucracy's role in the social system. All proposals to reform the social structure, from whichever fraction of the bureaucracy they derive, envisage a perhaps modified, but similarly paramount, function for the state-class, in which it will continue to control the extraction and use of the surplus.

In such a situation, any transformation of the economic or the ideological system will naturally be opposed by the representatives of state authority. In particular, if an alternative mode of organisation of the economy is proposed which implies the appropriation of surplus by non-bureaucrats, the state-class will be threatened both as a group which risks losing part of its revenue, and because the system which supports its existence as an administrative class will be threatened. Inasmuch as the state-class can act as a class for itself, it would be expected that it will attempt to protect both its revenue base and the system which legitimated it as serving an important function. The historical proliferation of market relations, and the growth of a merchant class beginning to receive a share of the agricultural surplus, occasioned precisely such a response. Not only did merchants emerge as a social class with a rival claim on the surplus, but the proliferation of market relations also threatened the very foundation of the social system. From this point of view the bureaucracy – akin to any ruling class – possesses a double nature. It is, on the one hand, made up of state functionaries whose task is to perpetuate the conditions for system reproduction; hence it must protect and maintain its own legitimacy which in itself requires that the internal articulation of the system is reproduced without major disruption. On the other hand, it constitutes a class within the system it helps reproduce, with its own structural claim on the surplus. Ordinarily, when the reproduction of the system is not threatened, the two natures and their respective requirements need not come into conflict. When it is no longer possible to fulfil the prescriptions of the 'circle of justice', however, the bureaucracy's concern for its own share of the revenue may override its fervour in defending various components or even the total functioning of the traditional order. I propose to analyse the Ottoman bureaucracy's insertion and behaviour in the world capitalist system, and the relative importance, success or failure of various mechanisms of capitalist economic penetration within this perspective.

The integral insertion of the Ottoman state into the European political system did not occur until the eighteenth century. Until then Turkey had inspired fear and curiosity, but was essentially an alien force to be contended with only when hostilities could not be avoided. This attitude was reflected in the world view of the Ottoman Palace, which, not unlike Chinese emperors, treated European envoys with disdain and condescension. The unilateral and revocable granting of capitulatory concessions during the sixteenth and seventeenth centuries was an instance of such disdain disguised as magnanimity. After a succession of military defeats at the end of the seventeenth and beginning of the eighteenth centuries, however, Ottoman attitudes began to change; treaties were imposed on the Palace and bureaucrats began to get involved in the intricate system of alliances and balances which characterised European diplomacy. It was during the eighteenth century that the civil bureaucracy, especially as a group dealing with the external relations of the Empire, came to be differentiated from religious officials.[3] The new civil servants who were not *medrese*-trained upheld a relatively more secular conception of state power, and tended to struggle against the military and religious conceptions of authority which had provided justification for the earlier relationship with European states. They were thus pragmatic in their approach to the inter-state system, in the sense of accepting the parameters within which bargains were to be struck. Through this acceptance, however, they also unwittingly limited the potential success of their own internal efforts at reform: future reformers in the Empire would derive from the ranks of this secular wing of the bureaucracy, whose conceptions of the possible were circumscribed by the narrow limits of European power diplomacy. This early, gradual and orderly insertion into the European state system, through which a new 'modern' faction within the bureaucracy defined and legitimated itself against a previously dominant one, might provide a clue to explaining the generally more accommodating behaviour of Ottoman civil servants when compared with, for example, Chinese antagonism, or Japanese revanchism towards Western penetration. In the Ottoman Empire the secular bureaucracy accepted and justified their adhesion to European models and principles in the name of progressive reformism. They welcomed the institutionalisation of economic integration into Western capitalism as a victory over the retrograde tenets of old Ottoman statecraft. Even when reformism acquired a somewhat more radical tint, it was closer to the Italian and Russian models than to the Chinese or Japanese; and it proclaimed its heritage within the European paradigm of social progress. In other words, the bureaucracy accepted a version of reformism which accommodated its class nature by allowing it to be the principal intermediary of incorporation, while they sacrificed, rather too readily, various social groups privileged in the traditional order and the overall integrity of this order. This is not to say that a Chinese-style xenophobic and conservative option was available, given the geographical position of the Empire, the importance of the Eastern Mediterranean for European capitalism, and imperialist designs on the Levant.

Within the narrow space left to the bureaucracy, its manoeuvres tended to favour a model of capitalist integration promising to uphold the claims of state functionaries as a surplus-receiving class. Alternatives to restoration of the traditional order were overridden by the attraction of the European paradigm of statecraft. In effect, growing integration of the Empire, both into the European inter-state system and the capitalist economy, made attempts at self-extrication from that paradigm increasingly difficult. By the end of the nineteenth century any freedom of action that the bureaucracy enjoyed was due to conflicts within world capitalism and rivalries internal to the inter-state system.

The first important step in institutionalising the Empire's integration into the political-economic logic of European capitalism was the trade convention of 1838 with England. No overt aggression had preceded this treaty, as, for example in the Nanking treaty of 1842. The Ottoman administration, however, had found itself having to curry favour on account of recent conflict with Mohammad Ali, the governor of Egypt. Mohammad Ali had approached perilously close to Istanbul with his army, and only British support had enabled the Ottoman bureaucracy to escape unscathed. The 1838 treaty was partly the *quid pro quo* of this intervention, and its provision that all monopolies granted by the state would be prohibited struck at one tenet of the traditional order which had allowed Egypt's governor to carry out his statist reforms. In addition, British merchants were allowed to purchase and export goods without the payment of any taxes except the single *ad valorem* duty of 12 per cent. Similarly a duty of 5 per cent was to be levied on all imports.[4] Within a few years other European states had signed treaties with similar provision: the Ottoman Empire had become an area of free trade. The joint effects of increasing industrial production in the West, cheaper transportation, aggressive commercial policy, especially of the French and British states, and institutional lubrication through treaties, were to substantially increase the volume of trade. Aided by the world upswing the volume of trade grew by 3.5 per cent per annum from the 1830s until the onset of the world depression in 1873. Growth was especially rapid during the 1840s and 1850s.[5]

Throughout the eighteenth and early nineteenth centuries Europe's trade with the Middle East had been characterised by a consistent difficulty, giving rise to frequent complaints by French and British merchants: the Ottoman Empire lacked a sufficient volume of exportable output.[6] In fact, the Empire's undeclared policy had always been that of its consuming bureaucracy: imports of luxury items and raw materials had been encouraged, while exports were discouraged with the fear that the provisioning of the realm – and especially the large cities – would suffer. The policy of granting trade monopolies to palace-appointed merchants had been used most apparently towards this end. It is also possible, however, to detect a more substantive aim of controlling production and division of labour under these apparent concerns. Exports, especially of raw materials, threatened to disrupt the entire productive structure and sever the links between various stages of production. The cumulative effect of such a disruption would be unemployment and a break in the reproductive system of the society with its dreaded social consequences. Imports, on the other hand, were consumables. Since they were mostly destined for the consumption of the state class, they could be encouraged without threat to the reproduction of productive balances. The 1838 agreement, by abrogating trade monopolies, and favouring foreign merchants in their competition with Ottoman merchants, created the conditions for such social disruption and unemployment. From the point of view of British capitalism, the abolition of monopolies served a simpler logic: the emphasis on prohibiting exports had contributed to the difficulty experienced by European merchants in finding goods to exchange for manufactured imports. Thus the lifting of all trade monopolies would allow the expansion of trade until it reached its more 'natural' limits, which, given the agrarian structure, were not very extensive either.

The dominance of small peasant property limited both the volume of the marketable surplus, and the pace at which production could shift from subsistence to export crops. The difficulty in establishing large-scale commercial farming implied that trade volume would mostly expand through the marketisation of the independent peasantry, which in turn had various implications. First, it would be difficult to induce a traditionally subsistence-oriented peasantry to switch to commercial production even if relative prices favoured export crops. The natural reaction of the peasantry would be risk aversion, especially since so many lived precariously, their subsistence subject to annual changes in weather conditions. At best, therefore, it would be a slow process to increase the volume of exportable commodities deriving from the peasant sector.[7] Secondly, the tendency with the start of trade would be to mobilise existing crop surpluses, instead of attempting to establish one dominant crop as the principal export commodity. When there are numerous producers, each avoiding risk, the switch, if any, from subsistence products to mono-crop commercial production will be difficult and slow. The tendency will be to further exploit a spectrum of already existing commercial crops, over a geographically more extensive area.

These implications as to the volume and nature of the export trade are illustrated in the nineteenth century commercial accounts of the Empire. Trade volume increased after the 1820s, and gained a new momentum with the advent of steamships to the eastern Mediterranean. The treaties of 1838 and following years ratified the new level of integration into European markets by formalising the trade regime and abrogating the imperial right to grant trade monopolies. By mid-century the trade pattern had attained a composition reflecting the core-periphery division of labour underlying the free trade doctrine: imports consisted in large part of manufactured consumer goods, while various foodstuffs and raw materials – none of overwhelming importance – were exported.[8] The volume of trade had in fact increased rapidly from a small base only to grow less rapidly in the second half of the century. The initial boost to Ottoman exports derived mostly from the diversion of existing marketed surpluses of raw materials from local to export markets. This diversion resulted in the disruption of the social division of labour and led to unemployment in urban manufacturing, rural crafts and domestic industry. Two parallel factors were prominent in gauging the impact of trade : the onslaught of cheap manufactured imports – especially of cotton goods – and the increase in raw material prices for domestic industry, mainly owing to alternative export markets. As for rural producers, whether they produced for their own consumption or to fulfil contracts with merchants, their shifting to more remunerative primary goods production was economically rational. Urban manufacturers were hit the hardest: accounts of the time are full of statistics showing a precipitious decline in the numbers of looms, yards of cloth produced, and craftsmen. Especially during the initial rapid increase in trade, British exports of cotton goods to the Ottoman Empire grew fivefold between the mid-1820s and late 1840s.[9] The displacement of local production, caused by the shifting of consumption to imports, continued to be effective during the mid-century Victorian boom.

It would be theoretically unjustified to argue that the destruction of local industry proves the systemic impact of capitalist integration to be reversal and blockage of potential evolutions. A crude argument equates the status of manufacturers in the periphery with the position and function of proto-industrial activity in the West. It suggests that without capitalist integration, these manufacturers would have created the accumulation necessary for the development of industry.[10] This is of course a technicist argument which tends to ignore the social system in which the activities take place and identifies capitalist development with quantitative accumulation of techniques. Even if peripheral manufacturing and European proto-industry had been similar in terms of their internal organisation, their articulation into the economic system and their capacity for transforming the system were very different. In addition, the relationship with the political authority condemned manufacturing activity in the Ottoman Empire to a prescribed division of labour which precluded unbridled accumulation. Therefore de-industrialisation did not destroy a potential dynamic towards capitalist industrialisation in the Western mode. It did, however, in disemploying tens of thousands of craftsmen and manufacturers create substantial social upheaval. It thus became a demonstration of how the traditional order was sacrificed to bureaucratic reformism.

The social upheaval following the destruction of an internally integrated division of labour was accompanied by the development of new activities and the rise of new social groups. The already mentioned comprador population, often carrying the protection and immunity afforded by foreign passports, prospered in port cities such as Salonika, Izmir, Trabzon and Istanbul, which became new centres of commercial activity.[11] These cities provided the points of linkage with commodity and credit circuits originating in Europe. Banks and merchant houses were established in the ports, and constructed communication networks to reach the interior. Such networks consisted of merchants, agents, petty traders and moneylenders. The implication of the growth of trade in its destructive and constructive moments was a substantial restructuring of the social division of labour. While manufacturing groups, who had provided the traditional order with an urban petty bourgeoisie, were rapidly becoming superfluous and were eliminated, a new class, finding employment through external trade, was beginning to flourish. Geographically, too, the economic space was being restructured: traditional maufactures undergoing destruction were mostly in the old trading cities of the interior, seats of the provincial bureaucracy. New activities, however, were located in ports, obeying the logic of the market. Their networks were established to emanate from central points where the link with European markets could be maintained. Thus restructuring implied an unbalancing of the geographical distribution of economic activity to favour coastal regions, market towns on principal arteries and their immediate hinterlands.

Most of what has been described as restructuration reflects a common experience of capitalist integration in the periphery. What was specific to the case of Turkey was the overdetermination of the class conflict accompanying this restructuration with religious and ethnic differences. The two major classes of the traditional system, the small peasantry and the bureaucracy, remained intact during this period of transformation. Certainly the small peasantry were subject to fundamental changes from the point of view of the degree and nature of their integration into commodity or money markets, with implications of unequal exchange and exploitation through circulation. Since they were increasingly integrated in the market, fluctuations in prices began to influence their production strategies and even constrained them to temporarily lose their independent status. Nevertheless the overwhelming majority of the peasantry continued as small producers whose degree of marketisation could vary, but whose mode of organisation, and use of family labour, remained constants.

The class whose status had been immediately threatened was that of the Moslem manufacturers and merchants. There was probably no decline in the absolute number of merchants; even in industry, destruction would be succeeded by the development of a new kind of manufacturing, located mostly in port cities. Within the ranks of merchants and maufacturers, however, there had been a rapid circulation of ethnic groups. Moslem traders, whose institutional guarantees had been the Palace's granting of monopoly rights, were left in an under privileged status. By and large, Moslem merchants survived in a subordinate capacity; they could not benefit from the increase in trading activity, particularly that part of it connected with world markets.[12] Foreigners and Christian populations of the Empire created, advanced and seized these opportunities on account of their economic (lower taxes) and political (extraterritorial) status. Nor should the importance of the cultural element in this process be ignored. It was certainly true that non-Moslem merchants and moneylenders were privileged through their affinity of tradition, religion and language with European businessmen. (Or, at least, they had the potential of thus being singled out. Certainly, the majority of Greeks and Armenians were difficult to distinguish from Moslems, and shared with them a common culture; when the occasion arose, however, part of the Christian population could respond to and benefit from the new opportunities, while the Moslems were in no position to do so.) During the nineteenth century the European view of the Ottoman Empire did not attain colonialist overtones evoking civilising missions, but remained heavily tainted by a romanticised crusader perspective, professing as its object the liberation of Christian populations under the yoke. Thus the formation of an intermediary class of Christians coincided with a cultural mission; their co-optation by European business constituted a total project designed to solve the Ottoman problem.

From a systemic point of view there were two reasons establishing the material basis for a conflict between the bureaucracy and the new intermediary bourgeoisie. First, the merchant class was the physical agent of capitalist integration, threatening to change the very principles of the traditional system which was guarded and defended by state functionaries. It did not require great foresight to comprehend the implications of the replacement of a bureaucratic system by market rationality for the traditional role of the bureaucracy. Secondly, even if the bureaucracy were willing to transform its traditional role, through transforming the whole social system during this process, it would have to preserve a degree of legitimacy in the eyes of the social groups making up the traditional order. In other words, it would have to maintain its alliances in order to retain the ability to undertake the transformation and restructuring of the social order. During most of the nineteenth century, the bureaucracy did not state its goal as being a transformation designed to maintain its status while adjusting to new world conditions. Nevertheless, the social disruption caused by the growth of a bourgeoisie threatened the bureaucracy's legitimacy, and placed it in an ambivalent position *vis-à-vis* the displaced social groups of the traditional order. We shall see below that when a process of bureaucratic social change was finally embarked upon, the ambivalent attitude towards Moslem merchants and manufacturers had to be resolved in favour of retaining legitimacy in the estimation of the traditional social groups.

The growth of a Christian intermediary class was a more immediate threat to state functionaries in their guise of a class receiving, ideally, the bulk of the economic surplus in the Empire. The growth of trade naturally increased the value of production; both because more resources were put to use and because there were shifts in production towards more remunerative products. In time, new techniques were introduced as well, increasing the peasantry's productivity. The taxation system of the traditional order was based on assumptions of simple reproduction, where neither techniques nor the volume of production would change appreciably from year to year. The new situation was that of a growing economy, and the traditional tax, fixed in money terms for a number of years, was not equipped to capture the larger amount of surplus. Furthermore, the new surplus was appropriated to a large degree by the class which engaged in the circulation of money and traded commodities. While the system of taxation provided for some extraction of merchants' revenue through internal customs, the new class engaged in trade were exempt from this octroi, thanks to privileges granted to European powers in trade agreements. Responding to newly forming consumption habits, they were also able to sell imported luxury consumption goods to the bureaucracy and thus extract a share of the surplus already appropriated by the state. State officials thus unwittingly became intermediaries in the appropriation of peasants' surplus by the merchants. In other words, while the income and output of the Empire were growing the bureaucracy's share was decreasing, and the new class's share increasing.[13] As long as it remained impossible to impose a new tax on protected merchants (all such attempts were countered by strong protests from European states), the situation could not be rectified in favour of state officials.

The existence of potential or actual conflict between a class representing the traditional order and a bourgeoisie nurtured through the dissolution of that order, was due to the mode of peripheralisation of the Empire. In pure colonial situations (such as that of India) the traditional ruling class was reduced to an appendage of the merchant-state, precluding a conflict either at the level of surplus appropriation or system definition. In countries of white settlers as well, political rule had similarly been established in accordance with the requirements of a merchant, commercial-landowning class. The Ottoman Empire, on the other hand, together with a few other cases such as China and Japan, had never been colonised, nor had it been drawn into the domain of 'informal empire'. It is no coincidence that the two most prominent examples of non-colonial peripheralisation were similarly inheritors of rich political traditions and, more importantly, of state officials cum ruling classes. Non-colonialisation allowed the status of traditional bureaucracies to be perpetuated during the process of capitalist integration; more precisely, during the period between the 1840s and the Great War. There was also mutual determination between the absence of colonisation and the importance of imperial rivalry. Various candidates among imperialist powers vied for greater influence and control over the Ottoman and the Chinese states: thus rivalry afforded greater manoeuvring space to the state officials, enabling the traditional ruling class to better oppose a colonial-type transformation of the social structure. In other words, imperial rivalry, the absence of colonisation, and the relative strength and autonomy (*vis-à-vis* imperialist pressure) of the traditional bureaucracy constituted an interdependent set of definitional parameters which guaranteed that the process of peripheralisation would be accompanied by an ambivalence at the level of the definition of the system; and that this ambivalence would be reflected in real or potential conflict and struggle between the representatives of the old order and the agents of the new. The social project of the bureaucracy, whether of transformationist or restorationist nature, would come into conflict with the system definition implied in capitalist integration and mercantile activity. Nevertheless, the maintenance of the strength of the bureaucracy did not imply a coherent class strategy. Its ambivalent position from the point of view of system preservation and immediate class interests frequently led the bureaucracy to adopt policies with unintended consequences of a paradoxical nature. A case in point is the policy of official borrowing which was overdetermined by the location of the Ottoman economy *vis-à-vis* imperialist economies, and by the class intentionality of the bureaucracy. Its consequences strongly affected the process of peripheralisation and class formation in the Empire.

As long as traditional, pre-capitalist modes of labour organisation survive, peripheral structuration according to the needs of capital is a process of orientation carried out by merchants and moneylenders. We have discussed the organisation of trade and the workings of merchant capital in establishing the links between European markets and peasant production, and remarked that the institutionalisation of the trade relationship was largely imposed on the Ottoman bureaucracy through the inter-state system. The establishment of the link with the European market of international loans was not an imposition of the same nature: state officials were willing to accept this relationship in their own short-term interest. There were, however, palace officials of a more conservative cast who voiced hesitations in this regard. Their misgivings were overridden by the reformist wing, which was convinced that the salvation of the Empire could only be negotiated through a more complete incorporation into the European system.

Until the mid-nineteenth century, the bureaucracy had relied on loans from bankers located in Istanbul; and at times the original provenance of such funds was the banking centres of Europe. The immediate reasons for borrowing had always been temporary shortages of revenue and deficits in the imperial budget.[14] During the nineteenth century, however, the requirements for state expenditures had risen conjointly with the modernisation of administrative and miltary structures, as well as with more integral insertion into the arena of European wars, necessitating further military engagements. The discrepancy between rising expenditures and insufficient revenue was manifested in the central authority's endemic revenue crisis. From the revenue side, the crisis signalled the underlying reason for the bureaucracy's declining share in the surplus; on the expenditure side, the costs of reform, especially military, were prominent. Formalisation of the debt relationship seemed to respond to several needs simultaneously: European moneylenders would now confront the central authority, rather than local bankers who did not have the power to collect their claims from a reluctant Palace; budget revenues could be supplemented, and the bureaucracy would increase its utilisation of funds. From the point of view of the lenders, advancing loans to the Ottoman government reinforced the decision to strengthen the imperial centre against centrifugal tendencies. Not only did the centre thus gain the ability to protect territorial integrity – when this was needed – but also to undertake institutional or material investments itself, and to guarantee the undertaking of such investments by foreign investors or concerns. Loans served to legitimate the Ottoman functionaries from the point of view of European diplomacy. They also served to perpetuate its weakness. While lending to the Ottoman state (and expecting the loans to be repaid) was tantamount to recognising its legitimacy, its perpetual indebtedness provided a leverage European governments felt free to exploit. Debt imperialism frequently served to force the Ottoman state to agree to concessions or to instituting desired measures and policies. In time, bureaucrats found themselves at the mercy of lenders.

From the point of view of accumulation of capital on a world scale, the repayment of loans by the central authority was equivalent to a conversion process whereby the peasants' surplus, received in the form of taxes, served the valorisation of interest-bearing capital of European origin.[15] In fact, after the bankruptcy of the Porte in 1875 this role of mediation was eliminated in favour of a direct interaction between representatives of European creditors and the peasantry. Despite this relationship, which served to structure the economy, the debt receiving-servicing ratio on the whole favoured the Empire. If the Ottoman economy is taken as a mercantilist unit there were long periods when it was a net receiver of loans, and for the 1856–1914 period as a whole, inflow of loans was roughly equal to the outflow of debt servicing.[16] From a strictly arithmetical point of view, the Ottoman economy did not suffer from the indebtedness episode by repaying more than the external finance it received. The argument we advanced earlier concerning the difficulty of constructing an export economy in the Empire is relevant in this context. It seems that while failing to develop an export sector, the Ottoman economy served as a market for manufactures more than as a supplier of food and raw materials. Throughout the nineteenth century, there was a trade deficit rather than a surplus.[17] The earlier complaints were still valid: since exports did not provide them, funds had to be injected into the Ottoman economy by European lenders so that European merchants could find buyers for their wares.

Once again, this is a specificity of Ottoman peripheralisation which needs to be explained through the location of the Ottoman economy and state in the world system. The fact that the Porte enjoyed the privilege of receiving loans without having to repay an excess did not result from a unified decision-making process of European capitalism, nor from the political preferences of a single hegemonic power (as would be the case during the post-World War II period). On the contrary, the privileged position of Ottoman bureaucrats was due to rivalry among imperialist powers. During the Victorian boom, France and England were the contesting powers; the depression of 1873–1895 was a period of consolidation when the Ottoman economy was under the tutelage of an imperialist consortium; the pre-war boom, however, once again witnessed rivalry intensified by Germany's late entry onto the scene. In their competition for political or economic advantage, European politicians were willing to use their influence on stock exchanges and bond markets in order to get the financiers to float yet another Ottoman loan.[18]

The first official loan that the Ottoman administration received was in 1854, during the Crimean War. This was followed quickly by another loan in 1855, and eleven more until 1875 when the Ottoman government announced its inability to continue making interest payments. Between 1875 and 1881 the Ottoman bankruptcy was negotiated among representatives of bond holders and Palace bureaucrats, resulting in the formation of the Public Debt Administration (PDA) which enjoyed considerable control over the finances of the government. The terms of these loans varied considerably, the rate of issue and the rate of interest changing according to the state of the money market, the complicity and encouragement of the governments involved and popular feelings in Europe about the Empire. Nevertheless, as long as the boom continued, European merchants and investors, who had come to depend on the Ottoman market, constituted a lobbying group for the extension of loans to the Porte. Since loans were frequently used to make payments on earlier loans, or to guarantee returns on private foreign investment, such lobbying was usually directly remunerative. After the financial crash of 1873, however, like many other states in similar position, the Ottoman government found new loans to be much less readily forthcoming, and the rates more prohibitive. The declaration of bankruptcy led to the Porte's virtual relinquishment of a part of its fiscal sovereignty.

The PDA was formed to safeguard the rights of European investors holding Turkish bonds.[19] To this end it was supposed to administer certain revenues, including some duties, the salt tax, the silk tithe and the tobacco tax, which were earmarked for debt servicing. Soon, however, the function of PDA was extended: it began to act as the intermediary between the government and foreign investors – both for direct investments (such as railroad companies) and public loans – to actively encourage and accommodate foreign enterprise and to represent merchant capital *vis-à-vis* peasant producers of tobacco and silk. In time, the organisation built by the PDA was large enough to rival the Ottoman finance ministry, and controlled about one-third of the total public revenue of the Empire. The PDA served as an alternative to the formation of a colonial apparatus: it reflected a compromise among rival imperialist powers in establishing a degree of stability in the financial relationship of the Empire with European sources of credit, while the commercial sphere remained open to competition. As sole intermediary between merchant houses and peasant producers (in the case of tobacco through forming a monopoly known as the Régie Coïnteressé des Tabacs) its activity was primarily directed towards the valorisation of loans. The formation of the PDA signalled for the bureaucracy a loss of fiscal sovereignty and, consequently, legitimacy in the eyes of its subjects. Like the Fermiers Généraux of the *ancien régime*, the PDA represented a committee of creditors of the Sultan, and like them constituted a barrier against fiscal reform. In defending the rights of European creditors, the PDA adopted the same ambivalent attitude towards the Ottoman central authority as characterised earlier European support of centralisation: on the one hand it rendered the Porte a more credible (and creditworthy) interlocutor in the international scene, while at the same time it prevented any radical internal change or fiscal reform. Again, like the Fermiers Généraux, the creation of the PDA was an adequate innovation to convert peasant surpluses to interest payments on money capital – in the Ottoman case of foreign origin. What was formerly achieved by the Porte itself was now taken over more directly by the actual representatives of European creditors. This was especially true in the case of tobacco and silk, where producers were pitted against the monopsonistic purchasing position of the PDA, which represented the intertwined status of merchant and money capital.[20]

The PDA did have one unexpected effect on the ideological development of the bureaucratic class: as its organisation grew to rival that of the Ottoman administration itself, it also came to personify the nefarious impact of the European connection on the traditional functions of the state. Through this concrete representation, the bureaucracy was, by contrast, absolved of its responsibility in the process of incorporation. Against the PDA the bureaucracy became defensive, and it was pushed to embrace the resentment of traditional orders against the European impact. When foreign borrowing started during the Crimean War, there were still factions within the bureaucracy who, in the name of the traditional order, had opposed the idea.[21] These factions were, however, primarily remnants of the old, non-secular orders, who had already suffered a decline in status. The proponents of the strategy which could be called reform with the social function of the bureaucracy intact had carried the day over the restorationists. With the formation of the PDA the reformist bureaucracy attained a new ideological consistency: its aim of transforming the Empire from above while retaining its own class position came to contrast sharply with the strict economic rationality and capitalist accounting of the PDA. In this confrontation the bureaucracy emerged as the paternalist defender of a normative social order while the PDA, as the servant of European capitalism, represented the rule of the market.

While the Moslem population could ideologically quarantine Christian merchants and moneylenders – the more immediate carriers of market rationality – from their everyday concept of reality, a new breed of organisation men (the personnel of the PDA) who performed very much the same functions as the palace bureaucracy, was harder to dismiss. In fact the extension of the market had already instigated a gradual drift towards an 'economic' mentality in the formalist sense. Towards the end of the nineteenth century a new group was emerging within the Moslem population, whose material conditions – whether as petty producers or specialists in accounting and maximisation – allowed them to acquire a notion of the social system substantially different from the traditional Ottoman one. This group, although later participating in the Young Turk and Kemalist projects, and supporting the Turkification of the economy, found itself in conflict with the mainstream of the bureaucratic class, precisely because of its more liberal conception of the social and economic order. The mainstream of the bureaucratic class thus became more uniform in the face of this development; the PDA had been instrumental in contributing to the creation of the bureaucratic movement of étatist social transformation that we shall discuss in the next chapter.

The story of the Ottoman debt highlights many of the aspects of capitalist integration, and its shaping of class structures and class action. Although clearly an arm of nineteenth century imperialism, debt also served the short-term interests of the state class anxious to preserve its economic status. The traditional social order and the class map, however, were changing under capitalist incorporation, and the bureaucracy unwittingly served to accelerate this change. Not only did indebtedness further the transformation of the traditional order; it also deepened the dilemma of the bureaucracy, caught between its allegiance to the crumbling normative order and its interests as dictated within the new world represented by capitalist rationality and the logic of the European inter-state system. Consequent to this confrontation, which was brought out in sharper contrast under the presence of the PDA, the mainstream of the bureaucracy opted for an alternative outside the immediate field of action defined by their European relations. They attempted to create an autonomous space in order to cope more effectively with the exigencies of European integration.

There was a third mechanism of capitalist integration which the bureaucracy did not willingly permit, but was required to agree upon through diverse pressures – direct investment of foreign capital aimed at the employment of local labour. A discussion of direct foreign investment is important within the context of the growth of domestic production. The development of a productive sphere entails a differentiation and frequently a division within the bourgeoisie, with manufacturing capital coming to represent interests other than trade-oriented compradors, and with different demands from the political authority. Such a manufacturing bourgeoisie usually starts its accumulation under the aegis of foreign capital, and becomes increasingly autonomous. In the Latin American case, for example, it is possible to trace the conflict between urban manufacturers and the exporting oligarchy to an initial differentiation within the merchant bourgeoisie whereby a fraction became involved in production, and were later transformed into defenders of national industrial development. For this reason, the presence or absence of direct foreign investment in the peripheralisation process, and the consequent differentiation of the merchant bourgeoisie, are important historical data: they condition the potential conflicts which may arise within the dominant class and the political struggle over the nature of the economic policy practised by the political authority.

In order to analyse the nature of foreign capital, we may begin by distinguishing between capital which arrives in the country as merchant capital, but finds it expedient to engage local labour in the production of commodities, and productive capital which arrives carrying the wage-labour relationship with it. In the first category are diverse forms of trading ventures, usually oriented to exports. These range from contracts with small producers to deliver the future harvest (a purely monetary arrangement which involves no control over the labour process) to *verlag* type contracts, as characterised by, for example, the organisation of export trade in domestically produced carpets. When merchant capital is involved in organising production its role is limited to reorienting existing forms of production. Depending on the general tendencies in the social formation as a whole, such an orientation may quickly lead to, or only marginally affect, the 'liberation' of labour from traditional modes of organisation. In the putting-out case as observed in carpet-weaving, for example, only one or a few members of a family were actually engaged in such contracts, while the rest continued as small peasant producers.[22] In such instances, the impact of integration into the circuit of merchant capital did not rapidly dissolve the old forms. When we consider contracts with agricultural producers involving future harvests (*à livrer* contracts), despite the degree of dependence such arrangements could engender, we can readily see that such dependency did not lead to a dispossession of the peasantry. Such examples do not only demonstrate the mode of articulation between merchant capital and small producers: they also signify a certain resistance of the social structure to the creation of capital-wage labour relationships.

Proletarianisation was unlikely because the central authority attempted to defend the independent peasantry through its policies. The reluctance to extend land ownership rights to foreigners could be seen as an example of this policy rather than a xenophobic reaction. Nevertheless, the Porte was forced to recognise a diluted version of private property rights on land in 1858, and under the pressure of European envoys, land ownership rights were extended to foreigners in 1867.[23] This legal innovation initially induced foreigners to purchase considerable stretches of agricultural land, especially in the Aegean area. The agrarian structure, however, did not allow for the inception of capitalist relations envisaged by the foreign landowners, since a dispossessed peasantry was not available as a free proletariat. With the failure of agricultural capitalism, merchant capital took over, and most of this land was rented out to family producers in arrangements that were very similar to *à livrer* contracts engaged in with the landowning small peasantry.

When direct investment in production was successful, it served the needs of merchant capital. The most obvious cases, which also account for the largest component of foreign investment, were railroads and ports. Railroads began to be developed in mid-century, but the pace of construction was exceedingly slow compared to India or Latin America, owing perhaps to the limited potential of export production. Entrepreneurs were reluctant to invest except when kilometric guarantees (i.e. an agreed sum of annual profit to the company per kilometre of railroad) could be obtained from the bureaucracy. Initially projects were undertaken only in the Aegean area, connecting the hinterland with the major port of trade. Only during the period of PDA, when imperialist rivalry intensified and more credible guarantees were forthcoming, was there a new wave of investments which did not simply aim at exploiting an existing market. The famous Bagdadbahn project was undertaken during this period.[24]

The composition of foreign direct investment reflects the argument that the economic integration of the Empire was dominated by the requirements of trade. French capital was the most heavily present in the Ottoman Empire. If we exclude financial placements, 62 per cent of total French capital in 1895 was found in railways, 16 per cent in ports, and 18 per cent in municipal services. In 1914, the proportions were similar and French capital comprised approximately 50 per cent of all the foreign direct investment in the Empire, while the German share was around 25 per cent. In the case of German-owned capital, however, the concentration of direct investment in merchant capital directed ventures was even more evident: 86 per cent of the investment was in railways, 5 per cent in ports and 8 per cent in municipal services.[25]

It is evident that railways and ports serve to increase the volume of trade and open up previously local market-oriented producers to world commercial networks. Municipal services encourage and increase the volume of trade in a more direct manner. By creating the physical environment in which the new merchant bourgeoisie lived, such services fashioned life styles in the model of distant metropoles. These life styles required increasing proportions of luxury consumer goods imports. This indirect impact of investment in municipal services was most clearly visible in the 'Europeanised' sections of rapidly growing port cities – especially Salonika, Izmir and Istanbul. In these cities the operation of trains, electricity networks, and passenger boat services were totally controlled by foreign capital. It may be argued that most of the new economic activity in urban areas was in fact trade-complementing; either in the sense of actively participating in imports and exports, or in the sense of catering for the needs of the Levantine population.

The old manufacturing activity serving urban demand continued in a more or less transformed fashion. Such activity, however, did not ordinarily articulate with foreign capital except in a few cases where new commodities which were too bulky to trade were produced. When local production did not compete with imports, such investment (as in beer and cement production) was undertaken by partnerships of foreign and local capital. The local capital for such joint ventures usually derived from the non-Moslem merchant bourgeoisie. In fact, we may argue that the new merchant bourgeoisie replaced the Moslem manufacturing concerns of the traditional order during the second half of the nineteenth century. This new manufacturing sector, however, was the product of a post-incorporation environment characterised by the ready availability of imported manufactures. As such it only complemented imports in satisfying the Europeanised consumption demands of the bourgeoisie itself.

As we shall discuss below, the weight of the manufacturing sector was quantitatively insignificant. At the turn of the century, there were probably around one hundred manufacturing concerns employing more than ten workers; and these were heavily concentrated in Salonika, Istanbul and Izmir.[26] Their ownership was probably more than 90 per cent foreign and non-Moslem. In other words, a very small fraction of the bourgeoisie was engaged in manufacturing. This small manufacturing sector existed almost entirely outside the Moslem population, because industrial workers were also non-Moslems. Thus the social differentiation resulting from capital-labour confrontation obtained exclusively within the non-Moslem population.[27] Even if this industrial class conflict had gained ascendancy – as it did for a few years prior to World War I – it would have been relegated to subordinate status under the ethnic and religious dislocations of social strife which came to characterise the Empire. The role of manufacturing in the economic structure of the Empire at the turn of the century was insubstantial, however, and for this reason, merchants determined the colour of the bourgeois class. Had the nature of export trade been different, requiring greater processing at the source, it is conceivable that a larger amount of capital might have been invested in production. It is also conceivable that this greater volume of direct investment might have generated linkages within the domestic economy to induce the transfer of merchant capital to more productive ventures, as was the case, for example, in Argentina and Brazil. As it was, foreign capital remained confined to trade-related activites, and very few among the bourgeoisie ventured outside of the already cleared tracks.

In the absence of productive capital as an important category, the internal differentiation of the bourgeoisie did not advance sufficiently to create a class fraction occupying the objective position necessary to oppose merchant and money capital. In other words, there was little opposition from the ranks of the new class itself to the capitalist penetration of the Empire. The political implication of this argument is that there was no bourgeois fraction demanding a share in political power in order to alter the conditions of integration into the capitalist system. Furthermore, the position of the manufacturing fraction within the bourgeoisie implied that the sociological conditions for its becoming a political actor were even more lacking. Since towards the end of the Empire ethnic hostility and conflict between Moslems and non-Moslems were paramount in social life, the fact that merchants, bankers and manufacturers were all minorities served to congeal this group as members of a single bourgeois class. Had there been a Moslem preponderance of manufacturers agitating against Christian merchants and moneylenders, the political situation might have been different. As it was, state functionaries were confronted by a seemingly undifferentiated group with economic policy demands in the direction of further and more complete integration into the world economy. Thus the bureaucracy had no natural allies to aid it in attempting to formulate policies required to change the mode of integration of the Empire into the capitalist system.

The preceding argument is not intended to imply that the non-Moslem bourgeoisie were simple extensions of foreign capital, employed as mere instruments in the hands of British and French merchants and investors. On the contrary, the mid-nineteenth century boom seems to have created conditions for the independent evolution of Ottoman intermediaries who emerged sufficiently strong to defend their own economic space. This evolution, however, did not imply a challenge to the structural parameters of incorporation: the Ottoman bourgeoisie took over some of the positions that foreign capital had created. Especially during the later period when the European economy was in a crisis, Ottoman merchants and manufacturers in a few cities, including Salonika, Izmir and Istanbul, became active to gain government support for their endeavours. Nonetheless, there was no translation of these demands to a search for political rule. When merchants and manufacturers, in their overwhelming majority Greeks and Armenians, became political, the inter-state system had already condemned the Empire to dissolution. Under different conditions, with higher odds in favour of the survival of the Empire, they might have taken a different tack. As it was, their politics gambled on the break-up of the Ottoman realm.

The mechanisms of nineteenth century integration of the Ottoman economy into capitalist networks, namely those of trade, debt and direct investment, reveal that the development of the Ottoman Empire as an economic periphery allowed for the rapid expansion of a class engaged in intermediation between the local economy and the European system. The coincidence of the social limits of this new class with the ethnic differentiation of the Empire's population exacerbated the potential conflict between them and the bureaucracy as representing the traditional order. State functionaries found themselves restricted in their attempts at reform, especially since the intervention of the inter-state system in bureaucratic policy-making required the institutional guaranteeing of the privileged status accorded to Christian minorities. Because of the welcome extended to trade and political modernisation, the bureaucracy could not secure the support of the mass of the population, nor could they rely on the new class for any attempt at changing the parameters of economic integration. Nevertheless, the bureaucracy remained a class whose location in the social system allowed it to attempt the transformation of that system while maintaining its location. In the next chapter we shall investigate the internal social and ideological conditions which led to such an attempt, and the changes in the inter-state system which precipitated it.

III

The Young Turk Restoration

We have so far talked about the bureaucracy in structural terms, discussing above all its systemic location, and its political capacity for class action. While the reformism which character-ised most of the nineteenth century could be seen as derivative and well within the space accorded to Ottoman bureaucrats in the European inter-state system, the Young Turk movement towards the end of the century was of novel character in breaking away from immediate imperialist impositions. It is important to discuss briefly the composition and the quantitat-ive strength of the bureaucracy in order to understand the new capacity for action it exhibited after the turn of the century. It was already mentioned that the eighteenth century had consti-tuted a threshold in the constitution of a secular bureaucracy. The separation of the religious institution from the secular branches of administration had been a decisive development in the growing adjustment of state officials to their changing context. The next stage in the transformation of the Empire's administrative structure came during the centralisation efforts of the 1830s. It was then that a civil bureaucracy, physically located outside the Palace (in what is known as the Sublime Porte), began to develop alongside the Palace secretariat.[1] The relationship between the two branches of the bureaucracy depended very much on the personal power of the Sultan: in the several decades preceding the accession to power of Abdülhamit (1876), the Porte grew in importance as well as in numbers. Although during the last quarter of the century more power was invested in the Palace, new departments of government and modernisation of local administration served to inflate the numbers of functionaries associated with the central administration. At this time, the numbers involved in civil bureaucracy (excluding the military and the Palace secretariat) may have reached one hundred thousand.

There were qualitative changes within the bureaucratic class as well – that component of it which supplied the ranks of both reformists and revolutionaries grew in size and importance, mainly owing to the educational institutions established to reproduce their cadres. The graduates of imperial schools of engineering, medicine and administration founded around the middle of the century joined the bureaucracy either to serve in the military or in central government.[2] Technical schools as well as military academies had originally aimed at the modernisation of the army, but they quickly became recruiting channels for all branches of the bureaucratic class. Another important aspect of these schools was their increasingly imperial character. Students derived from all regions of a retrenching Empire; and during the latter part of the century Moslem Turks, recently migrated from the Russian Empire, gained special importance in the academic and intellectual life of the imperial capital.

'Intellectuals', who initiated both the reformist and the revolutionary movements, were that stratum of the bureaucracy who received a higher education, either abroad or in the newly established schools. In contrast to their Western counterparts, they were often products of a technical or military education designed to serve the state, but they were also influenced by the contemporary currents of European political tradition. Although oriented to state administration, they were not, in a strict sense, a technocratic cadre aiming at efficient management. Nor, however, did they represent a humanistic or critical culture. Their primary purpose always remained the reform of the state in order to better cope with internal conflict and external pressure. Their class position or the fact that all intellectuals belonged to the bureaucratic class – not only in a genealogical sense but also in terms of their employment and location within the surplus extraction relationship – endowed them with a state-centred perspective. There was not a single Ottoman intellectual, even in letters, whose immediate concerns lay outside this framework; debates and differences were played out within the narrow field of salvaging and strengthening the state. This perspective ensured that there was an ample organic intelligentsia serving the bureaucracy, formulating its projects and politicising its members whose interests lay in controlling the transformation of the social structure while safeguarding their privileged position.

Before bureaucratic activism evolved into its revolutionary version with the Young Turks, it went through several stages. At first recentralisation of the Empire was the predominant concern, following upon the attempts of the Sultan during the 1820s and 1830s. A conciliatory attitude toward the West was paramount during this stage, since threats to the centre could only be opposed with the active support of European powers. Accordingly, reformism served to respond to demands by the West to curb the absolutism of the political authority, and to institute guarantees of citizens' rights and equality. The dominance of political liberalism as an ideal was apparent in the intellectual heritage claimed by upper bureaucrats and the Sultans who, at this period, were largely under their influence.[3] During this period, reforming bureaucrats went unchallenged not only because they held power over weak Sultans, but also because world conditions allowed for a fulfilment of the promises contained in Westernising reforms. It seemed both that the Empire could remain intact, and that economic integration with Europe would bring immediate benefits (in the form of loans) as well as long-term prosperity. But the disturbing aspect of this integration was also becoming visible, through the creation of a privileged Levantine class. The bureaucracy attempted at various points to reinstate the governability of all its subjects, in other words, to bring the Levantines under the centre's legislative authority, but the Great Powers were adamant in defending extraterritorial privileges. Despite failure on this count, there was, until the last quarter of the century, no radical disillusionment with reformism following Western guidelines.

During the next stage, official disillusionment with the results of integration into the capitalist system began to reflect the resentment of displaced craftsmen and Moslem merchants. The period coinciding with the downturn in the world economy (1873) was followed by a disastrous famine in Anatolia in 1874 (whose distant causes could be sought in the new orientation of the economy) and the bankruptcy of the Porte in 1875. The Russian war and the 1878 Berlin treaty following it served to awaken Ottoman bureaucrats to the external threat of dismemberment of the Empire, especially since Russia obtained the right to intervene in Ottoman affairs in order to oversee the Palace's treament of Armenians. It was now evident that foreign markets and international funds, and even wars, obeyed an external dynamic which could not be much influenced by sincere declarations in Istanbul of the liberal creed and good behaviour in general. The forcing upon the Porte of the Public Debt Administration (PDA) must have appeared to less suspecting Westernisers as the undeniable manifestation of cold capitalist logic.

The careers of the first generation of Westernisers ended as part of the shift of power from the more autonomous civil service in the Porte to the Palace secretariat under Abdülhamit (1876–1909).[4] The new Sultan and a strengthened Palace bureaucracy maintained a certain suspiciousness toward the West in excercising the old statecraft of the balancing act, which had become appropriate to the times. This was because Britain no longer supported the integrity of the Empire and, by the 1880s, intense imperialist rivalry targeted various territories within it. The world scramble for territorial acquisition and influence, which was occasioned by a relative decline in British hegemony, was reflected in the Ottoman mirror as ambassadorial politicking to curry concessions at the Porte. The Palace's tactics in response to this rivalry were essentially conservative: they sought – none too successfully – to maintain the integrity of the Empire, while seeking to restore some of the social dimensions of the traditional order. Such tactics were pursued with the help of a bureaucratic faction whose members found Islam to be the requisite fulcrum in extolling the virtues of the traditional order.[5] The less critical Westernisers were excluded from this scheme, and having fallen out of favour, they experienced a transformation, after which they were reincarnated in a more radical version as the Young Turks. As Young Turks and later members of the CUP, their attitudes towards modernity evolved in a much more ambivalent and nuanced manner. At the same time the restorationist bureaucracy and the Sultan enjoyed an ideological success at the popular level which had been withheld from the administration for almost half a century. Not only had economic transformations disturbed the essentially static order, but the Moslem masses and peasantry, as well as the urban petty bourgeoisie, had found it difficult to accommodate the hastily transplanted tenets of equality and constitutionality – especially since these seemed to serve the immediate needs of mercantile (and non-

Moslem) interests. Under such circumstances conservatism propagated from above, doused with religious legitimation, must have been reassuring; this probably explains the otherwise difficult to comprehend continuing popular appeal of Abdül-hamit to this day.

If the conservatism of Abdülhamit and the bureaucracy could be seen as an essentially palliative measure designed to gain time during a crisis period of world capitalism, the current of reaction culminating in Young Turk activism, based on a desire to change the political system, was also strong, and probably swayed the majority of the bureaucratic ranks. This stance had evolved out of the position previously assumed by the reformist bureaucracy, and was sharply defined by its opposition to the conservative flank in power. It was, however, also informed by the intellectual and political currents of late nineteenth century Europe, and was, therefore, no longer characterised by an unsuspecting adulation of French republicanism and British parliamentarianism. Its activism derived not from socialism, which was at the time only beginning to attain ideological hegemony among revolutionary intellectuals, but from a radical 'positivism' acquired through contact with French Comtians.[6] While sharing the social engineering perspective of most intellectual movements in less developed contexts, their under-standing of the Empire and its problems was not based on an analysis of the social structure, nor on a study of the mechanisms of imperialism. Instead, their discourse was pri-marily anti-absolutist, tinted with an ill-defined resentment of economic dependence. Anti-absolutism was, of course, a platform which could appeal to democrats in Europe, and could even articulate into policies of the Great Powers which aimed at establishing spheres of influence in a loosely federated empire. This double attraction explains the enormous popularity en-joyed by the Young Turks in European (intellectual and official) public opinion – prior to their coming to power.

There was, however, a second facet to the intellectual constitution of the Young Turk movement which supplied its activism with an ill-understood desire to overcome economic backwardness. Since the middle of the century, a neo-mercant-ilist platform of 'national economic' development had been current among radicals of middle-European and Italian origin. In the case of the Listian doctrine as appropriated in Germany, the idea of a 'national economy' could provide a programme for a bourgeoisie preparing itself for the world stage. Similarly, in

Italy, backwardness was seen primarily as a problem of technological catching-up, and it was in terms of industrial development that the Risorgimento had interpreted the idea of 'national economy'. The location of the Young Turks in the social structure was quite different from such proponents of Listian doctrines in Germany or Italy; rather than constituting a group within the society whose immediate interests would be served through the establishment of a protected domestic market, and who sought to influence the political structure, the Young Turks were in a position to actually take over the state mechanism itself. They lacked, however, precisely what their European counterparts possessed: there was as yet no manufacturing bourgeoisie in the Ottoman Empire whose interests could be served through the construction of a national economy. Since, however, it was the state mechanism which was aimed at, this all-powerful position could be used to create a client group which would serve as a surrogate bourgeoisie. It was primarily important to take over and defend the state in order to safeguard its privileged status in the social structure; if the state mechanism lost is structural dominance the bureaucracy would no longer be in a position to save the Empire, nor would it be able to protect its own class interest.

In fact, it was this latter political activism, aimed at 'saving the state', rather than at an economic programme, which was in the forefront of Young Turk thought. Observing the slow and inexorable dismantling of the Empire, the growing success of various nationalist separatisms and the increasing bondage of the Porte under PDA tutelage, their immediate concern was to re-establish the autonomy and the geographical integrity of the Ottoman state. Thus 'saving the state' became the symbolic formula for safeguarding the traditional order with the privileged status of the bureaucracy. This concern, however, was not accompanied by an analysis relating the forces causing the dismemberment and loss of autonomy to economic subordination to Europe. European influence and presence were also interpreted at an exclusively political level and at that level they were evaluated positively because of Europe's readiness to condemn the autocratic power and repression of the Sultan. It is for this reason that the analogy between the Young Turks and the Meiji restorationists is not generally valid: the Meiji were much closer to an ends-means scenario where obtaining state power was a step towards economic restructuring. The Young Turks, on the other hand, prescribed administrative reforms as the cure to the ills they could diagnose while remaining ignorant of their economic aspects. We will take up the Japanese analogy again after discussing the seizing of power by the activist faction of the Ottoman bureaucracy.

The beginnings of the Young Turk movement coincided with a greater involvement of the Western powers in the Ottoman economy. This was due in large part to the upturn in the world economy and the growth of world trade. For the Ottoman economy, the boom translated into increasing exports, improving terms-of-trade and a greater inflow of foreign direct investment. It is important to recognise that the pre-war boom was not accompanied by the establishment of a new political order in the world; on the contrary, imperialist rivalry and the scramble for spheres of influence continued even more intensely, and constituted one reason for the increase in direct investment. The struggle for influence extended to the social sphere as well: all the great powers attempted to cultivate client groups within the Ottoman mosaic. Schools, cultural centres, missions and hospitals were established by each of the powers, building on regional and ethnic differentiation. The consequence was the exacerbation of the conflicts deriving from such differentiation. National and ethnic consciousness seemed to be directly related to the level of education, and various minority groups dis-covered their own ethnicity and separatist activism within the new cultural milieu. The 1878 Berlin treaty, following the Ottoman defeat by Russia, had formalised Great Power intervention in minority affairs, through the famous article stipulating that the Ottoman government would institute religious and civic equality for the Armenian population under Russian supervision.[7] By the end of the nineteenth century special relations had been established with the Armenians, at the political level by the Russians, and at the cultural level by the Americans; Catholic minorities were under the protection of France; and the Greeks, depending on European politics, were close to both the British and the French. Of course, there was also an independent Greek state, and it was no secret that a majority of the Greek population of the Empire placed their allegiance with this state, even if they chose to stay in their current abode. When Germany entered the scene, Moslems seemed to have remained the only candidate for a privileged relationship.

The new German state was regarded with sympathy and hope

by the Ottoman Sultan. In his Islamicist policy Abdülhamit found support in the Kaiser, who had a clean record because Germany did not possess any Moslem colonies. German business circles considered the Ottoman Empire as a perfect dependency, close enough geographically, rich in agricultural land and resources, and poor in population. After Deutsche Bank obtained the Anatolian railway concession in 1888 German business literature propagated countless colonisation schemes whereby German immigrants would be settled in the agricultural lands made accessible by the railroad. These schemes did not materialise, but political relations advanced at a rapid rate and the Kaiser embarked on a 'public relations' tour of the Near East in 1898, during which he declared himself (and Germany) to be the 'closest friend of the 300 million Moslems in the world, and their Caliph, the Sultan'.[8]

Economic relations proceeded at a less exalted rate: the establishment of the Deutsche Bank and its intermediation in German direct investment, although helping increase German presence, was not sufficient to offset the weight of French and British investment or trade. Nevertheless, trading shares of France and England declined between 1898 and 1913 (from 17% to 12.5%, and from 37% to 20% respectively) while Germany's share increased from 1.8% to 9.3%. During the same period German capital increased its share from 20% to 30% of total direct investment, while the French share increased from 40% to 45% and the British share declined from 23% to 13%.[9] Concessions obtained regarding the construction of railroads, and an investment plan to irrigate one of the largest plains in Anatolia (concession obtained in 1907 – Konya valley irrigation), indicate that German finance capital was engaged in long-term planning of a division of labour where Anatolia would serve as the supplier of raw materials and foodstuffs to an industrial Germany. While British investments in the Aegean littoral tapped existing surpluses, and long-term prospects did not seem to play as great a role in other British and French investments, German capital deliberately engaged in projects with long gestation periods which would qualitatively alter the trading potential of the country. Complementary investments in the form of trading companies aimed at increasing the agricultural output, which would then be carried on the new railways. Anatolische Industrie und Handelsgesellschaft, for instance, imported agricultural machinery to sell on credit to settlers along the Anatolian Railway. This company and its counterpart in Çukorova, Deutsche Levantinische Baumwollgesellschaft, were engaged in campaigns to educate the producers, to start model farms and to modernise agricultural production in general.[10] The well-known characteristics of German industrialisation under concentrated finance capital were reflected in the network of German investments orchestrated by the omnipresent Deutsche Bank. Under the establishment of such an extensive network, German investors would be in a position to engage directly with direct producers, bypassing the mediation extended to French and British trading houses by indigenous merchants. It was therefore more likely that German investors and agents would confront the Moslem population directly, thereby underpinning the political understanding between the Kaiser and the Sultan. Similarly, this special understanding would give the German government greater reason to support the integrity of the Empire, which depended on both the strength of the central authority and the weakness of the minorities and their patrons. A slightly different interpretation would hold that in the implicit bargaining among the Great Powers, Germany had placed its bid for the non-Arab Islamic core of the Empire (i.e. Anatolia) as its sphere of influence, which would imply that in the eventual dismantling of the realm a Turkish core would remain. This view assumes, however, that Britain and France had designated primarily non-Turkish zones which could be clearly delimited as to geographical extent. Needless to say, such a harmonious relationship did not exist among the Great Powers on the eve of World War I, nor were claims to spheres of influence non-competing.[11] It is more credible to impute to German policies the intention of preserving the Empire intact under German suzerainty, while France and Britain seemed increasingly inclined (after the 1870s) to force its dismemberment.

The new alignment in the inter-state system allowed the Young Turks room to manoeuvre, both before and after their advent to power. Before 1908 they represented to British and French governments, and to European public opinion in general, the promise of freedom from a despotic Sultan. They were to continue with the reformism of 1838–1876, along with the restoration of the constitution, secularisation of the state, and extension of equality to the Christian minorities. Their platform of Ottomanism was widely interpreted to mean a federalism with a weak centre. Against arbitrary repression under the Sultan, the Young Turks were champions of liberty and progress.[12] No doubt this assessment owed much to the coincidence of interests between Christian minorities, British and French governments, and the Young Turk movement; when the Sultan was forced to accept the CUP bid for power in 1908, European public opinion saw this change as the defeat of Germanophile Islamicism. In fact the Young Turks were openly pro-British, as became apparent in their appointment of pro-British functionaries to high government posts, and in their seeking an alliance with Britain against the Austro-Hungarian Empire and its ally Germany.[13] Despite fluctuations this pro-British and pro-Entente feeling continued until the very beginning of the war. During the intervening years, however, the CUP leaders were continually disappointed with Britain's (and France's) adverse policies. Starting with the 'counter-revolution' of 1909, which the British embassy was suspected of having supported, and continuing with the Porte's unsuccessful attempt to float a loan in Paris and London, sentiments began to change.[14] The British government maintained strict neutrality in the face of Bulgarian and Greek attacks on the Empire's European territories, and when the Istanbul government made repeated attempts to enter the Triple Entente it was rebuked, both Britain and France estimating that such an alliance would constitute a *casus belli* in the eyes of Germany. In a world where neutrality was increasingly impossible, the CUP government seemed to have no choice but to take its place among the Central Powers.[15]

At a more substantive level, however, it cannot be forgotten that alliances made in anticipation of the war also reflected conflicting designs for the post-war world. As discussed above, the place of the Ottoman Empire, according to the German vision, corresponded much more closely with the Young Turk desire to save the state and protect the integrity of the Empire. It gradually became clear, after the deposition of Abdülhamit in 1909, that reforms aimed at restoring the authority of the state would conflict with the increasingly secessionist aspirations of the Christian minorities. Confronted with the Austro-Hungarian annexation of Bosnia and Herzegovina, the Italian campaign in Tripoli and the Balkan Wars, Young Turks were naturally more inclined to strengthen the centre rather than carry out reforms which might lead to more powerful secessionism. German policy towards the Empire supported this vision, both because of the desire to protect the integrity of the Empire, and as a tactic for thwarting British and French designs on the Arab provinces and the Russian project to establish an Armenian protectorate in Eastern Anatolia. In short, imperialist rivalry in addition to its growing economic presence, determined the Young Turks' alliance with Germany, thus temporarily forestalling the growing momentum for the dismemberment of the Empire.

Although the leaders of the CUP were members of the bureaucratic class, and represented an educated and intellectual cadre, they were unprepared for their sudden accession to power. They had no specific programme to implement, nor had they yet discovered the social group whose interests could provide an orientation for future policies. Consequently, they changed and evolved rather rapidly in the face of events. Once in power, their attempt was to safeguard the centrality of the state authority, and their policies derived primarily from this consideration. It was a persistent purpose rather than an ideological consistency which informed the formulation of these policies. The ideology was incidental in that it resulted from an interaction of the desire to save the state (and to safeguard the position of the bureaucracy in the social structure) and the material conditions of the Empire in the international capitalist context.

It is important to recognise that the initial purpose of saving the state was cloaked in various principles of cohesion between 1908 and 1918. At the outset Young Turks were considered, by themselves and others, as Ottomanists whose struggle aimed at equality and federation among the various ethnic and religious groups of the realm. When confronted with the reality of secessionism and the impotence of government against European intervention (ostensibly aimed at protecting the interests of foreigners and the minorities) the naïve version of Ottomanism soon ceased to exist. Implementation of policies which attempted to establish uniform practices in the Empire, for example, in the field of education and language of instruction, were prevented by European embassies who invoked the rights obtained through capitulations and the late nineteenth century treaties. Administrative reform was limited by the insufficiency of state revenue; an insufficiency resulting from an inability to raise customs duties and tax foreigners, and the necessity of ceding close to one-third of the revenue to the PDA. The bureaucracy's attempts at constructing a political entity based on the European model of the nation-state were opposed by the same statesmen they were trying to emulate. All of these obstacles appeared as extensions of the social heterogeneity of the Empire, or the consequences of coexistence with Christian minorities.

In addition, the Young Turk accession to power had genuinely occasioned a cultural renaissance among the non-Moslem bourgeoisie. Emerging from a period of censorship and oppression, the Christian population were in a position to give cultural expression to their new social status. The most active groups in this cultural effervescence were Greeks and Armenians. Theatre, literature and journalism were fields that experienced veritable explosions, which tested the limits of the newly constructed public space. In Armenian communities alone more than two hundred journals began publication between 1908 and 1914.[16] Greek communities experienced a similar upsurge in cultural and educational life. Freedom of political expression necessarily followed this belated enlightenment: a full spectrum of organisations and publications varying from Ottoman socialists to religious irredentists soon began to challenge the government. Greek Orthodox workers organising a strike against French employers and carrying both Ottoman and Greek flags could not readily be dealt with in the cognitive universe of the bureaucratic elite. In fact the entire notion of bourgeois freedoms, athough rhetorically defended, was not easily assimilated into the perspectives of the ruling class in a state-centric empire.

The Balkan wars constituted a turning point in CUP relations with Greeks and Armenians. Armenian political parties had reneged on their support for the CUP, and were convinced of the necessity of internationalising the Armenian problem; Greeks were becoming 'Venizelists' – followers of the 'megale idea' and Venizelos, who advocated a summary solution to the Ottoman problem through annexation of Christian-populated regions by Greece.[17] It was in this political context that the CUP leaders veered rapidly towards a policy of Turkish nationalism.

Without delving into the intellectual background of Turkish nationalism, we might mention briefly that a majority of the proponents of this ideology had recently arrived from outlying Turkic areas of the Empire, and had received their nationalist schooling mostly in Europe. The CUP leaders themselves knew next to nothing about Anatolia, the supposed motherland.[18] It was, however, becoming apparent that Moslem Turks constituted not only the largest ethnic group, but also, by default, the most loyal. If the state were to be saved, such a loyal group was a necessary prerequisite even if it had so far remained silent on the historical scene. It did not take long for the CUP to advance from this diagnosis to an active policy of Turkish nationalism which excluded the minorities. In the process of cultivating the Moslem-Turkish element, the CUP enjoyed special freedom during the war years owing to the absence of inter-state constraints on bureaucratic policy-making. When the principal imperialist powers controlling the Empire became active enemies, the CUP leaders had the occasion to freely pursue their ideological design. The German alliance provided the autonomous space they needed, and actively supported the nationalist goals.

The CUP government's first important war-time policy was the unilateral abrogation of capitulations. The decree announcing this abrogation explicitly stated that the effect of immunity from taxes granted by the capitulatory regime had been to weaken the state, rendering the Porte unable to secure the means to implement reforms, and forcing it to resort to foreign loans for its routine administrative needs.[19] In addition the protection of foreigners through the extraterritorial regime had been an instance of apparent privilege, which hurt the autonomy and pride of the state. With the abrogation of capitulations, the government was then free to introduce a new trade regime, and protectionist duties were quickly instituted. At the same time measures were taken to abolish the privileged status of foreign firms by bringing them under Ottoman jurisdiction and tax legislation. Such measures of unification were obviously not sufficient for the implementation of the bureaucratic project. More specific policies were felt to be necessary in order to pursue the goal of national development. The overwhelming political theme of the war years was the creation of an indigenous bourgeoisie, with its proponents arguing the necessity of state policies designed to further Moslem enterprise. Nationalist intellectuals and activist bureaucrats alike attacked liberalism as the doctrine of free trade, economic dependency, and the comprador class. It was necessary to acquire a national consciousness and to further economic goals from the top; freedom of enterprise for individuals would come later. The best example was provided by German development and its anti-liberal, Listian policy of national economy based on protection. Yet the bourgeoisie of the Ottoman Empire, like the bourgeoisie of Poland, was not national and therefore could not be trusted. For this reason a new class of entrepreneurs had to develop from among the Moslem population who had so far been confined to posts in the military-civilian bureaucracy and to tilling the land. Only after the development of such a bourgeoisie could a national state be constituted.[20]

In accordance with this vision, government policy during the war was directed to increasing the profitability of Moslem business. The field of economic activity where it would be easiest to succeed was trade. Shortages imposed by the war meant that even the most minimal favourable treatment would yield high profits. As belligerence and mobilisation continued, political control over the distribution of foodstuffs and military material increased, and within this war economy, political privilege came to make even more of a difference in terms of mercantile profit. The Turkish government was certainly an important source of demand, but the German Central commission of Purchases (ZEG) was also active in Istanbul, procuring the local produce for the needs of the German army. In addition, the newly completed Anatolian Railroad helped create market opportunities – for the first time the capital began to receive its wheat and flour from the interior of Anatolia (its newly designated 'hinterland') rather than importing them from Black Sea ports. It might be imagined that the combination of expected shortages in a war economy and increasing demand would create conditions for an active black market and political patronage mechanisms. Such was in fact the case, with the natural result of accelerated accumulation of mercantile profits.[21]

More importantly, however, the new nationalism was put to practical use through attempts to promote employment and enterprise of Moslems in business. A 'language reform' in May 1915 prohibited the use of French and English (and later German) signs on the streets, and decreed that all business correspondence and official accounting would be conducted in Turkish. This measure sought to increase the employment of an educated Ottoman cadre and, although not fully implemented, was obviously aimed at the Levantine population who did not speak or write Turkish. The CUP government extended its Turkification policy by changing the directorate of foreign-owned railways, and by attempting to control foreign banks. A German observer of the scene commented that this was all very commendable from a patriotic point of view, but it meant that

Germany would lose the lucrative fields of business that it planned to exploit when the war ended.[22]

Under the guise of making provision for the capital city and the army, the CUP instituted allocation mechanisms which totally bypassed the market. The Ottoman trade monopoly system had returned in all but name, making use of the newly available technology: since means of transport were scarce, political favourites who could obtain the use of a railway freight car became instant magnates. At the same time, attempts were made to organise retail merchants and urban manufacturers in corporations, again in a manner similar to the Ottoman government's handling of the urban economy in its classical period. Workers' organisations which had been active during the 1908–14 period had already been banned. In provincial towns the politically led process of promoting Moslem enterprise was even more transparent: market centres witnessed the establishment of new merchant companies organised along cooperative lines. Moslem businessmen were brought together under the aegis of the party organisation to found 'national' companies for the financing and carrying out of trade. There was usually one-to-one correspondence between the roster of the CUP local organisation and the shareholders of the new companies. The government had no qualms about totally supporting such national concerns, and in effect required the identity of the party organisation and the newly emerging network of the national bourgeoisie.[23] Through this identity, the period during the war fulfilled the Ottoman bureaucratic ideal of political control over the economy. The autonomous sphere, that creation of imperialist incorporation and the bourgeoisie, suffered a decisive reversal. The market yielded to the domination of the economic life by political decision.

In addition to the bureaucracy's growing willingness to utilise its position to strengthen its control over the economy, this domination was due to the increasing number of control mechanisms available. Even before the war, there had been tax reforms which had instituted direct collection of taxes to replace the tax-farming system. This and other administrative reforms had increased budgetary revenues; the new customs duties also became a source of added revenue. More importantly, the beginning of the war meant that the PDA could no longer function. A majority of its directors and shareholders were nationals of Entente countries, whose creditor positions were suspended when hostilities began. Thus the Ottoman government could exercise control over that portion of the revenue which had previously been devoted to the amortisation of the public debt. At the same time, the Ottoman Bank's operations were also suspended. This Franco-British institution had been conceded a charter in 1863 which made it into a *de facto* central bank. The suspension of this charter meant that for the first time the government could implement monetary policy, in the sense of printing paper money. This was done by the CUP government, with some help from German financiers. A formula was found whereby paper money was printed, presumably backed by gold stored in Berlin. This gave the government enormous purchasing power (equivalent in nominal terms to about three-quarters of the total credit received by the Porte between 1850 and 1914) even though paper liras depreciated in relation to gold liras soon after their issue.[24]

We might then see, in the short period during the war, the victory of the bureaucratic class in establishing itself as master of the social structure. It achieved this through politically reversing the process by which market mechanisms had replaced traditional political mechanisms of control. The rupture caused by the war in the relations which had previously ensured the Empire's unequal integration into the international capitalist context allowed the bureaucracy to supplant the market with direct political control over the economy. It was thereby able to re-establish itself as a class controlling the productive structure, thus fulfilling the promise of bureaucratic revolution.

It might eventually have been possible for the bureaucracy to recreate its hegemony in the social structure through the establishment of political control over the economy, had it not been that its class struggle with the bourgeoisie was displaced ideologically to a level of ethnic and religious conflict. The Greek and Armenian minorities were seen not only as carriers of the logic of the market, and as bourgeois agents of a capitalist social system which would eventually dispense with the traditional ruling class, but also as the internal support of an imperialism preventing the bureaucracy from reconstituting the traditional class balances. This vision had been formed under an ideological perspective whereby minorities become totally identified with impositions on the Ottoman state. The evolution of Greek and Armenian relations with the Porte was due in some measure to this identification, which had come to be shared by both the bureaucracy and representatives of the minorities. When the war started the reformist bureaucracy felt two simultaneous needs: to neutralise the minorities in order to prevent a resurgence of imperialist impositions; and to find for itself a client group in the economy without running the risk of this group becoming another internal support mechanism for external pressure. Therefore the economic constituency of political control by the bureaucracy could not be Greeks or Armenians: they had to derive from other ethnic groups which did not pose any threat to the integrity of the state.

The constituency which appeared to fit the description were merchants of Moslem Turkish origin. Not only did they satisfy the requirements of not having ties with external powers, but they also constituted an essential element in the new nationalist ideology. To a lesser extent, Jewish businessmen also fitted the bill. They could become part of the national programme, because they were not identified with a particular external power, and they were not a secessionist group. In fact, Jewish participation in the formation and pre-1908 activity of the CUP had been considerable, with Jewish intellectual tradition and radical bourgeois political activism contributing to both the ideas and the organisation of the Young Turks. The CUP, prior to 1908, was based in Salonika, which was a predominantly Jewish city.[25] Under Abdülhamit's despotism, Salonika had remained relatively independent of the capital owing to its European character and to its population's close contact with both French and Middle European cultures. Not only did Salonika supply initial impetus and an important number of the CUP leaders, but after the city's conquest by the Greek state in 1912, some Jewish, Moslem and Dönme businessmen moved their operations to Istanbul. These groups of merchant bourgeoisie fitted the CUP specifications rather well: in Istanbul, they constituted a good part of the clientele of Young Turk economic policy during the war.

More significantly, the war period also witnessed the cultivation of small merchants of Moslem and provincial origin. A group whose fortunes until then had depended on their relations with rich, well-connected Christian merchants was elevated to a more significant role by becoming *grands commerçants* linked to the CUP and the state mechanism. Those Moslem merchants who benefited from the new nationalism while retaining a provincial base played a very significant role in the post-war national movement.

This constitution of a Moslem and, to a lesser extent, Jewish privileged merchant class, although important as a reflection of Young Turk nationalism, would not of itself have made a significant impact on the social structure alongside the over-whelming presence of Greeks and Armenians. In terms of numbers, the CUP protégés could not have exceeded a few thousand, regardless of the size of their individual windfall gains. It was unlikely that they could capture the terrain of merchant capital from a long-established and well-entrenched Christian bourgeoisie, whose numbers and networks suggested quite a different order of strength. In other words the bureaucracy, even if it could establish political domination over the realm of the market, would still need to confront a distrusted Greek and Armenian bourgeoisie in carrying out its economic policy. To avoid such an obstacle, the 'national' bourgeoisie – favoured on account of its exclusive internity – had to be elevated to primacy and perhaps to being the sole economic interlocutor of the political class. This is not to imply that ethnic destruction and exclusion, which lasted from 1915 to 1923, were determined solely by the social project of the bureaucracy. As has already been mentioned, the struggle between the traditional ruling class and the challenging bour-geoisie was ideologically displaced to the realm of ethnic and religious conflict. At this level, what was proclaimed amounted to the inescapable interdependence between saving the state and neutralising the minorities; while, in the vocabulary of class and class project, what was being contested was the nature of the social system and class domination within it.

The principal conflict between rival classes attempting to establish hegemony and its ideological displacement emphasis-ing ethnic difference had given rise to mutual antagonism among Turkish, Armenian and Greek populations. At times hostilities had been occasioned mostly by official policy and by growing nationalist sentiment among Armenians in Eastern Anatolia. There was, however, also a deep-seated conflict, grounded in material interest, unfolding due to shifts in land ownership. Increasing production of export crops in Western Anatolia had implied growing numbers of Greek petty pro-ducers in agriculture who for the most part had migrated from the Anatolian interior, and from Aegean islands. Especially after the success of the central authority against *ayans,* fertile lands in the Aegean littoral came under the ownership of Greek peasants, whose primary orientation was to the export market.

This colonisation by Christian Greeks of the west coast of Anatolia had been in progress at least since the early nineteenth century.[26] More recently, Armenian merchants had also started purchasing land in Eastern Anatolia and in the fertile plains of Çukurova. Immediately before the war, observers remarked on the extent of the concentration of land in Armenian hands, and the parallel decline in Moslem peasants' fortunes.[27] The urbanisation of the nineteenth century, which was instigated by a growing volume of trade, had resulted in shifting population balances in favour of Christians in all the market centres of Anatolia. A more general observation concerning the differential impact of economic change, was that the Moslem population, in demographic and economic terms, had fared badly during the nineteenth century. Unequal development was reflected in the changing demographic composition of Anatolia: the Moslem population increased slowly because of high mortality, and especially because of the frequent wars which periodically decimated the young adult male population. Until 1909 Christian minorities were exempt from military service; and life on the coastal stretches was certainly easier. The urban population was disproportionately Christian, especially the newly urbanised population of the nineteenth century, who also enjoyed better health conditions. All these factors, including the Greek immigration, contributed to a rapid change in the demographic structure which, although not constituting a pressure on natural resources, must have been perceived as an infringement of the traditional Moslem monopoly over the principal source of subsistence and surplus.

What precipitated the CUP policies against the Armenian minority was of course the war. Immediately prior to the war, demands for autonomy in the eastern provinces, and British and Russian willingness to establish an Armenian protectorate, had reached a high pitch. The Ottoman military were also wary of Armenian defection to the Russian army on the eastern front.[28] These conjunctural concerns brought to the surface the question of minorities, and the evacuation of the Armenian population especially from Eastern Anatolia was undertaken in 1915, resulting in a staggering loss of lives. A similar treatment of the Greek population (although there were deportations to the interior for military purposes) was prevented for various reasons. The Greek Patriarchate in Istanbul were against an enlarged Hellenic state which would include parts of Anatolia; until 1917 the Greek state was undecided about entering the war, and the German military were concerned about its neutrality. Consequently, the Greek community were divided in their preference for the warring parties while Armenians were believed to be supporters of the Entente. In 1917, however, Venizelos came to power and the Greek state entered the war against the Ottoman Empire, extracting from the Allies the promise of occupation of Western Anatolia after victory.

The Central Powers lost the war and the Ottoman Empire signed an armistice with the Allies. The peace treaty, however, took much longer to prepare and sign. When it was signed in Sèvres in 1920, the Greek occupation had already resulted in a widespread resistance movement and the signatory Ottoman government had lost its legitimacy. Besides, the treaty itself remained vague and indeterminate concerning the fate of Anatolia and Istanbul. The Greek government had occupied the Izmir region based on a promise that the area would be administered by Greece after the war, although none of the parties had expected the military occupation to be carried out by the Greek army alone. Not only the Ottomans, but also the Italians and French were dismayed at the prospect of Graeco–Turkish confrontation; and in fact a new war was triggered immediately after the Greek landing, a war which would not spare the Greek minority in Anatolia.

The Greek army's occupation of Western Anatolia in May 1919 was the culmination of a century-old dream; the *megale idea* which would re-establish Hellenism in a greater Greece. As the Ottoman Empire grew weaker, and the Greek bourgeoisie within it stronger, the intelligentsia and the politicians of Greece had regarded the re-establishment of 'Hellenism in Asia Minor' as a foregone conclusion. In 1919 it did seem as if no obstacles would confront the occupying army, especially since the local Greek population served to consolidate the rule of the invaders, and its ranks swelled with the enlisting of the local Christian youth.[29]

Despite skirmishes with local opposition operating as loosely organised resistance groups, the actual invasion proceeded to cover an area greater than the originally mandated Izmir sanjak. As the Greek army extended its front towards the Anatolian interior, however, Turkish nationalist opposition quickly organised its military wing, started to control local resistance and was successful in arresting the Greek advance. After more than a year of uninterrupted battles and near victory for the Greeks in 1921, by mid-1922 the nationalist army had forced the enemy into a hasty retreat, which terminated in most of the occupying troops leaving Anatolia from the quay of Izmir, their port of entry.

With the turn of fortunes in the war, the Greek population of Anatolia had started fleeing to the occupied zone, and the retreat of the Greek army led to massive departures towards Izmir from abandoned areas. By this time the occupying forces were demoralised and in total disarray: they burned all towns they were forced to evacuate with much loss of life and material damage. Within one month of the capture of Izmir by the nationalist army (September 1922) close to one million Ottoman Greeks had escaped to Greece. During the talks at the end of the war a compulsory exchange of populations was agreed upon whereby 450,000 Moslems from Greece were sent to Turkey and 150,000 Orthodox Christians from Turkey to Greece. Only those Greeks living in Istanbul and Moslems in Western Thrace were exempted from the exchange.[30] When the exchange was completed in 1924 a total of 1.2 million Greeks had moved to Greece. A decade after the start of the war the Christian minorities had been effectively eliminated from what remained as the territory of new Turkey. About 2.5 million Greeks and Armenians had perished, departed or been expelled, a number which probably contained 90 per cent of the pre-war bourgeoisie. The subordination of a class had occurred under unexpected circumstances.

IV

Looking for the Missing Bourgeoisie

For Turkey, World War I ended in 1923. The defeat suffered by the Central Powers had occasioned a reluctant occupation of Anatolia by the Entente, but it was clear that no government would risk resuming active belligerence. Confusion reigned at the political level as well, as to the administrative mode to be applied to occupied areas. It seemed most likely that after the separation of Arab lands and the remaining Balkan territories, what was left of the Empire (mostly Anatolia) would be conceded to the heirs of the Porte. It was important, however, that this be a docile and pro-Entente administration, preferably headed by the Sultan and his devout servants. Even the establishment of an Armenian protectorate, so prominent in the pre-war agenda, was discussed half-heartedly, owing largely to US reluctance to assume any responsiblity.[1] International politics reflected the absence of a stable inter-state system: the war had not helped to resolve the rivalries of the earlier period. Britain was unable to impose its hegemony, and the US was as yet unwilling to do so. Rivalries among the victors continued: for example, the Italian government made no secret of its designs on the coastal areas of Anatolia, while the French aimed foremost at limiting the spread of British influence. When the Italian army began to occupy parts of the southern coast and started its advance toward the Aegean, the British decided to support Greek expansionism and the French reluctantly agreed. The post-war confusion and rivalry among the great powers provided Venizelos with the freedom to calculate that the Greek state would succeed in inheriting the spoils. Accordingly, in May 1919, the Greek army landed in Anatolia and occupied most of the Aegean coast, an area whose population was perhaps up to one-quarter Greek, although the proportion in urban areas was usually larger.

It was the Greek army's advance towards the interior of Anatolia which apparently decided the bureaucracy's attitude towards defending what remained of the Empire. The CUP leaders had, by the end of the war, been discredited due to the disastrous military defeat, and had either been arrested or fled – mostly to Germany. There was an Ottoman government in the occupied city of Istanbul which had very little autonomy, and the army, although much weakened, was still mobilised on the Eastern front. It seems that the CUP at the end of the war had organised an underground resistance organisation in Istanbul and the Anatolian provinces against an impending occupation. Although not very substantial, it was this organisation which later provided both an essential network and arms caches to the nationalist movement.[2] Ideologically, the legitimating notion of protecting the Empire's integrity was totally bankrupt. Ottomanism had been given up even before the war; during the war, a short-lived attempt at mobilising the Islamic elements in the Empire under the holy flag of the caliphate had to be abandoned in the face of the 'Arab betrayal'; pan-Turkism that sought to include in its purview Turkic peoples to the East had found its dénouement in the timely treaty with the Soviet Union. The bureaucracy, therefore, could not rally to any of the old platforms, although pan-Turkic velleities persisted in the CUP leadership, and notably Enver, who fought in Turkestan against the Red Army. In fact, ideological discord ruled among the intellectuals – some preferred British or American mandates, some advocated independent states of various geographical reach.[3] It was clear, however, that whatever the outcome, Anatolia, the recently discovered heartland, would constitute the principal territory within the new entity. For this reason, the Greek occupation stretching towards the interior – to the heart of the heartland – served to unify and mobilise the military-bureaucratic class. They joined the movement, led by Mustafa Kemal, which aimed at collecting the still mobilised units of the army in order to fight off the Greek invasion.

The military defeat and the flight of the CUP's ruling faction had left a political vacuum in the country. Kemal, who had been a successful general, notably in defending Gallipoli against the

British navy, gained prominence in this atmosphere as a likely leader. There is evidence that a group within the civilian bureaucracy and CUP circles regarded him as a possible commander of the Turkish nationalist forces against the Greek army; it was in fact a Palace order making him inspector general over the eastern army which provided him with a cover when he embarked on the Anatolian struggle in 1919. After a series of coups within the military hierarchy, at which time he also attempted to exercise administrative control over the provincial bureaucracy, Kemal emerged as the uncontested leader of the Turkish resistance. The resistance movement rapidly gained momentum with the participation of a good proportion of the provincial CUP organisation and the Moslem bourgeoisie. In 1920 there was a new government and parliament in Ankara, composed mostly of bureaucrats and deputies who had previously belonged to the Istanbul assembly, and also of provincial notables for whom the Greek occupation of Western Anatolia had provided the occasion for deciding on a nationalist course. It seemed, in the early days of the Ankara parliament, that the path to negotiation with the occupying powers was still open. When it became clear that the elections for the parliament in occupied Istanbul had returned a large majority of deputies who sympathised with the Ankara assembly and the Anatolian movement, the occupying administration in Istanbul started to arrest and exile the deputies. It was then that the bureaucratic class was driven to join in large numbers the newly constituted seat of power in Ankara. It soon became clear to the Entente powers that it was the new seat of government which represented the traditional governing class, rather than the secretarial staff of the now totally impotent Sultan. Accordingly, the Ankara government was recognised as the legitimate interlocutor.

In the general mood of war-weariness and isolationism, none of the Entente powers was willing to risk a new war by supporting the Greek army. France and Italy preferred instead to conclude cease-fire agreements with the Ankara government, and Britain abandoned the Greeks to their own resources. The French government in particular had started to interpret the Greek occupation of Anatolia as part of the British scheme to realise its long-standing imperialist goals in the Middle East. Public opinion and the Quai d'Orsay pressed for an early settlement with the Turkish army, especially since Mustafa Kemal was widely regarded as a reasonable proponent of a Western alliance, unlike the CUP leaders who were seen as both pro-German and, after the war, pro-Bolshevik. By mid-1921, the French press was celebrating the nationalist leader as 'the objective ally of the West' (some French officers in fact fought on the nationalist side),[4] and Italy was engaged in large-scale arms sales to the Ankara government. The new Bolshevik regime in Russia had not only concluded a separate peace treaty with the Ankara government, but supported the nationalist effort by sending financial aid and arms to the Turkish army. When the British predictably decided against active engagement, it was a matter of time before the Turkish army could drive Greek forces back to the western coast and, literally, into the Aegean.

After several battles and countless local engagements, Turkish forces occupied Izmir and succeeded in pushing the Greek army out of Anatolia in September 1922. They then continued their march towards Istanbul to claim that section of Thrace which had been designated by the nationalist movement to be part of the new Turkish political entity. The Entente called for a new peace treaty, and the resulting Lausanne convention of 1923 served to ratify the existing state of affairs. In July 1923, the present borders of Turkey (save the disputed area of Hatay-Alexandretta whose fate would be decided in 1938) had been drawn.

Through the period of its retrocession the Ottoman Empire had been carved into nation-states; its final demise arrived during the protracted war that ended in 1922. In 1925, in what remained of the old Empire, Moslems represented some 97 per cent of the population, and Turks were by far the dominant ethnic group. With secessionist threats dispelled, the new unit could function as a nation-state. The upheaval of the war period had, however, greatly altered the social structure and the balance of class forces within what remained of the Empire. The actors who were to be involved in an attempt to impose their projects on the social system had changed greatly on account of geographical and demographic dynamics. The class conflict which was described above and whose outcome, under a more orderly historical evolution, would have determined the social structure of the new political unit, had taken an unexpected turn through displacement and annihilation.

Any change in class balances, either radical or gradual, may only become comprehensible through an analysis of pre-existing conflicts. Such an analysis, however, does not by itself indicate the manner in which conflicts reach their dénouement. It was certainly the case for the Ottoman Empire that, without the impositions of the inter-state system and the ravages of the war, the conflict between the bureaucracy and the Christian bourgeoisie would not have culminated in such complete expulsion of the latter party from the field of struggle. It may be suggested that despite the expression of class conflict in ethnic and religious terms, under more peaceful conditions, the Young Turk policies would have resulted in the attainment of greater political control over the market, and in the relative ascendancy of the non-Christian elements in the bourgeoisie. To continue exploring the implications of these counterfactual premises: without World War I, the bureaucracy might have succeeded in reconstituting itself as the dominant group in an altered social structure. In other words, with economic policies aimed at achieving a degree of political control over the process of economic integration, it might have located itself in a position to appropriate and control the surplus more efficiently. All of this, however, would have occurred in a socio-economic context with increasing economic weight of the market, and a growing commercial bourgeoisie. Thus the bureaucracy would have had to accommodate, and retain its domination over, a class of traders, manufacturers and urban professionals whose ranks grew in tandem with the market. Would it have been possible to achieve a capitalist transition while the state apparatus protected its privileged status?

From the perspective of the relationship between the bureaucracy and the commercial class, the situation resembles the Japanese restoration, when an autonomous state class established tutelage over burgeoning capitalist interests. It has been argued that the specificity of the Japanese transition was due precisely to the fact that the bureaucracy was not identified directly with either the landowning or the bourgeois class. This allowed it to employ its control and mobilising ability over state resources to promote new forms of economic organisation.[5] In the Ottoman case as well, centralising bureaucrats, prompted by external threat and internal disorder, had organised to seize political power in order to strengthen the state apparatus. Like their Japanese counterparts, Ottoman bureaucrats attempted to use public resources to support and orient particular factions of the commercial class. However, while Meiji bureaucrats sanctioned and accelerated the proletarianisation of the peasantry, the Ottoman governing class tended to protect and bolster small property land ownership. In other words, whatever transition was to occur in the Ottoman Empire, it had to proceed slowly, on the edge of the dominant protected social relation between the bureaucracy and the independent peasantry.

The development of a commercial class in the Ottoman Empire had not been accompanied by significant proletarianisation. Capitalism in agriculture was non-existent (except in the form of seasonal wage labourers, most of whom also possessed their own plots), and outside agriculture, wage workers in services and manufacturing numbered no more than 200,000–250,000 at the beginning of the twentieth century (a much smaller figure if the present borders of Turkey are considered).[6] The commercial class, then, was engaged principally in the marketisation of the surplus from small commodity production, with the bureaucracy tending to resist the dissolution of peasant production in agriculture. From this restricted vantage point, the similarities between the Ottoman case and the French transition to capitalism may be worth exploring. In France the central authority resisted – more or less strongly – the expropriation of the peasantry, and attempted to perpetuate the dominance of small property. When the central authority was strong, its success in protecting peasant proprietorship was palpable: thus, except in a few isolated geographical areas, enclosures of land accompanied by proletarianisation of the peasantry did not occur. In France too, therefore, capitalist relations of production developed outside the basic agrarian structure, while the commercial class principally handled the surplus of small commodity production.[7] It was the French Revolution which broke the continuity of the state apparatus and eventually allowed for the direct political representation of the capitalist class. While consolidating the status of the peasantry, the Revolution replaced the bureaucracy of the old regime with state functionaries more or less given to serving capitalist interests.

Without a revolutionary break the Young Turk attempt at social change from above could only represent continuity in the state's role. Thus the political apparatus would not be totally responsive to capitalist needs until the bureaucracy was conquered from within by the interests it sought to nurture and keep under its tutelage. On the other hand, the political support given to the independent peasantry would prevent a rapid growth of the capitalist sector, sanctioning instead a mediated development of and a complicated articulation with capitalism. It must be remarked that an alternative scenario to what the Young Turks sought to achieve would have been a 'middle class' rebellion – akin to the Latin American trajectories. This possibility was excluded, however, for two reasons. First, the 'middle class' in Latin America often included a section of the landed oligarchy who had themselves diversified into industrial production. The rebellion, therefore, had an aspect of intra-class struggle, where the political authority was not totally opposed to the new contestation. In the Ottoman case, however, the bureaucracy derived its *raison d'être* from the petty producers, the stratum whose existence would be most threatened under capitalist development. Therefore it would not regard an unfettered capitalist project favourably, and its opposition would reduce the chances of success of the 'middle class'. Secondly, and more importantly, the commercial classes, like the bureaucracy, suffered the same ideological dislocation of their class conflict, in seeing their principal problem in religious and ethnic terms. For this reason the Christian bourgeoisie attempted to stage its struggle in the inter-state theatre, not principally through social demands designed to favour its access to political authority, but through demands for ethnic and religious autonomy. From this point of view, the Christian commercial bourgeoisie never entertained the idea of becoming a class in itself through exercising influence over the state. Especially during the later period, rather than looking at the Porte as a political authority to be swayed in the direction of its economic interests, it rejected the Ottoman state as a legitimate field to be conquered and utilised. Christian merchants, by opposing the legitimacy of the Ottoman state and advocating its dismantling, also relinquished the possibility of a bid towards political contestation and primacy through a 'middle class' revolution. More than any other single factor, this reluctance and inability on the part of the minority bourgeoisie to claim political power decided the subsequent development of the state and ruling classes in Turkey.

We may conclude that the peculiar status of the bureaucracy as a ruling class, which implied the absence of a landowning commercial oligarchy, prevented Ottoman social development from embarking upon any of the more familiar trajectories. In addition, the manifestation of the social problem (the conflict between class projects) in exclusively ethnic and religious terms, prevented both the bureaucracy and the comprador bourgeoisie from articulating their demands, especially regarding the role of the state, in the vocabulary of system transformation. Had it not been for the war, and the elimination of the Christian bourgeoisie, the most likely outcome would have been growing accommodation between the respective social projects of the two parties, culminating in a precocious neo-mercantilism. It must not be forgotten, however, that the commercial class would have brought into this equation not only its considerable quantitative strength, but also its recently acquired desire for cultural emulation of the European bourgeoisie. The vantage point of Republican Turkey tends to distort the historical importance of this development and leads to an underestimation of the level of (bourgeois) cultural development – albeit geographically specific – achieved during the period before the war. In fact, the modernisation attempts of the Republican period period may be understood in this context, as bids to substitute a nationalist ideology for the cultural germination which had taken place in Anatolian towns prior to the expulsion of the Christian bourgeoisie. We will now leave the realm of the counterfactual, in order to describe the balance of classes at the birth of Republican Turkey.

It has been remarked that the bourgeoisie could to a large extent be identified with non-Moslem merchants, bankers and middlemen. This is not to say that minority populations were all urban, or all in business. A large majority of the Armenians in the Empire lived in Eastern Anatolia, in conditions similar to the Moslem peasantry. There were also Greek communities in the interior and on the northern coast of Anatolia, which continued to practise traditional agriculture. The Greek agricultural population on the Aegean coast were predominantly producers for export markets. A majority of the urban wage-earning class were also Greek. Nonetheless, during the latter half of the nineteenth century, in all the important cities, starting with Istanbul, Salonika and Izmir, non-Moslem populations constituted the overwhelming majority of the commercial bourgeoisie. Even in the most 'traditional' towns of the interior such as Bursa, Konya, Kayseri, Sivas, and Ankara, not to speak of eastern cities with clear Armenian dominance, the resurgence of mercantile activity had meant the capturing of economically prominent positions by minority populations.[8] Ottoman population statistics, although geographically complete in coverage, have been challenged by contemporaries and historians alike, especially when it was thought that the dismantling of the Empire would lead to the establishment of separatist states based on ethnic affiliation. Nevertheless, it now seems that the official figures, even if not exact, are usable, particularly since they derive from a series of consistent censuses conducted during the second half of the nineteenth century and before World War I.[9] According to the census of 1906, the Ottoman population within the border of present-day Turkey was around 15 million. Approximately 10% of this population were Greeks, 7% Armenian and 1% Jewish. Moslems counted over 80%. Between 1914 and 1924 the composition of this population changed dramatically; according to the 1927 census the total population was 13.6 million, of which non-Moslems accounted for 2.6 per cent. There were 120,000 Greek speakers and 65,000 Armenian speakers. Part of the change in the figures was due to the ravages of the war. For instance, it has been estimated that 18 per cent of the Moslem population were killed between 1914 and 1922.[10] Of the Armenian population, a proportion perished as a result of expulsion or death in 1915, and another part migrated or was forced to migrate, to Syria, Russian Armenia and other countries. The Greek population suffered less in terms of actual deaths: according to the 1928 census in Greece, there were close to 1.2 million refugees from Turkey, and Greeks had also migrated to other parts of the world.[11] Thus slightly over one-quarter of the 1913 population of Turkey were no longer there in 1925: compared with the 18 per cent of the Moslem Turks who perished, only one-sixth of the non-Moslem population remained. To express it differently, before the war, one out of every five persons living in present-day Turkey was non-Moslem, after the war, only one out of forty persons was non-Moslem.

What this drastic development indicates is that during the war years Turkey lost most of its commercial class, such that when the Republic was formed, the bureaucracy found itself unchallenged. Whatever remained of the bourgeoisie was too weak to constitute a class with an autonomous stance against the bureaucracy. Furthermore, the surviving commercial class of pre-CUP vintage was now concentrated – to a greater degree than before – in the two cities of Istanbul and Izmir, now pale reflections of their former glory. The provincial cities, where economic change and cultural awakening had begun to occur only at the end of the nineteenth century, lost most of this momentum and reverted to their sleepy incarnations as administrative centres. The impact of the expulsion and annihilation of the provincial commercial classes served to destroy all the cultural emoluments that the bourgeoisie had come to desire, create and support. The beginnings of a civil society were thus suffocated before their fruition, and once again the rule of the state threatened to become compact and supreme. Reflecting this development were population trends in urban areas. Istanbul, for instance, had dropped from a population of one million to 700,000, and Aydın vilayet, which included Izmir and contained a population about 30 per cent Greek prior to the war, declined from 1.6 million to 1.3 million.[12] It has been estimated that at the end of the nineteenth century urban dwellers constituted 25% of the total population – probably higher immediately before the war.[13] In the 1927 census this figure had dropped to 18 per cent. Within this general ruralisation, all the cities, and primarily the commercially important areas, lost some of their population; the exception that proves the rule is Ankara, the new capital and a boom town, whose prosperity was due entirely to its designation as the new seat of the bureaucracy.

These population trends and their implications for the social structure would have been all the more adverse had it not been the case that Anatolia also received Turkish-speaking Moslem immigrants. Most of these immigrants came from former Ottoman territories now captured by Russia; an estimated half-million persons of Crimean origin had arrived in Anatolia during and after the Crimean War. Again in the 1877–78 war another group of one million migrated.[14] Another half million migrants from the north were settled in what is now Turkey between 1880 and 1923; and arrivals continued during the 1920s.[15] In addition more than one half-million Moslems had arrived during the Balkan wars and the exchange of populations with Greece. Aside from contributing to the Moslemisation of Anatolia, these migrations also served to alleviate the economic loss suffered through the disappearance of the majority of the commercial class. The immigrants from Russia in particular, although overwhelmingly of peasant stock, contained an important number of Moslem commercial groups in their ranks. These bourgeois families, with sons educated at Russian and European universities, provided intellectual leadership in most of the political movements of the dying Empire. As might be expected, owing to their newly attained status, they were more than willing to support nationalist attempts and desirous of replacing the non-Moslem bourgeoisie. Because of this tendency, most of this group identified strongly with the political class carrying the nationalist banner, and failed to constitute a rival political estate. Nevertheless, during the 1920s, in league with more autochthonous candidates, they were ready to fill the positions left empty by a departed commercial class.

The allegiance of Moslem merchants and landlords to the cause gave the nationalist mobilisation a clear social base, defined by opposition to the expelled and departing bourgeoisie. For the bureaucratic class it was a question of protecting its patrimony and possibly fulfilling the aims of its late nineteenth century reformism. The Moslem merchants and businessmen sought to defend acquired privileges and wanted to prolong the CUP period when political patronage had effectively favoured them, in order to capture the lucrative positions prepared and abandoned by Christian minorities. In addition, a substantial transfer of wealth had taken place during Armenian deportations and the Greek war. In 1915, Armenians had been allowed to take with them only their movable property, while they were forced to sell – no doubt at low prices – their urban holdings. As to the population deported from the villages, their more fertile lands were immediately seized by Turkish landlords and Kurdish tribes. The Greek population sent during the war to the interior from the west coast and from the region around Trabzon on the Black Sea, and those who chose to migrate to Greece before the end of the war, must have also left their land behind, or sold it at a fraction of its value.[16] It might be conjectured that this war-time transfer of wealth to the Moslem rich constituted a strong impetus to support the nationalist cause. In fact the amount of land and wealth transferred after the defeat of the Greek army (with one million prosperous farmers and city dwellers leaving) must have been at least as much as the war-time transfer, thus fulfilling the more material aspects of what could be expected of a nationalist victory.

The locally based support for nationalist mobilisation in Anatolia had been organised in 'defence of rights' associations, established by Moslem businessmen in cities under occupation. The military-based movement led by Kemal had taken over the local strength of these associations in ensuring financial and personnel support. After the end of the Greek war, the first issue to be negotiated in Lausanne was the status of the remaining Greek population. According to the provisions of the compulsory exchange of populations, the property left behind by emigrants would be considered nationalised and used to compensate the refugees.[17] A crude calculation, which is certainly an underestimate, suggests that the departure of the Greeks implied the transfer to Moslem landlords of close to one-fifth of the best land in Western Anatolia. In cities, the abandoned property and wealth, not to speak of the business positions thus made available, were surely of even greater value. In this sense, then, the nationalist option had become immediately remunerative, for often it was a political decision as to who would benefit from the division of war spoils. It is not clear how the nationalised property was divided, although it does seem that arbitrary local schemes were employed to favour demobilised soldiers and war widows. An important amount of land was distributed to new arrivals from Russia and Greece; but especially in the urban areas, the allocation mechanism was openly political. Those burghers who rallied early to the nationalist cause (as mentioned earlier, these were usually the same individuals that had benefited from CUP policies of nationalisation) were the prime beneficiaries. This was the first instance of a symbiotic relationship between the new state and the native bourgeoisie.

Having established the conditions within which the nationalist struggle was conducted, it would seem that the years immediately succeeding its accession to political power would exhibit the bureaucracy in unrivalled supremacy over the social structure. Yet for a variety of organisational and institutional reasons, the political class in power established an authoritarian regime without a clear tutelage over the native commercial class. For half a decade, this latter group was allowed to enrich itself until the conjuncture of several developments, including the world economic crisis, brought the bureaucracy back to its position of the 1930s, that is, of full suzerainty. Nonetheless, during the 1920s, the growing commercial class did not enter any political or cultural conflict with state functionaries: it simply expressed its gratitude, and hesitantly put forth demands that would bring immediate pecuniary returns.[18] Nor did it continue with the cultural traditions of enlightenment which had begun flourishing in the pre-war period. In other words, it exchanged the right to establish (even the faint traces of) a civil society for (what seemed to be) the privilege to make money.

Even when political alternatives existed to accommodate the putative demands of a bourgeoisie in formation, it chose the safer alternative which it found in the faction in power. Although this timidity may be ascribed to the bourgeoisie's numerical weakness and to its inability to attain a critical mass, it also brings to mind the subservience which characterised Ottoman merchants in relation to the Palace. As was already argued, this atavistic equation had found novel expression in CUP policies aiming to create an indigenous bourgeoisie. In other words, 1920s merchants had only recently been brought to age under the protection of the political authority. Despite their rapid maturation, they were far from opting for autonomous power, being in full knowledge of the need for continued political protection. During the 1920s then, the bourgeoisie did not constitute an autonomous political force, and the economy did not emerge as an autonomous sphere with its own institutionalised rules of conduct. The bureaucracy, meanwhile, concentrated on 'superstructural' reformism, attacking the institutions of social life and the traditional world of popular classes. In analysing the implicit political philosophy behind the cultural reformism of the 1920s, we shall also investigate the factors that led to the bureaucracy's temporary inability to dominate the economy, despite its unchallenged status.

Although the war against the occupation armies was won in 1922, and the Republic established in 1923, territorial integrity was by no means assured. The most important challenge to the Ankara government came between 1924 and 1925 with what is known in Turkish historiography as the Kurdish rebellion. This was a full-scale insurrection with religious and separatist overtones, which aimed at challenging the tribal oligarchy and the central authority which was in implicit alliance with it. Although there were no clear territorial demands associated with the rebellion, it did serve as a potent reminder that, despite the Armenian deportation and the Greek exchange, the new country still had not attained the degree of national homogeneity desired by the bureaucracy. This rebellion put the government back on a war footing, with independence courts enjoying extraordinary powers to repress Kurdish demands in the east, and using them with impunity. A new Law for the Maintenance of Order provided the government with an institutional framework for authoritarian rule, at the same time eliminating potential channels of opposition. After 1925, with the exception of a brief period in 1930, these channels were to remain closed during two decades of single-party rule.[19] This closure also meant that even if the bourgeoisie wanted to organise autonomously, a challenge to the regime may not have been possible. A measure of the impact of the Law for the Maintenance of Order was the decline in the circulation of daily newspapers. In 1925 there was a total circulation of 120,000 whereas in 1926, after the introduction of strict censorship, the figure had declined to just below 50,000.[20]

At the same time the government was proclaiming a series of reforms at a startling pace, with the attendant consequences. There was substantial opposition which, although only rarely becoming active, served to justify constant vigilance on the part of the bureaucracy. For instance, seventy people were hanged because of their opposition to the 'hat laws' which banned traditional head-dress.[21] This vigilance also reflected a division within the bureaucratic class which clearly originated in the ideological and personal rivalries of the CUP period. Mustafa Kemal, although close to its leadership and a member of the committee, had not been part of the ruling faction within the CUP. During most of the war he had been absent from Istanbul in active military duty on various fronts, which fact had protected him from being arrested by the British under the occupation. When the nationalist struggle began there were a number of Ottoman generals of equal standing leading the forces in Anatolia. Gradually, however, Mustafa Kemal succeeded in dominating the allegiance of the existing networks of resistance with his greater organisational ability, perhaps partly due to the covert support by underground remnants of the CUP. Kemal also benefited from the existence of a tightly-knit group of close associates foremost among whom was Ismet (Inonu) which constituted a veritable junta. The divisions and personal rivalries within the nationalist leadership were kept at bay until the end of the Greek war. Yet when the Republic was established, and the nationalist movement had to reconstitute itself as an administrative cadre, it became more and more difficult to maintain both collaboration with former CUP leaders and the loose alliance with other nationalist generals, each of whom commanded his own forces and had his own allegiance within the military. After 1924, the Kemalist party behaved in an increasingly exclusionary fashion, first in an attempt to isolate and eradicate the CUP veterans, then in forcing Kemal's potential rivals into passive positions. This was achieved in two stages: in 1924 an opposition political party was organised within the parliament which aimed to check and limit Kemal's personal power and his clear tendency towards one-man rule. This (Progressive Republican) party wanted separation of powers, greater control over the government by the assembly, and an end to the rather random judiciary as represented by the independence courts. The Kemalist faction found an opportunity to close this party during the Kurdish rebellion, and brought to trial many of its high-ranking members, former heroes of the nationalist movement. In 1926 an attempt on Kemal's life provided the occasion to concoct a conspiracy and to implicate the CUP members who were still considered to pose a threat to the ruling faction.[22] Their trial was successful in eradicating this rival heritage, for although some of the accused were acquitted (and some notable CUP figures were hanged) they left the country and political life until after Kemal's death. Again in 1926 another group of potential rivals were exiled and could not return to the country unless they received personal forgiveness.[23] It was not until 1929 that the Kemalist faction felt sufficiently entrenched to suspend the Law for the Maintenance of Order which had allowed such repression.

By this date the process of forming a single-party political regime had been largely completed. There was an assembly to which deputies were appointed through a mechanism euphemistically known as elections, but an electorate was lacking. A system of two-degree elections amounted to the designation of a group of men (women did not have the vote) who then ratified the names sent to them from Ankara. Deputies found themselves representing unlikely reaches of Anatolia which they had never seen. Despite this degree of control (or rather, because of it) there was not much need for the deputies to function in any legislative capacity, since the government felt neither accountable to the parliament, nor seemed to be in need of legislative initiative. Deputies worked very short hours, and voting on each law took a matter of minutes.[24] Not only had the more visible rival factions been eliminated within the bureaucratic class, but also all mechanisms of control or opposition. Although the rank and file of the administrative apparatus were inherited directly from the imperial bureaucracy of the Porte, the government which enjoyed unchallenged power came to represent one particular faction within the bureaucratic class. The evolution of this intra-class struggle was perhaps the most important factor determining the relative inactivity of the bureaucracy in controlling the new commercial classes.

The course of the struggle within the bureaucratic class had a substantial impact on reformist zeal, both directly and indirectly, and was one of the determinants of the degree to which various components of this reformism were upheld to the detriment of 'bourgeois' freedoms. In this sense it was the rift within the old bureaucratic class which led to the search for a new mode of legitimation of the ruling group. With each reform, the past consensus around the notion of 'saving the state' became less solid: the state had now been saved, and its perpetuation was no longer uncertain. Differences thus rose to the surface and conflicts became apparent, especially as to the manner and pace of importing Western forms. There could not have been much debate over the absolute desirability of most of these reforms: the urban population, especially the bourgeoisie, had had Westernised life styles for at least half a century. Nor was it the case that the public discussion of such reforms would come as a total surprise, because they had all received attention and discussion during the Young Turk period. Nonetheless, the earlier reformism of Ottoman bureaucrats had been gradual and orderly, although the purport of the reforms during the nineteenth century had been at least as great as in the Kemalist period. In the fields of legal and administrative modernisation, the 1838–1876 period had achieved as much as the Republican period, and Abdülhamit's reign, despite the Sultan's despotism, had done much to strengthen the apparatuses of a centralised state.[25] The 1908 Constitution had done more for parliamentary democracy than the entire Republican period between 1925 and 1945.[26] What distinguished Kemalist reformism from its precedents was the concentrated effort to define a political system free of religious and dynastic legitimation. By abolishing both the sultanate and the caliphate, the Republic constituted itself on a secular-nationalist basis. This is not to suggest that the Ottoman system prior to its demise had exhibited anything approaching a successful legitimating ideology. The dynasty was weakened to the verge of perishing altogether after 1909, and any religious legitimacy invested in the status of the caliph was destroyed by the 'Arab betrayal'. It may be argued that the Empire could not adapt itself to being stripped of its multi-ethnicity. The dynasty had never presented itself as national, or thought of itself as such and therefore could rely only on religion in its ideological guardianship. Yet the status of the

Sultan and the Palace within the religious order was a curious one, the religious establishment becoming increasingly political and a-dynastic during the nineteenth century. It cannot be argued that secularism necessarily accompanied the abolition of the sultanate. Neither was it the case that the religious establishment as a whole had opposed the idea of reformism. The Ottoman *ulema* were part of the bureaucratic class as we have defined it, and during the latter half of the nineteenth century, the higher *ulema* had been instrumental in providing ideological justification for the reforms. During the CUP period these high religious officials had become active supporters of the constitutional movement and, according to some witnesses, had even joined the same masonic lodges as the CUP leaders.

It was mentioned above that Abdülhamit's restorationism had found wide support among the common people; later, at the beginning of CUP rule, an important rebellion had expressed discontent with the new constitutional regime in exclusively religious terms.[27] At that time, as was also to be the case later during the Republic, the rallying call was the presumed loss of the *şeriat* – the Islamic legal code. Now it is obvious that what was meant by that *mot d'ordre* was not the (perfectly correct) suggestion that the old code was being replaced by a new one, but rather that the reforms were infringing upon the established order, and, more importantly, on the life-world of the groups rebelling. Islam emerged as the binding principle of that life-world, that sphere of existence which had not been penetrated by the political society. Islam became a banner of defence against the political centre whose guiding principle was believed to be militant reformism. Accordingly, the type of Islamic faith and organisation employed under this banner was not of the orthodox official variety: it was a version easily articulated with local traditions, pagan cults, accounts of the exploits of legendary heroes and mystical sects. A Byzantine country priest would have felt at home with this popular concoction.[28]

In contrast to popular Islam, which constituted an essential vocabulary in the life-world of the masses, the orthodox version, that of the religious establishment, had never been organised in an institution independent of the state. As well as the caliphate being invested in the person of the Sultan, the head of the religious establishment, the Şeyh-ul-Islam, was an appointed functionary and a member of the cabinet until 1916. The CUP had acted to divorce the political establishment from its religious legitimation by secularising all Islamic courts, schools and foundations.[29] The Kemalists followed this by abolishing the caliphate and adopting a state policy of strict laicism; they had to confront a social reaction, similar to what the CUP had faced earlier. Combined with the Kemalist faction's sectarian zeal, this popular reaction convinced a group within the political class to distance itself openly from the administration. Responding to the malaise among the peasantry, and more importantly among the urban petty bourgeoisie, this group challenged the Jacobinism of the Republican government. It would be wrong to label this current within the political class as restorationist: it was primarily anxious about the unmistakable drift toward the elimination of opposition, and it sought to anchor its own current within what it identified as the feelings of the masses. Otherwise, it lacked any coherent ideological platform.

What the successive waves of secularisation achieved was to reconstitute the Ottoman/Turkish state along European precepts. Nineteenth century reformers, Young Turks, and Republicans clearly saw that a state which would claim its place in the concert of nations could not be based on religious rules and legitimation. The teaching of the French Revolution, that sovereignty is based in the nation, was well digested by Ottoman bureaucrats and they believed (perhaps to an exaggerated extent) that European statesmen judged any candidacy to the imagined league of nations with those nineteenth century criteria such as national sovereignty, positivism, secularism, and faith in progress. At home, however, the political class faced a more severe test. The militant secularism of the state amounted to a repudiation of what used to be its principal ideological apparatus. The consequence of this repudiation was a separation between the state and society, for which Islam continued to be the popular cohesive principle.[30] The bureaucracy was forced to cope with this separation not only because it would have liked to legitimate itself in the eyes of the people, but also because it sought to pre-empt uncontrolled ideologies from filling the vacuum created by the divorce of the ruling and popular belief systems. On the other hand, with the rejection of orthodoxy as a pillar of state authority, Islam in the society had a chance to coalesce around an increasingly unitary basis.

It may therefore be argued that the reformist zeal of the bureaucracy became uniquely instrumental in coalescing the various elements of popular culture into an 'Islamic reaction'.

In response, the ruling faction was concerned not only with eradicating all rival principles of association, but also sought to achieve a formal appearance of uniformity, presumably reflecting the individual bereft of any local affiliation. The bureaucracy sought to delocalise and departicularise, exhibiting the same centrist attitude which had characterised nineteenth century reformism. The implicit ideology to which all the reforms referred was nationalism. Now that a state had been established, the population living in it had to be forged into a nation. Individuals were supposed to find meaning in their belonging to the national unit, and alternative affiliations, sub- or supra-national, were regarded with suspicion. Religion was doubly suspect, because it was the legitimating principle of the old Empire, as well as the vocabulary most commonly available to the opponents of the new legitimating principle. Nationalism was a modernising ideology, specifically concocted for purposes of 'late-comer' states in nineteenth century Europe. World War I and the League of Nations had ratified it as *the* state-building ideology for the many political units carved out of the Austro-Hungarian and Ottoman Empires. The attempts of the Turkish nationalist regime were in the direction of reforming the population to prepare them for the new model state. This preparation involved precisely the creation of individuals who only submitted to universal associative principles.

Nationalism also implied an anti-liberal economic philosophy, as it did in the original German and Italian versions. In both examples, the creation of a national economy had been the primary goal of the bourgeoisie who saw in liberalism a threat to their survival and world-wide expansion. In the nationalism of later architects of nation-states, anti-liberalism lacked support in the person of a developed national bourgeoisie. For Turkey this absence was even more pronounced, and the bureaucracy was therefore led to search for a concrete form in which the anti-liberal prerogative would be implemented. The CUP experience provided a clue but it had been both too haphazard and overly dependent on war conditions. Only towards the end of the 1920s, with the contemporaneous Italian and Soviet examples in view, did Turkish Republicans begin to envisage new state–society linkages other than liberalism, which would both safeguard the status of the bureaucratic mechanism and achieve the desired national development. During the 1920s, however, such alternatives were not yet visible, and their absence became a factor exacerbating the

intra-class conflict within the bureaucracy. As a result, the
1920s witnessed a return to the characteristic authoritarian
equation: a politically strengthened centre combating rival
principles of social cohesion, while allowing the development of
the market and its implicit organisation.

V

State and Capital

The preceding chapter gave an overview of the bureaucratic class and the difficulties it confronted during the 1920s. Now I wish to consider the new commercial groups constituting themselves, in the aftermath of the war, and their relation to the economy. It was argued above that, during the five years following the formation of the Republic, the functionaries were incapable of significantly altering, or transforming, the principal structures of the economy. In other words, the economic networks created during the pre-war boom continued to function, except that most of the commercial bourgeoisie who had motivated the networks were now absent from the scene. It is surprising in fact how much continuity in economic flows there was, despite this removal.

The Turkish economy emerged devastated from the war, especially with regard to the labour force. The agricultural labour force decreased by more than 20 per cent, although we might argue that the decline in the number of mainly subsistence peasants was not of great consequence to the commercial classes. In fact most of the conscripted men killed in the war probably came from the interior and eastern parts of Anatolia – areas of predominantly subsistence agriculture.[1] During the 1914–18 period, the Aydın vilayet, comprising Izmir and the fertile valleys of the Aegean, had been spared the ravages of war, except for the military conscription of Moslem and Greek males alike. Nonetheless, commercial agriculture continued relatively undisturbed partly because of the cushioning influence of a governor of known Entente sympathies who ran the

91

province as a virtual fiefdom. During the Greek invasion (1919–22), however, and the subsequent Turkish-Greek war, there was widespread destruction. Apart from those killed in the war, at least half a million Greeks, engaged to various degrees in commercial agriculture, were forced out of the Aegean countryside. Then the Greek army, in flight from the Republican forces, destroyed and burned everything it could, including entire towns.[2] Gutted structures, which used to serve as warehouses or processing plants for raisins or olives, can still be seen in the countryside. The great fire of Izmir, following the Turkish capture of the city, destroyed the commercial infrastructure of Western Anatolia's principal export outlet.

The Black Sea coastal strip – a region predominantly given over to export agriculture of tobacco and hazelnuts – also suffered economically, although the war did not cause active destruction. During the nationalistic struggle and later in the exchange of populations, close to 200,000 Greeks, mostly merchants and commercial farmers, left the area. In Çukurova, the third most important region of commercial agriculture after Western Anatolia and the Black Sea coast, Armenian farmers performed an important role prior to the war and their fortunes continued to grow until 1915. When Armenians who had fled to Syria during the war came back to the region under French protection in 1920, they faced stiff resistance from the local militia.[3] By that date, farms and businesses had already been transferred to Turkish landowners, merchants and exporters.

Since export-oriented commercial agriculture was disproportionately undertaken by Greek farmers, the departure or exchange of 1.2 million Greeks signified substantial economic loss, with a consequent impact on the potential of commercial activity. The overall decline in the number of commercial farmers was compensated to considerable degree by the inflow of immigrants from Greece[4] and from Russia. There are no figures available for the Russian *émigrés* but 90 per cent of the immigrants from Greece were skilled farmers, primarily tobacco growers.[5] Although there was no systematic effort to match previous specialisations with the new settlement areas, these migrants must have contributed to the quick recovery of pre-war levels of output.

The main export crops of Ottoman Turkey had been figs, raisins and tobacco from the Aegean, tobacco and hazelnuts from the Black Sea, and cotton from the Aegean and Çukurova. Of

these crops only figs and raisins lost their relative importance
during the 1920s; levels of output in cotton, tobacco, and
hazelnuts were quickly recovered between 1925 and 1927.[6] In
the case of figs and raisins, departing Greeks had transferred
both the cultivation and the commercial organisation (credit
and sales) of these crops to Greece. Nevertheless, even in these
two crops, 1920s export performances were not far from pre-
war levels. The surprising fact is that despite the loss of the
labour force, and the connections and organisational ability of
the merchant class, commercial agriculture retained at least
some of its importance. There are two complementary developments during the 1920s which explain this performance.

It would be misleading to discuss commercial production in
agriculture as if it could be conducted simply through a
combination of technical inputs. The crucial element in commercial agriculture carried out by independent producers had
always been, and continued to be during the 1920s, the
organisation of markets and credit. In other words, the various
ranks of the 'commercial class' were integral elements of
market-oriented production. There were two developments
which compensated for the removal of the Christian elements in
this commercial class: one, a greater involvement of foreign
capital, and, two, the rapid coming-of-age of the Moslem
commercial class.

The bourgeoisie in the Ottoman Empire, despite its structural location as intermediary between foreign capital and
domestic production, still constituted a local bourgeoisie, well
placed to capture the lucrative fields of enterprise. As such, it
was an obstacle to greater involvement of foreign capital in the
local economy. A. Emmanuel has argued that white settlers and
foreign capital were historical rivals, since they were armed
with competing developmental projects.[7] A similar argument
can be made concerning the local merchant bourgeoisie, who
contain the potential for independent development and therefore represent a historical alternative to imperialism with
foreign capital. The expulsion of the Christian bourgeoisie
invited greater involvement of foreign capital in the Turkish
economy. Through trading ventures, merchant houses, banks,
and direct participation in the distribution of credit, foreign
capital in the 1920s became immediately instrumental in
encouraging and organising export-oriented agriculture. Foreign merchants had already monopolised the final stage in
export trade; during the 1920s they made efforts to substitute

other mechanisms for the intermediaries who traditionally had handled the connection between the producer and the foreign purchaser. With the active assistance of banks, foreign merchants began to contract directly with producers, using the producers' growing indebtedness to effect more complete subordination.[8] This method seems to have been successful, particularly in the case of tobacco and cotton production. Another instance of foreign capital replacing the Christian bourgeoisie was in the growth of banking activities, with credit oriented to external trade constituting the principal element of this expansion. Between two-thirds and three-quarters of all credits were extended by foreign banks who had been spurred on by competition with newly formed Turkish banks. Foreign capital was also prominent in new manufacturing firms. Of the sum invested in manufacturing corporations between 1923 and 1929, foreign capital accounted for exactly twice the contribution of Turkish capital.[9] In addition, certain foreign firms obtained monopoly rights to import and sell particular goods in the domestic market through concessions given by the government. All this activity pointed to a greater and substantively different involvement of foreign capital in the economy, as compared to the Ottoman period which was characterised by a much stronger local bourgeoisie.

This extensive involvement of foreign capital, however, did not prevent the rapid development of a Moslem commercial class. Although subordinate to Christians, Moslem merchants and bankers had found new impetus through the political patronage of the Young Turk period. Especially during the war, and with the abrogation of capitulations, the CUP government's attempts at nourishing a Moslem bourgeoisie had met with relative success. This initial impetus must have resulted in a sufficient accumulation of organisational ability such that, when the Greeks and Armenians left the stage, Moslems could perform most of the roles. From the point of view of material accumulation, the episodes of the Armenian deportations, the Greek flight and the population exchange had been doubly important: not only did positions thus become vacant, but the physical property that was left behind was made available and seized by a Moslem bourgeoisie-in-formation. Thus the original accumulation of the previous period (1914–23) served to provide greater profit and expansion during the early years of the Republic.

Within the accommodation reached with the bureaucracy,

the issues dominating the period were those concerning the appropriation of positions and privileges by the citizens of the new Republic. Since there were still third-party resources to be expropriated, the relationship between the bureaucracy and the Moslem commercial class could continue without engendering a conflict over distribution. On account of their own internal fracture and the reformist task they had assumed, the bureaucrats were in no position to direct and orient this process of 'nationalisation'. On the other hand, they did welcome, and respond positively to, various demands by the new merchants. Such a welcoming stance towards the 'national' bourgeoisie did not, however, extend to assuming a negative attitude towards foreign capital. As has been described, the status and weight of foreign capital increased during the 1920s, and various trading concessions were offered to foreign concerns.[10] The principal organisation of Turkish merchants – the Istanbul Chamber of Commerce – did not insist on the exclusion of foreign capital. With the exception of a few fields (most notably coastal shipping which was still dominated by Greek ship-owners) they did not ask for government-enforced nationalisation. On the whole Turkish merchants already enjoyed greater opportunity than they could cope with, and were content to remain on the receiving end of a division of labour organised by and favouring foreign capital. Insofar as they could to some degree replace the departed Christians as intermediaries, they were happy to accumulate; since this accumulation had not yet reached a critical minimum requiring more active political intervention, they were content with the bureaucracy's constrained stand.

If the nascent bourgeoisie of the 1920s cherished any hopes of participating in political power, these were shattered brusquely by the crisis. Starting in 1929, the commercial sector suffered a drastic downturn in its fortunes, an outcome already adumbrated on various occasions since 1926. The health of the economy had depended exclusively on the flow of traded goods and the procurement of funds for this flow. In 1926, 1928, and again in 1929, agricultural crises and short-term credit shortages highlighted this dependence and the fragility of the system.[11] The Great Depression starting in 1929 was an affair of much more permanent impact and greater penetration. The prices of Turkey's exports suffered an abrupt downturn, and merchants' credit, which alimented commercial production in agriculture and covered short-term balance of payments deficits, ceased to

arrive. The result was an exchange crisis, a fall in the value of
the Turkish lira, which increased the importing merchants' debt
burden, and widespread bankruptcies in the commercial sector.
In 1930, less than a year after the 1929 harvest, more than one
thousand firms in Istanbul and Izmir declared bankruptcy, and
some peasants had to sell all their belongings to fulfil their debt
and tax obligations, which were fixed in money terms.[12] Within
this atmosphere of economic confusion, the weakness of the
bourgeoisie was highlighted: it became evident that it had
depended excessively on foreign markets to an extent that the
material base of its activity could disappear at a moment's
notice. It was also apparent that its relationship with the
political authority had served only to further its cause within
this precarious framework. There was no possibility of utilising
the existing links towards a structural transformation: for that,
the political authority needed at its disposal a different set of
instruments and policies.

By 1929, the bureaucratic faction in power had emerged
victorious from the intra-class struggle, and seemingly felt
sufficiently in control to suspend the notorious Law for the
Maintenance of Order. Reformism had subsided with potential
and actual rivals for the leadership dead or exiled. It seemed
that the forthcoming task of the bureaucracy was to prepare the
ground for transforming the economic system such that its own
position within it would conform to that envisaged in the Young
Turk project. In addition to the political preoccupations that
beset state functionaries during the 1920s, there had been an
important obstacle inhibiting the implementation of economic
policy: there was a clause in the 1923 Lausanne treaty according
to which Turkey had to live under the Ottoman trade regime
unil 1929. This clause, by itself, did not preclude protectionism,
because the government could have bypassed the restriction by
instituting state monopolies over particular commodities when
it wished to protect domestic industry.[13] Nevertheless, a new
trade regime with specific duties was instituted at the end of
1929, and the coincidence with the crisis allowed the government to embark on a restrictive trade policy. It was fortuitous
that political developments and the economic cycle were
mutually reinforcing, thus allowing the bureaucracy to concentrate on economic matters. The years 1930 and 1931 were
periods of feverish economic innovation; they also became
years of major transformation in the political regime. On the
one hand, after years of internecine strife, the bureaucracy had

once again found the wherewithal to instal itself in the class equation – this it did through changing the dimensions of state administration – while on the other hand the crisis and the difficulties faced by the commercial bourgeoisie invited the formulation of a new set of economic policies. It was the intersection of these two developments which determined the character of Turkey's political economy in the 1930s. A new state form (the range of state functions and the nature of the relationship between the political power and the economy), together with the set of measures originally formulated to combat the crisis, resulted in a regime which represented the culmination of bureaucratic reformism. In its basic dimensions, this regime, and consequently the bureaucracy-bourgeoisie balance, remained in force until the end of World War II.

The policy measures which initially responded to the disruption of economic life followed the currency crisis of 1929, and sought to minimise the permeability and the external dependence of the internal market. With the onset of the crisis it became apparent that the political authority did not have at its disposal the administrative apparatus and the instruments of control required to combat the situation at hand. Most importantly, from the point of view of the short-term confusion experienced during the fall of the Turkish lira, there was no monetary authority equipped either to control foreign exchange or to withdraw and issue the local currency in an attempt at some sort of stabilisation. During the Ottoman period, the French-British-owned Ottoman Bank had enjoyed the monopoly of issuing currency, and despite the war-time usurpation of this privilege by the CUP government, the charter of the 'Imperial' bank had been renewed in 1925. The Ottoman Bank was still the largest bank in Turkey, but in 1930 the government felt sufficiently independent to institute a national bank, the Central Bank, to assume the functions of controlling and concentrating transactions in foreign exchange.[14] A first attempt had already been made during the previous year, with an interbank consortium in which the government controlled only a minority share. Both the 1929 consortium and the Central Bank, which began its proper functioning in 1930, were conceived primarily as instruments of control over transactions in foreign currency, rather than as implementing substantive economic policy. The instinctive bureaucratic response to economic difficulties had been to step up prohibitions and

restrictions and to barricade the internal economy. A culprit
had already been identified in the merchant who speculated
against the Turkish lira and in foreign banks which preferred to
hold reserves in foreign currencies. The direction of the new
measures became clearer when a government-organised Association for National Economy and Parsimony was established and
started its activities in 1930.[15] The aims of this association were
to promote frugality, to reduce the consumption of imported
commodities by encouraging the production and consumption
of local products, and generally to promote the ideology of
economic self-sufficiency.

The mode of organisation of the Association for National
Economy and Parsimony is of interest on account of its para-
governmental nature. Although the entire project was conceived and carried out by the government, with all the deputies
as members, the Association was formally private. This
arrangement was continued into the 1930 Industrial Congress
convened by the Association, which proceeded to recommend
the organisation of Turkish manufacturers on a sectoral basis,
reminiscent of Italian *corporazioni*. One significant aspect of
these undertakings was the emerging propensity of government
activity to colonise the society; not only directly but also
through the formation of strictly ideological apparatuses which
were *de facto* under the control of the central authority. It also
became clear that Turkish republicans had discovered the
organisational innovations brought to the European scene by
Italian fascism. This was most apparent in the self-conception of
the ruling party and its place in the society, with the 1931 Congress
defining the political order as a single-party regime where the
party assumed the responsibility to rule in the name of the
nation.[16] In doing so the party would abide by 'populist'
principles, vigilant against special privileges that sought to
divide the population. In fact, 'a main principle' was to consider
the 'people of the Turkish Republic not as composed of
separate classes but divided into members of various occupations for the purpose of individual and social life'. Hence the
party would aim at 'establishing social order and solidarity
instead of class struggle'. This solidarity would be immediately
instrumental in 'involving the State directly in activities required by the general and supreme interest of the nation –
especially in the economic field'.[17]

The combined administrative and economic policy innovations indicated that the bureaucracy had succeeded in unifying

itself around the principle of politically led social change. A new institutionalisation of the state, with party organisation doubling as an administrative apparatus, would implement policies in accordance with the implicit goal of establishing the bureaucracy's status above the society. This goal required both a defensive and an active stance: the first led to the elimination of all societal autonomy while the second invited attempts at economic planning and ideological conformity. Within the defensive rubric proscriptions arrived rapidly. In 1931 the Turkish Hearths, a legacy of Young Turk nationalism, were closed down. This association, consisting mostly of an intellectual elite with a self-styled civilising mission, had reorganised itself under the new Republic, and in 1931 boasted 32,000 members in 267 branch offices.[18] The membership consisted of young professionals who felt that the Hearths would educate the masses in order to fill the gap left by the departing minorities. In the early 1920s the Hearths were mostly active in Western Anatolia, but were subsequently encouraged by the government to increase their presence in the East following the Kurdish rebellion. Their principal activity was offering lectures and courses to explain the tenets of the new regime. Despite a blatantly elitist and colonial attitude, and the fact that they were obviously working within the purview of the nationalist regime, the new orientation of the government found the Hearths overly independent. Accordingly they were ordered to dissolve the association and transfer all their property to the party.

Again in 1931, a new press law gave the government the right to close newspapers and magazines for publishing anything that 'conflicted with the general policies of the country'. Of course this legislation came to be used to prohibit opposition press and to secure a uniform voice of praise and approval broadcasting government positions. In 1933 a university 'reform' expelled two-thirds of the hundred and fifty teaching staff at the only institution of higher learning, the Istanbul University. Once more the new arrangement reflected a desire to eliminate independent shades of thought in order to achieve uniformity. In 1935 freemasonry was outlawed despite its roster of former and actual dignitaries; shortly after, the Turkish Women's Association was closed.[19] During this entire period party hacks wrote exaltedly about the requirements of the revolution, the need to be unified and the necessity of sacrifice. Their penchant for analogy was more revealing: examples were drawn indiscriminately from Italy, the Soviet Union, and later Germany.

The point was made repeatedly that in these countries the necessity for the press or the university to be aligned with government policy was recognised, and requisite measures taken. These three countries were seen as paving the way for a new social system (revolution out of a defunct liberalism). Liberalism and its understanding of personal liberty were considered bankrupt. The recognition of this bankruptcy led the proponents of the new regime to see as anachronistic the feeble protests originating in, for example, the university. In fact, by 1933 and definitely by 1935, the authoritarian nature of the government had been well established, with no channels of dissent remaining. Participants later claimed that its leaders were influenced at the time by a totalitarian conception of the party's status in the society; and the will to incorporate everything under the aegis of the party betrayed especially the Italian influence.[20] The crowning touch, which was really a pronouncement after the fact, came in 1936 when the prime minister, in his capacity as acting secretary general of the party, declared full congruency between state administration and party organisation. With this declaration all state officials in the administrative field became local party officials.

The nationalist intelligentsia have until recently interpreted the economic policies of the 1930s, known as 'étatism' in Turkish historiography, as exemplifying a strategy of non-capitalist development. We have already mentioned that the crisis was the stimulus which started the government on its path of both active and defensive measures; in fact the world economic situation was frequently cited as the direct justification for the growing statisation of the society. On a more conceptual level, the crisis was seen as signalling the failure of the market system and the need for new economic mechanisms. This anti-liberal attitude defending economic *dirigisme* was prevalent across the fairly narrow spectrum between the left and the right, whose views differed as to the mix of state and private enterprise. It must be added that among the bourgeoisie and the bureaucratic intelligentsia hardly a voice was raised contesting the social and political measures of authoritarian repression. The few who complained were promptly exiled while the intellectual debate was confined to the realm of the economy. At this level there was general agreement on the need to control foreign transactions closely, and on the desirability of statist protection of industry.[21] It gradually became apparent, however, that the state's intervention needed to be more direct, and more attuned to specific needs. Such specific policies first came on the agenda with price controls and other indirect measures, and later with the beginnings of state enterprise.

The years immediately following 1929 witnessed a crisis of merchant capital. Firms went bankrupt in the trading centres of Istanbul and Izmir, and workers became unemployed.[22] Both in current and real terms imports and exports declined from levels which, during the late 1920s, had represented the highest degree of world-economic integration that Turkey had experienced. An immediate impact was felt in the commodity-producing agricultural sector where producers had depended heavily on merchant's credit for their year-to-year reproduction. Failure of trading firms led many producers to switch to subsistence crops. But in subsistence crops too, the impact of the crisis was strongly felt, partly as a result of government policy. The government allowed wheat prices to decline following world prices, while the few items which small and middle peasants bought in the market became subject to customs and excise taxes.[23] At the same time new taxes were imposed on the agricultural sector, and old taxes which had been fixed in money terms began to weigh heavily when agricultural prices declined to less than half their pre-1929 levels. Tax collectors and creditors pressured the peasantry equally : many abandoned their lands and sold their animals, both in order to pay their obligations and to escape future taxes. These poorer peasants had to accept sharecropping tenancy on larger landlords' farms.[24]

Output in agriculture declined because of a contraction of the market and also because of the difficulty of obtaining critical inputs. The beginnings of mechanisation during the 1920s ceased abruptly with the high price of petrol and restrictions on machinery imports. Peasants also protested at the low prices in the traditional manner, slaughtering their animals – which increased meat output but deprived agriculture of its means of production. In addition to the decline in output, internal terms of trade evolved to favour manufactured goods: terms of trade for wheat farmers decreased from 100 in 1929 to 46 in 1934.[25] Part of this decline was due to the movement of world prices; the rest was a result of the government's protectionist policies and taxation on manufactured goods.

The second sector which definitely suffered was commerce. With greater state control over both internal and external trade, merchants had a narrower field in which to operate. During the first years of the crisis imports were tied to individual quotas, so manufacturers were able to purchase directly from foreign sellers. After 1933 bartering and clearing arrangements became more important. With Germany's increased share in Turkey's foreign trade, merchants could only participate in this market if they were in the good graces of the government. Together with the absolute decline in imports in 1933 to one-third of their 1928 level, there was a decline in the share of consumer goods from 52 per cent of imports in 1928 to 25 per cent by the latter half of the 1930s.[26] This decline meant fewer opportunities for the commercial sector, especially at the retail end. In the import trade, opportunity seems to have passed from small and retail merchants to large, government-approved traders, and to manufacturers themselves.

The absolute decline in exports would be expected to lead to a similar evolution in the commercial sector, particularly because of the dispersed nature of export production mostly in family farms which characterised the 1920s and which required a large number of intermediaries. The decrease in export trade, however, was relatively less substantial than that of the import trade, because the government's immediate policy after the payments difficulties of 1929 had been to curtail imports while attempting to promote exports. As a result Turkey's foreign trade registered an export surplus from 1930 until 1938, with the absolute level of exports declining less rapidly than imports. Once again, with the strengthening German connection, state involvement in the export trade, especially of wheat, became important, to the detriment of the commercial sector. It must be added that foreign trade may serve as a good measure of the activity of the commercial sector, because commodification in agriculture depended so directly on foreign markets. A study of commercial firms which were engaged primarily in foreign trade showed that profitability declined from around 10 per cent in the late 1920s to outright losses and profit rates of less than 2 per cent in the early 1930s.[27]

Of course this situation was not peculiar to Turkey. With absolute decreases in volume and declining prices, commercial sectors in all market economies suffered. What was significant in Turkish peripheral countries, was that the crisis primarily affected the commercial sector because the economy had been under its dominance during the previous decade. Since what there was of Turkish manufacturing was rudimentary, and since

economic policies quickly intervened to protect it, the crisis
actually benefited industry. According to the only detailed
calculation available, manufacturing's share of GNP was 10.5
per cent between 1925 and 1929. The ratio increased steadily as
the crisis began, to reach 16.6 per cent in 1935; it fluctuated
between 15 and 17 per cent until the end of the war.[28]
Manufacturing undoubtedly benefited from the steady move
away from free trade. In 1929, immediately after the five-year
period stipulated by the Lausanne Treaty, specific duties were
imposed on imports; then in 1931 the government adopted a
quota system. Only raw materials entering as inputs in
manufacturing were exempt from the quotas announced monthly
by the government. Such a stipulation invited pilfering of
foreign exchange, and 'factories' were established overnight,
producing import substitutes with minimal local value added.
Since these undertakings were privately very profitable, the
monthly announcement of quotas resulted in intense politicking
by importers, and equally intense efforts to establish factories in
order to benefit from the 'raw materials' exemption. As in any
bureaucratic allocation scheme, the operation of the quota
system increased the influence and status of state functionaries
while enabling the beneficiaries to make extra profits.

Already in 1927 a Law for the Encouragement of Industry had
been promulgated, improving the stipulations of a 1913 law put
into effect by the CUP government. According to this law a
minimum scale and level of technology would entitle manufacturers to customs exemptions, land grants and guaranteed public purchases in preference to foreign competitors.
Despite the number of firms encouraged by the Law, those
capable of competing against imports remained few. The Law's
impact was felt when it was coupled with protectionism: after
1930 the number of firms that received privileges decreased
while their scales increased. Gross output per firm was 2.4 times
the 1932 value in 1939. In 1939 those firms benefiting from
official encouragement employed one-quarter of all industrial
workers.[29]

There were frequent attempts by industrial capitalists to
organise in cartels in order to prevent 'overproduction', or in
order to safeguard the high profit rates they enjoyed.[30] The
government responded positively to these demands and permitted the formation of sector-based associations which openly
sought to fix prices and avoid competition. Manufacturers'

demands from the government were extended to include easy access to credit – a major problem of the previous decade when foreign and national banks alike preferred to provide short-term loans to the commercial sector. An industrial credit bank, although formed specifically to advance long-term loans to industry, never operated satisfactorily. Instead, the major semi-official bank of the day adapted itself to the conditions of the new decade by switching its loans from the now disadvantaged merchants to the favoured industrialists.

We have already mentioned that the internal terms-of-trade moved to favour manufactured goods. This ratio indicated that domestically procured raw materials would come cheaper to industrialists, and more importantly, since the principal wage good, wheat, declined in price, they could afford to lower their wages as well. While the industrial sector as a whole benefited from the crisis there was also a greater exploitation of the workers to increase the profitability of manufacturing capital. The political uncertainties of the period after 1925 had allowed the government to outlaw workers' associations and prohibit strikes. In the 1920s there was a real shortage of labour, especially in the urban areas where most minorities had departed, and where commerce continued to thrive. After 1929, this situation changed drastically: unemployment increased with the absolute decline in trade, and there may have been migrations from the countryside of peasants unable to pay their taxes or debts. In 1931 press reports in Istanbul claimed 100,000 unemployed (in a city of 800,000).[31] Loss of employment and attempts to lower wages led to workers' protests, with frequent disputes and strikes. Within this period of struggle, a labour law was prepared which sought to limit the hours of work and extend other privileges to workers, but the socially minded bureaucrat who drafted the proposed law was forced to resign and the proposal was killed off in committees.[32] Instead, various anti-labour decrees, such as the fingerprinting of all Istanbul workers in 1932, were promulgated. In 1936 a new labour law, based on Italy's 1935 law, was passed. Its aims were consonant with the new ideology of solidarity in the service of the state; it was supposed to eradicate the seeds of class strife that liberalism had sown.[33]

As a result of unemployment and legislation, workers' real wages decreased by 25 per cent between 1934 and 1938, according to figures compiled from statistics relating to 'encouraged' firms.[34] It must be mentioned that these represented the larger manufacturing firms, and wages in small manufacturing may have declined even more rapidly. With the war, deflation gave way to inflation. The statistics mentioned above indicate rising wages in 1938 and 1939, although taking the period between 1938 and 1943 as a whole, average wages in Istanbul, including those in small manufacturing and services, declined by another 40 per cent in real terms. Cost of living went up by 247 per cent while wages increased by only 114 per cent. As a result of this redistribution the industrial bourgeoisie enjoyed higher profits and rapid accumulation. That the shift in profitability was from the commercial sector to the industrial was apparent in the new attention given to manufacturing by foreign capital. Although foreign investment declined during the Depression, the number of manufacturing firms with foreign investment increased, in contrast to those in banking and trade.[36] As we shall see below, the state also invested in manufacturing, albeit for different reasons.

Between 1929 and 1934 state revenues increased from 10.8 per cent of GNP to 18 per cent of GNP.[37] In other words, within the great redistribution of the crisis, bureaucrats were acquiring a larger command over the national product. This was not an increase akin to the world-wide rise in state expenditures after World War II; there were hardly any redistributive schemes, and demand creation was confined to raising the salaries of civil servants. What appeared in the budget as social expenditures were payments in kind to state functionaries in the form of cheap housing and other subsidies. The bureaucrats, together with the industrialists, were the beneficiaries of the crisis. This is only a static conclusion: when we look at the interaction between the two groups, the system becomes even more transparent. While it is possible to observe the beginnings of state capitalism, it also becomes difficult to distinguish between the top ranks of the political class and the industrial bourgeoisie.

Already during the 1920s, the government had actively invested in the economy, notably in an ambitious campaign of railway construction and in two sugar factories. After 1929 it began purchasing foreign-owned railway and other concessions, such as the match monopoly, in addition to nationalising all foreign companies delivering public services. The new character of state capitalism appeared with what was called, in an obvious allusion to the Soviet experience, the First Five-Year Industrialisation Plan (1934). This plan was, however, no more than a list of fifteen investment projects and a programme for training the required technical personnel. The emphasis was on textiles and intermediary goods such as copper, ceramics, chemicals, and paper. Most of the projects were completed before the war, which also interrupted a second plan.[38] What distinguished these projects was their scale – obviously beyond the capabilities of private capitalists at the time – and the fact that they complemented existing industry. In fact the plan was the result of a complex bargaining process aimed at satisfying both parties in the ruling bloc. After a few years of protectionist policies, capitalists had graduated to industrial investment and they were ready to benefit from the linkages that state enterprises promised to provide. They could now obtain a greater proportion of their inputs domestically, through political arrangements. On the other hand, the officially promoted private bank, (İş Bankası) which represented the central intelligence behind private capital, remained vigilant in safeguarding the areas of activity which were thought to be the domain of the industrial bourgeoisie. This bank had been founded in 1924 under the auspices of Mustafa Kemal, by an ex-CUP person who later became economics minister, prime minister and president. In 1930 its participation in national industry had grown to 50 per cent of all national banks and by 1937 it held 38 per cent of the deposits in national banks.[39] İş Bankası provided a smooth interface between industrialists and the bureaucracy. Its board of directors consisted of thirteen deputies, and its links with public banks and state enterprises were intricate and strong. Industrialists regarded the bank as their platform when bargaining had to be carried out with the bureaucracy. The boards of directors in all the firms in which this bank held shares included high level bureaucrats and deputies. It was almost impossible to imagine a large manufacturing firm without such participation by the bureaucratic class. In 74.2 per cent of all firms established between 1931 and 1940 (and still surviving in 1968) the founding entrepreneurs were bureaucrats.[40] This high figure was partly due to the bureaucracy's growing share in national income and the opportunities it had enjoyed in public contracts and land speculation in the growing capital city. It mainly indicates, however, the currency which political influence enjoyed during the period.

The economic practice of 'étatism' led to an increase in industrial production, with the bureaucrats and the manufacturing bourgeoisie merged into a homogeneous coalition. The interests of the two groups seemed to coincide in a period when the growth of a domestic productive sector increased the political control over the economy which a bureaucratic class naturally desired. Neither party had much use for the peasantry and the working class since the stage of industrialisation did not yet warrant the nurturing of a broad internal market. Instead price and tax policies and labour legislation tended to lower the incomes accruing to farmers and workers, in an attempt to maximise the accumulation potential of the ruling coalition. Exploitation of classes remaining outside the ruling bloc allowed the symbiotic relationship to continue inside the coalition, with conflicts remaining at the level of dividing the spoils. The inherent contradiction between the principles of political allocation and the market could be held at bay as long as the number of actors remained small. Individuals who straddled the bureaucratic and the capitalist fields (they seem to have been a majority among the higher ranks) did not need to choose sides until diverging interests became irreconcilable.

'Etatism' was a label attached somewhat grandiloquently to a practice that appeared novel at the time. With the hindsight provided by Third World nationalist development schemes in the 1960s and the 1970s, it emerges as one of the first examples of what was to become a fairly general pattern. Under the guise of a novel social system, a political elite and a nascent bourgeoisie joined forces to isolate a national economic space for themselves in which heavy oppression of the working class and exploitation of the agricultural sector would allow for rapid accumulation – all this achieved under an ideology of national solidarity, more or less xenophobic, which denied the existence of conflicting class interests in favour of a corporatist model of the society. In the case of Turkey, the model, its administrative structure and ideological underpinnings, derived directly from the contemporaneous experience of European fascism. At the time, all four of the southern European states, Italy, Portugal, Spain and Greece, were dominated by varieties of fascist political systems, with Italian fascism providing the innovative laboratory.[41] It has already been remarked that the Turkish bureaucracy was well aware of the Italian experience, and did not spare words in declaring its admiration of the organisational methods of Mussolini's party. This admiration extended to wholesale borrowing of ideological and institutional motifs, as well as to a similarity in the declared goal, namely national strength through the construction of economic autonomy.

At the level of an instrumental interpretation of fascism where it becomes a version of 'developmental dictatorship', an alternative to socialism which seeks to achieve certain economic targets, it would be difficult to distinguish between European fascism, Turkish 'étatism', Peron's or Vargas's regimes in Latin America, or Third World nationalisms mentioned earlier. Beyond this instrumentalilty and the strict emphasis on economic achievements, however, fascism is born out of a particular class base and is nurtured on the transformation of a revolution-ary will. It is a reaction to a social evolution which threatens to disrupt the status quo and its social balances. Fascism promises to reverse this evolution and to conserve old values and symbols which concretise the social structure. At the same time it mobilises the masses towards the goal of establishing a new state which will exclude the vagaries of the old system. If the category of fascism is reduced to apply to political dictatorship and oppression of the working class, it becomes a catch-all concept referring to all non-parliamentary capitalisms. The Turkish experience of the 1930s shared certain dimensions of the fascist ideal; but these were entirely dictatorially imposed from above. The regime and the economic policy were conservative, attempting to impose control in order to stave off eventual demands for political participation and economic benefits. They could remain conservative primarily because there was no prior mass mobilisation for them to have to confront. Capitalism had not yet produced the divisions in political organisation and social life so characteristic of European societies emerging from the Great War. Consequently, a petty bourgeois or peasant reaction against liberal capitalism, ideologically refracted to establish an anti-socialist platform, was out of the question. Anti-liberalism remained an intellectual posture in Turkey, propagated by the bureaucrat-bourgeois bloc. Without prior social mobilisation, the authoritarian regime did not need to cope with a mass movement, and its aims were reduced to control and repression from above. Since bureaucratic particularism, inherited as a legacy of the ruling class of the Empire, distrusted the subjects it ruled, it appeared best to vigilate over unawakened masses. Besides, even if the bureaucratic elite had decided to induce a social mobilisation, an adequate platform was lacking. Unlike in Brazil and Argentina, the threat and potential damage of foreign capital was not evident; the more readily targetable comprador bourgeoisie had already been ousted; there had never been a landed oligarchy; and neither international balances nor the economy allowed a revanchist military adventure. Even the personality cult formed around Mustafa Kemal Atatürk remained cool and distant. We will discuss below the ideological reasons for this distance; nevertheless, it is striking to think that for all the adulation, there is not a single instance of Kemal addressing a popular rally in the style of a typical fascist or populist leader. Once again, the explanation can be found in the continuity represented by the Republican regime with the Ottoman past. There had been no social reaction to the traditional polity, no anti-oligarchic movement as in Latin America, and no mobilisation against the implications of economic development; for this reason the regime was devoid of the kind of social base characteristic of fascist or populist examples. It remained a regime established over a society which had not yet become a 'people', let alone citizens. 'Etatism' did not follow upon the breakdown of an exclusionary bourgeois system of restrictive parliamentarism, as was the case with fascism. It sought to extend bureaucratic rule, and devised a modality of coalition with a newly developing bourgeoisie in order to do this. Thus it was a regime where bargaining and political posturing remained within the confines of the elite.

Turkish social, economic and political development had not yet reached a level where fascism in the southern European sense or populism in the Latin American version, with their implications of social mobilisation and mass ideologies, were either palatable to or considered desirable by the ruling coalition. *Fascistisant* elements were present in the reaction of this coalition to the world crisis, but such elements could be discovered even in a reaction as far from 'étatism' as the New Deal. In the spectrum of adjustments to the breakdown of the world market, such similarities, basically stemming from a political recovery of the economy, were ubiquitous; but they were articulated into quite diverse political systems, depending on the histories and levels of national development. Turkey's position in the 1930s Depression was that of a society only just emerging into capitalism. *Fascistisant* elements were thus articulated into an authoritarian political system designed to further capitalist accumulation. We will have occasion below to analyse a genuine fascist movement in Turkey with genuine mass mobilisation and ideology. Arguably, it arrived at a period in Turkey's national development (the 1970s) which had much in common with inter-war Italy; but the world economy and the international political situation were in no way similar to those of the 1930s, and therefore not even minimally accommodating.

The beginning of World War II signalled an end to the 'étatist' success story. Between 1932 and 1939 manufacturing output had doubled, with about a quarter of this volume produced in state enterprises. From the peak of 1939 to the trough of 1945, there was a rapid decline with the 1945 figure only 20 per cent higher than 1932.[42] Agricultural production had also declined to 40 per cent of its 1939 level. Wheat output, for example, decreased from an annual average of above 7 million tons to 4 million tons. During the war years, especially under the impact of German commercial domination, Turkey registered an export surplus, accumulating currency reserves at the expense of selling more of its domestic product than it purchased through external trade. Thus, in addition to declining production, less of it was available for domestic use. The shrinking of the pie was accompanied by a typical war-time inflation rate (350 per cent between 1939 and 1945) which threatened urban incomes and even caused a decline in bureaucrats' salaries. While state levies increased in the form of various extraordinary taxes, expenditures were principally devoted to military mobilisation.

In the agricultural sector, rising prices after 1936 had somewhat ameliorated the situation of the wheat-growing peasantry. During the few years before the war, the government had increased its wheat purchases through a newly created Office of Soil Products and had transferred some of the favourable price changes to the farmer. The farmer, as well, was more willing to produce for the market, and the conditions of the wheat-growing peasantry probably improved during this time. With the war, however, the government adopted a policy of military mobilisation which harmed agriculture in various ways. First of all, close to one million male adults were taken out of the labour force, most of them from agriculture. Draught animals were confiscated for military use, and most agricultural inputs became impossible to obtain. At the same time price policy became blatantly exploitative, with the prices offered to farmers remaining almost constant while all other prices obeyed the inflationary trend. This drastic shift in government policies towards agriculture, and particularly against wheat farmers, was an important factor in the eventual estrangement of the petty producing peasantry from the ruling party.[43] The government sought to carry out its policy by enforcing the delivery of a designated amount of grain from each farmer by instituting a new 10 per cent tax on production, and by imposing collective responsibility on villages based an previous levels of output. Although the volume of grain purchased by the government increased, a parallel market with more realistic prices also developed in response to state control. Both of these consequences, the alienation of the peasantry and the formation of a black market, had important political implications.

The legislative package allowing the bureaucracy to conduct an extraordinary war economy was known as the Law for National Defence and equipped the state with total freedom to act in matters of the economy.[44] According to the Law, the government could set production targets for private industry and had the right to deny approval to investment projects; it could confiscate factories and mines, control prices in all markets and nationalise trade in certain commodities. The Law suspended labour privileges such as days off and fixed hours, and also stipulated that forced labour could be extracted from everyone. The bourgeoisie readily acquiesced and did not register any complaints.

During the entire war period both the bourgeoisie and the majority of the bureaucracy may have felt closer to the Axis powers. Although Turkey remained neutral, its abstention secured the south-eastern flank of German expansion and allowed Nazi armies to attack the Soviet Union with some freedom. The Allies considered Turkey implicitly hostile to their cause, especially since many promises to the British that war would be declared against the Axis came to nought, and the Turkish press was allowed to wax jubilant over German victories. Under such conditions, the war economy set up by the Turkish bureaucracy was perfectly consonant with the prevailing ideological atmosphere, and its similarity to the German model may have been reassuring to the bourgeoisie. A more direct impact of the German connection was a growing dependence on the German economy in foreign trade. After 1933 Nazi economic plans aimed at supplanting the international market with bilateral agreements based on barter and clearing. Turkish bureaucrats had already instituted similar measures in 1931, so the two systems coincided in attempting to bypass the crumbling international market.[45] Immediately before the war, Germany accounted for between 40 and 50 per cent of Turkey's foreign trade; similar levels continued during the war, although the exchange became less and less advantageous to Turkey. The unequal relationship obliged the Turkish government to sell strategic metals and wheat while domestic consumption levels were declining.[46] In exchange, instead of essential imports, war material and Germany's surplus industrial output were purchased. This pattern was hardly beneficial to the economy as a whole, but since trade was in private hands it served particular merchants in obtaining government contracts for military supplies, and in cornering sections of the export trade.

As I shall presently describe, war-time accumulation by merchants took on substantial proportions and became an important element in the breakdown of the bourgeois-bureaucrat alliance. Before the industrial bourgeoisie began to consider other political options, however, there were vocal complaints against war-time profiteering in black markets and against speculation. Debates in parliament reflected the discontent both of bureaucrats whose salaries no longer kept up with prices, and industrialists who had scant means of benefiting from the windfall opportunities. It was also obvious that the regime did not have at its disposal the means to prevent such profiteering. The rationing scheme by which bread and other essential items were allocated in towns was cumbersome and of limited effect. The populace was continuously confronted by parallel markets which became the established domains of the well-to-do. There were frequent articles in the daily papers describing operations yielding enormous benefits to their agents. In the general atmosphere of shortages and misery, this sort of awareness soon developed into a resentment of the government, and led to a search for culprits.

The desire to discover a scapegoat led the Ankara government to turn once more against the non-Moslem trading bourgeoisie in Istanbul. The old capital had always been identified with undesirable colonial links and a comprador bourgeoisie. The purity of new blood represented by Ankara had come to attain a significance beyond ethnic revanchism – it was being held up as the essence of national development. Within this ideological setting the identification of a colonial-merchant-Istanbul against a national-industrial-Ankara was not difficult to arrive at. In fact, although greatly diminished in numbers, the Jewish and Greek bourgeoisie of Istanbul had continued to be active, especially in foreign trade, and war-time shortages had certainly allowed them – like all merchants – to inflate their profits. It was not a difficult step therefore to revive the recent past in order to conjure up anti-minority sentiments and to combine these with demands for economic justice. In the 1930s, substantial industrial investment had taken place in Istanbul and some of the more important entrepreneurs in larger undertakings were Greek, Jewish or Dönme. This latter group were members of a Salonikan community, who had combined their earlier experience in imperial Salonika with the financial rewards of the population exchange in 1924 to become prominent in textile manufacturing. Ostensibly Moslem, they had converted from Judaism during the seventeenth century, preserving some of their Jewish traditions in both ritual and social life. Their liberal politics, close connections with CUP cadres, and industrial acumen had repeatedly invited the ire of conservative and Islamic (and, during the war, racist) opinion. In fact this small community, despite its political timidness, had emerged as the least 'étatist' flank of the bourgeoisie. Within the prevailing xenophobia of the war, the original goals of an anti-profiteering act thus became refracted to include non-Moslem and Dönme industrialists within its purview.

The Wealth Levy was proposed by the government in 1942, and despite its vague wording and an unusual procedure whereby the rate of taxation would be determined by local commissions empowered to assess each individual taxpayer's responsibility, it was accepted without debate in the parliament. Since most members of the parliament were potential subjects of this levy, it must be assumed that they possessed prior knowledge of the procedure which was later adopted by local commissions. Seventy per cent of the tax was collected in Istanbul, and 65 per cent from non-Moslems and foreigners.[47] Non-Moslems were assessed at ten times the Moslem rate, and Dönmes at twice. Christian and Jewish businessmen not readily able to obtain the sums needed were forced to sell their businesses and real estate to Moslem profiteers. Most of these businessmen left Turkey immediately after the war. Despite short-term gains by the Ankara government and the statist bourgeoisie (state revenues increased by one-third in 1943), and despite windfall gains by Moslem businessmen who were in a position to buy from the less fortunate Istanbul merchants and industrialists, the Wealth Levy seriously damaged business confidence in the years after the war. Once the extraordinary conditions were over the seriousness of the damage became apparent, with opposition politicians repudiating the experience and bureaucrats rushing to condemn it.[48] The bureaucracy's action had not been opposed by the industrial bourgeoisie; rather it had allowed an infringement which, even in an economy politicised to such an extreme degree, had violated the most elementary conditions of capitalist accumulation. In the midst of war-time frenzy and pro-German sentiments that spilled over into anti-Semitism, basic principles had been clouded over. The damage had been done, however, to the previously unassailable alliance, and the industrial bourgeoisie voiced its discontent at the earliest opportunity.

The last years of the war witnessed further instances of alienation between the bureaucracy and the bourgeoisie. A more radical wing of state managers had attempted to speculate about the post-war world, believing there would be an independent niche for Turkey between the two emerging world orders. Expanding upon the left version of 'étatist' ideology, they planned for a bureaucratically controlled post-war reconstruction.[49] However, neither the internal class balances, nor the ill-diagnosed state of the world would allow such bids at autonomous solutions. The final effect of this bureaucratic endeavour was to convince the bourgeoisie of the necessity to terminate the pre-1945 political alliance and to unambiguously declare Turkey's position in the world system. It must be mentioned that the modernising Western aspirations of the great majority of the bureaucracy meant that there was not much debate on the latter half of this package. Learning of the impending San Francisco meeting, Turkish bureaucrats had somewhat belatedly entered the war in February 1945; they had already declared their preference on the world order in Bretton Woods the previous year. Immediately after the war, when the *casus belli* of the Cold War was being discovered, a Soviet demand concerning territorial concessions by Turkey came to their aid, convincing the US government of Turkey's need for economic and military aid. Simultaneously, and in rather direct response to various American critics who expressed their misgivings regarding Turkey's previous pro-German attitude, the Wealth Levy, and the single party regime, the government announced that there was a pressing need for an opposition party in the parliament and that elections would be held in 1946.

It seems that the bureaucratic ranks in power greatly

underestimated both the strength of the bourgeoisie and the distance which now separated business circles from the statist policies of the previous period. What was hoped for was a party of loyal opposition that would work with the bureaucracy in order to evolve a negotiated set of policies to suit the new world situation. The political regime would remain essentially the same even if the economy gained some autonomy and some of the statist administrative apparatus were dismantled. A multi-party system in 1946 provided a rude awakening for the bureaucracy: the opposition party had gained surprising strength after only a brief period of organisation. With extensive allegations of fraud, the single party was returned to power and the main opposition party remained a minority in the parliament. Between 1946 and the new elections in 1950 accommodation and appeasement were the principal tenets of the government's behaviour. Public criticism was acknowledged in the form of new policies and new appointments; American experts were allowed to draw the post-war economic programme. Concessions were given even in the realm of religion, tainting a previously pristine record of militant secularism. The field that was conceded to the opposition, however, had irreversibly created a public space where all classes joined in to participate in the impending revolution. Agreements among the elite on the proper management of the economy would no longer be sufficient to contain the anti-absolutist current. A political solution to the débâcle was inevitable.

VI
Populism and Democracy

The elections of 1950 constitute a watershed in Turkish history. Until then politics had been the business of the elite, with power being transferred within the bureaucracy, or shared with a bourgeoisie who were few enough to permit face-to-face negotiation. Politics had not been differentiated as a profession within the bureaucratic polity; parliaments had served as an extension of administration, as had the boards of public and private business concerns. With the decision to introduce a multi-party parliament in 1945, however, universal suffrage and electoral politics arrived together to articulate the split in the ruling coalition. The parliament was transformed into a forum of debate, and when the ruling party attempted to constrain the opposition by decree, it felt itself justified in 'going to the people'. In the parlance of the 1946-1950 period, 'going to the people' became the formula announcing an entire constellation of novel political activity. Its practitioners implicitly denied that the parliament had any representative legitimacy and declared themselves to be the only politicians voicing the will of the people. They thus introduced to the scene new dimensions of populist contestation.

The two pillars of the opposition platform were economic and religious freedom, which upheld the market against statist intervention, and local traditions over the political oppression and ideological onslaught of the centre. That religion and the market came to constitute the dimensions of bourgeois opposition so belatedly is not surprising: movements with similar ideological equipment often crop up against bureaucratic

117

systems. In Turkey in 1950, this bourgeois platform succeeded in mobilising a mass following. I shall attempt to identify the particular articulations of these general principles, and their resonance in the Turkish social structure which accounted for their success.

The sudden discovery of the market was of course primarily due to the bourgeoisie's disenchantment with bureaucratic control over the economy. Having gained sufficient strength through politically mediated accumulation, and having reinforced its ranks through profiteering under war-time policies, the bourgeoisie could now differentiate itself from the bureaucracy at the level of ideology. Against a *fascistisant* corporatist solidarism which employed the 'national good' as a categorical imperative, it reached out to the tenets of market liberalism. Individuals were promised freedom from controlled prices, from gendarmes confiscating products, monopoly state enterprises, and a state whose principal concern appeared to be the collection of taxes. The market would be able to dismantle the structure of privilege built around the political authority in concentric circles. In other words, it would bring with it a field of opportunity where economic accomplishment could be pursued independently of the structure of privilege, even if this latter remained rigid. The promise of an autonomous economy carried with it the image of producers freely competing in the market without the interference of bureaucratic control. For the bourgeoisie which felt itself to have come of age, this would be a desirable state of affairs. It must be remembered, however, that the population which could be characterised as living within capitalist relations of production remained an extremely small minority. In 1950, out of a population of 20 million, 80 per cent lived in the countryside – the great majority being small producers. Self-employment was the rule in urban retail trade and in services. Even in manufacturing, 37 per cent of the workers were self- or family-employed, while only around 400,000 wage-earners worked for employers.[1] These figures indicate that the overwhelming majority of the population were petty producers who might well be expected to subscribe to the ideals of 'simple market society'.[2] In other words the market ideal did enjoy an objective correlative in the Turkish political arithmetic, and did not remain a purely ideological construct mystifying capitalist relations of production.

Subjectively as well, this vast majority of petty producers were ready to embrace market freedom as an avenue away from the traditional social balances which had changed little in recent decades. Their preference, in other words, was not only negatively determined as a reaction against bureaucratic interference; they also experienced the beginnings of economic development and personal enrichment, particularly rapidly after 1945. Per capita income had increased by 15 per cent between 1941-45 and 1950, and agricultural incomes by 30 per cent. The relative advance over the war years was especially remarkable.[3] This development was due in large measure to the ending of the war, when around one million men were demobilised, and some of the more deleterious government policies were abandoned. At the same time, an atmosphere of optimism was conveyed to the populace through the role which the US was supposed to play in economic reconstruction. In their new dominant role within the world system, American capital and the US government had devised a Recovery Programme for Europe, and this scheme of dollar grants for economic reconstruction was extended to Turkey in 1947. Having thus become part of the 'free world', Turkey was eligible for grants and aid in exchange for military dependence and economic liberalisation. American funds advanced to Turkey between 1946 and 1950 were equivalent to around 3 per cent of GNP, allowing imports to increase by 270 per cent over the war-time average.[4] The largest relative increase was in agricultural machinery (from 1 per cent to 8 per cent of imports) which was consonant with the new economic model counselled by American experts. According to this model, the Turkish economy had to live without protectionism and was to specialise within the world market; this new agenda implied investment in agriculture and agriculture-based industry rather than inefficient factories. One report by an American expert deplored the gap between isolated examples of 'twentieth century industrial technology' in state enterprises, and agricultural techniques which dated from Hittite times.[5] Instead of such inefficient investments, the government would do better to devote public resources to a road network and other infra-structural projects. The manufacturing of agricultural machinery and processed food would be another sector of importance if economic development were to be diffused to the general populace. It was argued by US experts that the average person's welfare had not been at all affected by the industrialisation effort and that the new priorities might redress the balance.[6]

Such a diagnosis of the Turkish situation coincided with the aspirations of several million petty producers, especially in agriculture, who were also aware that the costs of the industrialisation effort had been borne by the masses while its fruits were enjoyed by the elite. The implicit extension of this new prescription was decentralisation of the economy and geographical dispersion of the loci of accumulation. This implication accorded well with the aspirations of small town merchants and larger farmers in the more marketised regions, who had already received an impetus through war-time inflation. When US grants were translated into road-building machinery and 15,000 tractors (from the US economy ridden with market problems), the material counterpart to the rhetoric became concretely visible: transportation facilitated market access, and tractors opened up new land and increased production. There was therefore a coincidence of US prescriptions, bourgeois criticism of the bureaucracy, and the petty producers' aspirations, which was reinforced by the tangible fruits of economic reconstruction. The hinge which held together these diverse currents was the ideological platform centred upon the belief that the market was the mechanism to deliver material benefits. Until the new system hit bottlenecks, the prophecy was well placed to fulfil itself.

Together with the market, religion constituted the second focus of opposition during the 1946–1950 period. This was a more explosive issue because the particular version of Kemalist secularism had long been held immune from criticism and the bureaucracy was adamant in its defence of it, correctly recognising the potential of religion for populist mobilisation. As discussed above, the reformist current during the 1920s was aimed at eroding autonomous community traditions, seeking to replace such cohesive principles with centrally propagated rules of conduct. The 1930s witnessed intensified efforts to raise a nationalist consciousness in response to the crisis of liberal economics, which had proved destructive of the social fabric. Nationalism remained an elite ideology, however, employed more effectively as an instrument of control than as a mobilising platform. The implicitly adopted model was that of a network of cadres who would impose modernism from above to essentially reluctant masses. Not only did the threat involved in such a menacing imposition invite reaction, but the centre itself never attained sufficient economic and social dynamic to carry the urban petty bourgeoisie and the peasantry out of their historically rooted life-world. As a result the dominant forms of social transaction remained those of the imperial past, and this apparent conservatism came to define the ideological confrontation with the centre. When the centre became more oppressive in its ideological obtrusion, the peasantry and the petty bourgeoisie of small towns took refuge more resolutely in tradition, thereby inviting the bureaucracy conveniently to label their behaviour as obscurantist reaction.

The creation of a modern society according to Western norms had been an avowed goal of all reformers since the nineteenth century. What this project amounted to in context was the eradication of parochial and particularistic allegiances in favour of the constitution of a *gesellschaft* whose functioning would assure the cohesion of isolated but rational individuals. The target, then, was not religion per se, but those traditions, customs and rules of daily conduct which were claimed to be grounded in and legitimated by the maxims of Islam.[7] Islam in its Turkish version is not a particularly other-worldly religion; its lack of a separate religious institution is perhaps an indication that its realm is primarily that of the caesar. It seeks to define and provide meaning to a social universe: its believers thus identify as Islamic the meaning and the structure behind their entire lived relation with the socio-political sphere. It is curious that Ottoman-Turkish reformers identified their task negatively, as unseating, rather than constructing an alternative to, community-based social life; in other words, they were led to accept symbolic violence as the desirable course of action. The notion that a particularly intolerant attitude toward the symbols of traditional society would entail lasting and substantive changes at the level of practice was perhaps nowhere as fervently pursued as in Turkey. With Kemalism this violence assumed its most extreme form. Not only was religion repudiated as the basis of the political and ideological authority of the centre, but also popular Islam lost the whole of its institutional foundation through the banning of *tarikats*, or Islamic brotherhoods; the closing down of sacred tombs; and proscription of traditional dress. The Kemalist government created various departments within the bureaucracy designed to control from the centre all aspects of religious life. Thus secularism came to signify political control over religious life by bureaucrats, rather than separation of church and state, as the term usually implies.[8]

A corollary of such an understanding of the relationship

between religion and the state was that any oppositional mobilisation protesting against the oppressive political authority could claim to be acting in order to restore the status of Islam in the society. In the absence of an entrenched political tradition, resentment of the reformism of the state was expressed in the vocabulary of religious conservatism – the only language commonly accessible to the majority of the people. Consequently the Kurdish rebellion of 1925, the anti-government incidents in the south in 1930, and the Free Party episode (see below), as well as uprisings in Bursa and the east in the 1930s, were officially ascribed to religious fanatics and obscurantists.[9] All resistance to the centre was thus given a convenient label. The bureaucracy also attempted to classify the opposition party in the 1946–1950 period under this rubric of religious reaction. In fact the opposition (not only the Democrat Party, but also several smaller parties) had made religious freedom one of their important rallying calls. Although the RPP bureaucrats attempted to compromise on this issue by opening new religious schools, instituting religious education in primary schools, and withdrawing the ban on the visiting of sacred tombs, the platform of religious freedom continued to be effective, and the ruling party's compromise was all but ignored by the populace. Such a bias in the popular assessment of the two parties seems to illustrate how the issue of religious freedom came to be a metaphor for resentment against political and ideological obtrusion.

If the account of the opposition I have advanced above slides into the terms of a mass–elite confrontation, it is because the political contestation of the time was a declaredly populist one: 'the people' had been politically dominated, socially oppressed and economically exploited by the bureaucrat-bourgeois bloc. The two dimensions of the opposition platform reflected this antagonism in appealing to universal principles of economic and religious freedom, the ideological content of which did not readily reveal a class bias.[10] It was, of course, a former component of the power bloc, the maturing bourgeoisie, which acted as the mobilising elite, and probably stood to gain the most from a populist victory. Nevertheless, against the absolutist authority of the bureaucracy, resistance based on universal principles potentially unified elements of all social classes, whether or not they had become aware of their particularist class interests. Even the illegal Communist Party actively supported the Democrat Party in the 1950 elections. What is historically curious is that the organising principle of Latin American populisms, and of populism of a later vintage in Turkey, was anti-liberalism seeking to replace the rule of the market with political mediation of economic outcomes. In contrast the 1950 movement in Turkey took on the character of a latter-day liberal resistance to absolutist rule, except that a much larger proportion of the population (compared to seventeenth century England for example) was mobilised to form a common front with the bourgeoisie. In the following three decades the elements of this populist mobilisation remained an important dimension of Turkish politics even when class-based interests came to be much more fully articulated.

To illustrate the historical specificity of this populist mobilisation we may refer to a similar but unsuccessful incident in 1930, when the full impact of the economic crisis was most acutely felt. Aware of growing discontent, the ruling faction of the bureaucracy had decided to divert antagonistic sentiments within the populace by allowing the formation of a genuinely liberal opposition. A close friend of Kemal of known liberal convictions started to organise what was called the Republican Free Party, whose principal demands were free enterprise, abolition of monopolies (of which not many existed at the time) and free speech. Within twelve days of its incorporation the Free Party had received 130,000 applications for membership.[11] In the campaign for municipal elections which it entered after only two months of existence, huge crowds attended its rallies and must have embarrassed the ruling cadres who had never received such adulation. These crowds consisted of the same elements that made up the 1950 version of populism: small merchants, urban petty bourgeoisie, commercial farmers. In time, the peasantry might have joined in larger numbers as well. Like the 1950 movement, the Free Party had made possible the expression of resentment towards the militant secularism of the government. In 1946, when the Democrat Party was beginning to organise, it took over much of the Free Party's local leadership and found strength in many of the same towns where its previous incarnation had rapidly gained followings.[12] All the promises of populist mobilisation, however, could not split the ruling bloc in 1930. The bourgeoisie which led the 1950 movement to a successful conclusion, had in 1930 elected to remain in the bureaucratic alliance. With the assurance that the bourgeoisie would remain in the ranks and would not choose to ride the mobilisation of the masses, the bureaucracy felt free to close summarily the Free Party in 1930 after barely three months of existence. The bourgeoisie's choice, of course, was rational and understandable. With the crisis in full swing neither democracy nor liberalism appeared as likely avenues to economic salvation. Lacking the mobilising force of the bourgeoisie, the remaining elements of populist opposition did not unite into a movement. In 1950, by contrast, a more mature bourgeoisie had full confidence in the coming boom, which was, furthermore, ensured and underwritten by the world hegemonic power. The forces driving for a victory of liberalism were overwhelming. That is why, between 1946 and 1950, the movement steadily gained momentum and attracted growing numbers both of the bourgeoisie and of petty producers.

By any measure the Democrat Party's accession to power in 1950 constituted a fundamental break in Turkish history. For the first time a popular electorate expressed its political choice and voted against a statist tradition several centuries old. Paternalism, control from the centre, and reformism from above were decisively rejected while the market (and capitalism) were given free rein. Of course the large majority of the population were as yet ignorant of the implications of an unbridled market economy. Its immediate benefits appeared tangible, and the unknown seemed far more desirable than what had been recently experienced. The bourgeoisie, however, was politically the most conscious party in the populist mobilisation. It was aware that the new era heralded its political and ideological domination at the expense of the bureaucracy and its awkward attempts to propagate a statist system with a nationalist ideology. It must certainly not be forgotten that the bourgeoisie had engaged in a relatively easy battle, as the war had already been fought on a world scale and been won (as far as Turkey was concerned) by the proponents of free enterprise and the market. Nevertheless, it was this battle which signalled the transition from capitalism under bureaucratic tutelage to capitalism based much more solidly on market mechanisms. The bureaucracy for its part experienced a more momentous change than the bourgeoisie. As a class it had ruled Turkey according to its various successive projects for the entire duration of the Empire, and particularly through the reformist currents of the nineteenth century. Like members of any other class, the bureaucrats had been neither homogeneous nor uniformly favoured in terms of being able to carry out their intentions or of obtaining pecuniary rewards. There had been, however, a continuity in their location within the social structure, and, *grosso modo*, in their relations with the rest of the society. Of course, when they engaged in the task of supervising the transformation of the social structure while attempting to maintain their own status intact, they had had to form an alliance with a chosen bourgeoisie – given that they were not about to eradicate private property. During the CUP period and under the 1930s' étatism, this alliance had not meant that the bureaucracy was reduced to the accommodating role of state managers while the bourgeoisie had full control over the economy. On the contrary, the bourgeoisie was allowed to privately control portions of the economy only while it obeyed the rules of its association with the bureaucracy. Besides, the bureaucracy had established and retained control over a significant portion of the economy, not only through expenditure of revenue but also through direct control over the means of production. Despite all this, however, without full state ownership of the means of production, it appeared to be impossible to prevent rapid accumulation and consequent differentiation in the private sector. The 'external economies' provided by state enterprises through their investment and pricing policies were, in fact, a factor facilitating private accumulation. Another factor contributing to the development of the capitalist sector was the general policy pursued towards the peasantry and the working class to guarantee accumulation in the state sector, but which necessarily benefited the bourgeoisie as well. What ultimately constrained the bureaucracy was the sanctity of private property. Unlike its Ottoman predecessors, it could not simply confiscate the property and capital of a private individual. This inability clearly manifested the contradictions of the project: if the society could be transformed in the desired manner, with all the implications of capitalism, then the bureaucracy could not possibly retain its status within it. This meant that the common front of the two classes eventually had to split.

Such a split might have occurred in a number of ways – a socialist revolution with the bureaucracy mobilising the peasantry in the Chinese style was one alternative. Leaving aside the problems posed by Turkey's position in the world system, it was also true that state functionaries were individually implicated in the remunerative concerns of the bourgeoisie. It is doubtful that proponents of a non-capitalist solution would have won over the rest of the class. Furthermore a peasantry of which at least 80 per cent are independent petty producers does not have much revolutionary potential, save where the revolution promises market freedom. In this connection we may mention a curious episode of 'land reform' legislated in 1945.[13] At the start of its troubles with the bourgeoisie, the bureaucratic faction of the ruling party decided upon a land distribution project. With labour shortages being a perennial problem, there had never before been a demand from below for land distribution. As I shall discuss in subsequent sections, sharecropping existed to some degree, but this was due not to a lack of access to land but rather to a lack of access to oxen. Nevertheless, President Inonu was adamant, and pushed through a project of land reform in 1945 which involved distribution of state land to the landless and poor peasantry. The ensuing parliamentary battle was a milestone in the simmering conflict between the bureaucratic and bourgeois factions of the party. Between 1946 and 1950, during Inonu's presidency, land distribution was timidly pursued with 33,000 families receiving state land, while between 1950 and 1960, under the Democrat Party, whose eventual leaders had initially opposed the project, 312,000 families received land (20 per cent more land per family).[14] It is evident that land distribution amounted mostly to ratification of *de facto* claims on state land, and that these claims varied with access to material means of production, i.e. tractors and oxen. The question therefore remains as to the reasons why the bureaucratic faction in the party felt the need to legislate a land reform when other troubles were brewing and while there was no expressed demand for it by the beneficiaries. The explanation probably lies in the bureaucracy's attempt not at social revolution, but at forging a new alliance with the poorer peasantry against the growing challenge of the bourgeoisie. Rather belatedly, and no doubt prompted by the decision to hold real elections, the bureaucracy awkwardly began to search for a constituency. The poor peasantry had arguably suffered the most from étatist policies and war-time mobilisation: there was then some logic to their being selected as a target for appeasement, even if they had not voiced any autonomous demand for land reform. What characterised this attempt, however, was the caution and the care taken to preserve existing balances; unable to burn its bridges with the bourgeoisie the bureaucracy retreated without achieving its objective. It is difficult to imagine a different outcome: had all the bourgeois elements within the ruling bloc already distanced themselves from the ruling party, the isolated bureaucracy might have been bolder in carrying out a land reform.

The question that was not posed is whether there was sufficient need for such a reform to create a grateful constituency and a new alliance. While it is true that in Mexico a similarly bureaucratic polity had secured the position of the revolutionary party through land reform, the Mexican experience could not be repeated in Turkey, even if the bureaucracy had not run into opposition; this was principally because of the absence of a landowning oligarchy, the Anatolian countryside being populated instead by independent small owners.[15] It might have been possible to woo the poorer peasantry, but as became clear in the 1950s, they too preferred economic freedom in the form of market opportunity, although not as fervently as middle and rich peasants.

The bureaucracy's inability to forge a new alliance not only signalled its defeat in electoral politics, but also assured its subordination to the bourgeoisie during the subsequent phase of Turkish political economy. The bureaucracy lost its status as a social class with its own project and became a group of state managers whose level of autonomy depended on the nature of the accumulation process and intra-bourgeois balances. Despite the rich historical heritage of a state tradition, political power after 1950 remained in the hands of the bourgeoisie. From then on, the relative autonomy of the state managers could be understood in terms of the weakness of the dominant bourgeois fraction, conflict within the bourgeoisie, or by reference to Turkey's conjunctural relationship with the world system.

The first years of Democrat Party (DP) rule witnessed radical economic and political transformations. The parliament was both younger and more provincial; the deputies were locally based politicians deriving their strength from being in a position to represent their constituencies and from their promises to do so. Since most of the electorate lived in villages with close ties to provincial centres, it was understandable that the DP leaders would shift their attention to agricultural development. Besides, American aid continued to arrive in increasing volumes, and it carried specific instructions extolling the virtues of a market-based world division of labour. Turkey's part in such a market would be agricultural exports. Both American aid officials and DP politicians aimed at complementing rural development with a road network designed to facilitate the marketisation of agricultural products. The government invested in infrastructure, and the motor car was to integrate the national market. Industry would follow in orderly fashion, induced by rising income and growing demand in the countryside.

Once the market is accepted as the principal mechanism to allocate economic resources, this package contains no surprises. Considering the dominance of independent producers in agriculture, it is a scenario of understandable attraction and more defensible than would be the case had the Turkish countryside been characterised by oligarchic domination. In fact the first few years of DP rule witnessed a providential fulfilment of all expectations until the tide began to turn because of external constraints and adverse movements in world prices. The market ideal – at least inasmuch as it concerned international specialisation – was then abandoned to some degree. Instead the DP turned to economic policy to extend agricultural development in a typically populist, that is, inflationary, manner. By the second half of the 1950s, external constraints had become pressing and the urban bourgeoisie was increasingly discontented with the policy favouring agriculture. A new protectionism and the beginnings of import substitution eventually responded to their demands.

We can now turn to a discussion of the agrarian structure in Anatolia. It was mentioned in Chapter 2 that the re-centralisation of the nineteenth century had effectively combated the 'feudalising' tendencies of provincial landlords. Although some areas remained in which large holdings were still significant, the political-legal framework and the continuing availability of land meant that the peasantry remained independent. This independence was threatened during the 1930s Depression (and probably in earlier general crises as well), when declining monetary incomes forced the poorer peasantry to sell their animals and instruments of labour, with the consequence of increasing the incidence of sharecropping tenancy. This proved to be a temporary development, however, which was reversed once prices started favouring agriculture. With rising agricultural prices, wider availability of cheap credit, and a large inflow of tractors which made large-scale land reclamation possible, sharecropping dwindled to a small presence after the war and during the 1950s.

The absence of a landed aristocracy – or a land-owning oligarchy in more peripheral vocabulary – was a significant feature of the Turkish social formation which had allowed the bureaucracy-bourgeoisie bloc to adopt industrialisation policies unopposed by landed interests. The preponderance of small ownership played a determining role in the success of the opposition movement of 1946–1950, and the agrarian structure continued to be the key to the transformation of Turkish society during the following two decades. The nature of the agricultural economy, the specific qualities of urban migration, the particularity of the labour market and the constitution of the domestic market for manufactures may not be understood without reference to the agrarian structure and the nature of the peasantry.

The history of the agrarian structure we are discussing was conditioned by an abundance of land relative to the population. Anatolian soil was on the whole tired and not very fertile, with islands of irrigable areas, which has led some experts to describe Turkish agriculture as 'oasis type'. Average yields were not high and depended very much on rainfall. Technology had remained unchanged for centuries, with the result that an average family could only crop and cultivate an area of around five hectares. On the other hand, there was no shortage of land: reclaimable land at the margin was usually of the same quality as land already under cultivation. Thus it was always possible to move out of established settlements and start anew with freshly reclaimed land. This was an option which was exercised by villagers escaping from social unrest during the Ottoman centuries; and by several million immigrants settling on new lands in Anatolia during the latter part of the nineteenth century.[16]

During the last quarter of the nineteenth century agricultural production increased partly as a result of population growth and partly because of new commercial opportunity. Continual wars, and later the mass departure of minorities, reversed the trend. A significant revival, though short lived, was experienced during the 1920s, yielding to declining agricultural production until the mid-1930s. Although after 1936 the volume of production and area under cultivation increased, a low rate of marketisation was still prevalent. The entire period between 1929 and 1945 may be characterised by the closure of isolated villages when agricultural stagnation implied a substantially decreased level of economic integration with both national and world markets.

It was not until the end of the war that major transformations began to occur in the countryside. During the war, agricultural technology had regressed owing to shortages of petrol and parts. In 1946 the number of operating tractors barely exceeded one thousand. By 1955, with agricultural machinery provided through US aid, the number of tractors had reached 43,000, without any decline in the number of draught animals. This additional source of energy was initially used to expand the area under cultivation. Between 1946 and 1955 the total area sown increased from 9.5 million hectares to 14.2 million hectares, or by 50 per cent, while population during the same period increased by only 20 per cent.[17] The process of reclamation which was carried out through the utilisation of new tractors did not exacerbate the inequality in the distribution of land; in other words it did not serve only to increase the holdings of a few large landlords. First of all, tractors were not simply sold on the market: in most cases they were purchased on credit. In a 1952 survey, 93 per cent of households owning agricultural machinery were found to have financed their purchases by credit amounting to 60 per cent of their outlay.[18] Political patronage mechanisms played as great a role as strict credit-worthiness in the allocation of funds. Besides, cheap credit through official channels had become more readily available from banks and newly established cooperatives. Secondly, reclamation of land was not carried out unilaterally by politically powerful tractor owners. The village community frequently became involved in the decision-making process, and the opening up of new land led to a chain of events whereby most peasants benefited indirectly. In poorer villages the distribution of land was uneven owing to the small number of 'middle peasants' who survived the 1930s depression with their holdings and draught animals intact. A significant portion of the peasantry in such villages were bound to a richer landlord by ties of usury and/or sharecropping, with no likelihood of escaping their situation until the reversal of the economic conjuncture. When this occurred and village landlords purchased tractors, the new technology was used to replace the sharecroppers. The sharecroppers responded to the loss of their tenant status by taking action, either collectively or under the authority of the village government, to reclaim land from what until then had served as the village common land. Thus part of the state-owned marginal land came under the *de facto* possession of former sharecroppers. Given the expanding supply of credit mentioned above, the establishment of owner-occupied farms was not constrained by a scarcity of funds. Furthermore, the uncertainty associated with occupying state land was soon dispelled as *de facto* possessed land was formally distributed with proper titles. 'Land distribution commissions' established in accordance with the land reform act of 1945, travelled from village to village to formalise this transfer of newly opened state land to the least propertied peasants.[19]

A second type of 'opening up' occurred in more prosperous villages with a more even distribution of land and a greater proportion of 'middle peasants'. Such 'middle peasants', if they enjoyed political connections, or sometimes merely had entrepreneurial spirit, could obtain bank credit towards the purchase of a tractor. Most commonly two or more peasant households joined together to make the investment, and then agitated at village government level to reclaim land from the state-owned commons. Once again the occupation of state land was eventually formalised through cadastral ratification, but since there were relatively fewer sharecroppers driven out of these villages (i.e. fewer landless peasants) most of the village residents received a share of the new land. Contrary to more simplistic accounts, rich peasants purchasing tractors could not unilaterally seize the common land, except in south-eastern villages, reflecting a previous tribal structure. For the rest of the country, political balances and the general atmosphere of freedom experienced after 1950 required that the village as a whole consent to the opening up of the commons.

In both poorer and better-off villages, the dominant tendency was the extension of peasant property. The number of owner-occupied farms increased from 2.3 million in 1950 to 2.5 million in 1952, and to 3.1 million in 1963.[20] This constituted a growth of roughly 30 per cent in the number of petty producing units over the decade of the 1950s. The proportion of village families who did not own their land had declined from 16 per cent in 1950 to 10 per cent in 1960.[21] This latter figure does not correspond entirely to the incidence of sharecropping tenancy or wage-labour, since secondary occupations in the village increased during the same period. Together with expanding production, commercial activity became more prevalent. Villages which had consisted predominantly of subsistence households, with the nearest market in a small town that could only be reached by foot, now began to acquire motor vehicles and grocers. Such activites created secondary employment as well.

Developments during the 1950s reinforced the structure of

the agrarian sector in its predominantly petty producer orientation. The 'agrarian question' had never been an issue of
importance in Ottoman-Turkish history. If the solution of the
agrarian problem is taken to be an index of bourgeois-
democratic development, Turkey enjoyed a privileged position
from the very beginning, and during the evolution of the 1950s
registered further gains in this direction. Except in the south-
eastern region dominated by the Kurdish minority, precapitalist
practices were largely absent, or their presence insignificant. As
peasants became market-integrated petty commodity producers, the conditions for a capitalist transition in agriculture
also largely disappeared. The absence of a capitalist agriculture
had important implications from the point of view of the
relative success of democratic forms in Turkey. Not only were
party politics frequently tailored to woo the agrarian sector, but
at the level of ideological platforms as well, an independent
peasantry strongly determined the dimensions of political
contestation.

In the early 1950s agricultural expansion was aided by the
favourable price conjuncture of the Korean War. Terms-of-
trade for agriculture improved to reach a peak in 1953,
indicating that in addition to producing more, farmers would be
able to purchase more with what they produced.[22] In fact the
UN index number for Turkey's agricultural production indicates that when pre-war output is taken as 100, the 1953/54
harvest rates as 183. This is the highest increase for any country
for which data are available.[23] (The 1950/51 index number is
129.) The rapid increases in agricultural output brought about
general economic growth with per capita income increasing by
28 per cent between 1950 and 1953. As promised in the market
model, growth in agricultural output served to increase exports
by 50 per cent over the same period. Export earnings and
foreign aid were dedicated to buying tractors, road-building
machinery, construction materials and motor vehicles (between
1948 and 1953 passenger cars increased from 8,000 to 28,000;
commercial vehicles from 14,000 to 34,000 which in turn
increased commercial opportunities and market incentives.[24]
Only 20 per cent of the imports were consumer goods –
therefore it could not be argued that opportunities were being
wasted on spending sprees. On the contrary, government
policies exhibited a developmentalist bias: finding itself in a
favourable position *vis-à-vis* international markets and aid

agencies, the government attempted to import all the capital goods it could. It seemed in 1953 that all would go well and that a happy fulfilment of the liberal model of the economy, with its implications for modernisation, was just around the corner.

The tide turned rather abruptly: weather conditions and world prices seemed to conspire to undermine Turkey's new-found momentum. In 1954 agricultural output and exports decreased by 15 per cent, and per capita income by 11 per cent.[25] Such fluctuations in themselves may have reflected the vagaries of climate and the world market, and did not necessarily herald a fundamental change. In the case of Turkey, however, with its recent past of protectionism and inward directed economic policies, the disappointment with the international market had arrived too soon not to induce a growing suspicion of the liberal model. Prime Minister Menderes, leader of the DP, had already become a folk hero revered as a saviour, and the exuberance of such early success led him to behave in a manner typical of populist politicians: he wanted to extend the economic boom at any cost. The most obvious tactic was to exchange concessions in the accommodating market of Cold War politics for more foreign aid. Since 1945 Turkey had acted as a willing and loyal outpost of the West on the borders of the Soviet Union. The Menderes government attempted to prove the DP's allegiance with even greater panache, first by dispatching Turkish troops to the Korean War, then by insisting on joining the North Atlantic Treaty Organisation (NATO), and finally by granting the US army a number of military bases. The US's political and military expansionism, combined with Turkey's willing cooperation, served to make these years a period of US ascendancy. US Army personnel became visible on city streets and were much imitated, while the US embassy and aid officials were granted almost vice-regal status. Thus this bargaining for aid against political concessions did succeed for a period, but was insufficient to offset the poor export performance. Imports declined by 30 per cent between 1952/53 and 1956/57; and the excess of imports over exports, which indicates the extent of net externally financed trade (such as through aid and credit) declined from $165 million, to $78 million.[26] In other words, politically transferred foreign exchange could not keep up with Turkish demand, and since a larger percentage of the transfer was needed for debt servicing, the usable component of grants, credit and aid tended to decline.

Menderes was a politician of a genuinely populist mould; for him and for most of his party the mystique of development and the resonance it created among the masses rendered unthinkable the abandonment of expansionist policies. Inflationary finance was the most obviously available measure, through increasing credits to agriculture, price support programmes, and rapidly growing public investment. Menderes did not attempt as grandiose a scheme as the construction of Brasilia, but like Kubitchek he seemed to despise the ordinary constraints of accounting and was endlessly inaugurating public works projects without regard to cost.[27] These were financed by the Central Bank through the printing of money, causing prices to double between 1955 and 1959. Inflation was an illusory device to compensate for the slackened rate of growth, but it did mean rapid accumulation for the urban manufacturing sector.

The exceptionally liberal trade regime of the early years was abandoned in 1954 and some of the statist measures of control readopted.[28] Import restrictions once again provided manufacturers with sufficient incentive to produce for the domestic market. In the short term, the combination of inflation and protection served as a desirable policy to promote industrial profits. During the earlier period, orderly development led by agriculture had created a demand for those perennial mainstays of the early stages of industrialisation: both cement and cotton textile output had doubled between 1951 and 1955. At the same time most of the domestic supply of producers' and intermediary goods derived from imports. After 1955, when restrictions were imposed on imports, and the share of consumer goods dropped to only 10 per cent of a declining import bill, urban industry began to receive *de facto* protection. Thus all domestic manufacturing output could find markets and high profits. With such incentives the industrial sector began to grow faster than agriculture, and consequently industry's share in the national product increased from an average of 10 per cent to 14 per cent (with agriculture dropping from 49 per cent to 43 per cent).[29]

By the end of the decade, however, inflationary growth had become a liability because of its distributional implications. Although it was the prime beneficiary, the larger industrial bourgeoisie did not seem happy with the haphazard policies of protection and credit. On the external side both the US agencies and the Turkish desk at the OECD complained about inflationary finance, and annual demands for aid. Finally a stabilisation programme, a forerunner of the IMF packages of the 1970s, was imposed on the government in exchange for continuing aid.[30] In one of the first instances when international organisations forced a developing country's government to adopt more planning, World Bank and OECD experts urged Menderes to form a planning board in order to impose some logic and control over public spending and the allocation of foreign exchange. By the end of the decade it seemed that the hegemonic power had recognised Turkey's particularity in relation to other southern European countries in exempting it from the liberal market model. The protectionist scheme, aided by planning, could only mean a policy of import substitution, which had in fact been pursued rather inefficiently during the second half of the decade. A planning board was covertly formed in 1959, since Menderes had always denounced any such activity that had statist overtones.[31] In 1960, however, a military coup ended the preliminary phase of import substitution and inaugurated a period of an overt policy of industrialisation, complete with its State Planning Office and much respected technicians.

The decade of the 1950s introduced into Turkish society a mentality of geographical and social mobility which cannot be easily captured in statistics. Despite the growth in the number of family farms, agricultural mechanisation had driven some of the former sharecroppers out of the countryside and, more importantly, the new-found economic vitality of the towns promised more remunerative employment. Thus it was not necessarily the landless who migrated to the city, but also the lone young male whose family continued to cultivate its plot in the village. Since custom work carried out with tractors was quite common, especially after the end of the land reclamation boom, many families could afford to send part of the household labour into urban employment while engaging a tractor-owner to plough their lands. The first wave of urban migrants consisted mostly of former seasonal agricultural workers who had found temporary work in the cities. With the construction boom in private housing and public works (construction grew 21 per cent per annum between 1951 and 1953),[32] the previous pattern of migration was reversed: recent migrants now lived in the city and travelled to the village only at harvest time. First services, then industry, became important sources of employment after 1954. In the beginning it was small-scale manufactures; after the middle of the decade larger factories began to emerge, with the number of workers in plants of more than ten workers doubling from 163,000 to 324,000.[33]

As in most peripheral countries, the shanty town became a tangible correlative of the vast demographic movement, reflecting the opening up of the village and the consequent upheaval in social balances. The traditional city with its economic and cultural superiority as the seat of the governing class, and its special relation with European metropoles, was no longer. This was especially true of Istanbul which, as the imperial capital and the habitat of foreigners and the grand bourgeoisie, had epitomised late nineteenth century cosmopolitanism. The arrival of former peasants on the edge of the city, at first diffident, then assertive, reflected the new economic ethic; the social divisions of the previous era would dissolve when faced by an all-embracing market – as it was usually a short step from the edge of the city to the centre. This new economic ethic was precisely the reason for the migrants' arrival in the city. The ground in Istanbul was supposed to be paved with gold; in fact improvements in the income levels of immigrants were probably the rule during most of the 1950s, and 1960s. Compared to bleak Anatolian villages, urban life, although at the periphery of the urbis, was apparently preferable. The first settlements were imitations of village life: co-villagers stayed together and built shacks for each family, usually on state land. The quality of housing soon improved, both because the first wave of immigrants invested their urban earnings in new homes, and because the later arrivals brought a store of agricultural savings with them for the same purpose. Besides, on the eve of each election, politicians promised and then delivered to these burgeoning neighbourhoods some of the civic amenities and municipal services. Titles to the land soon followed, and the original shacks assumed the character of sturdy permanent housing.

In these early years, this new proletariat of the cities disappointed some of the more naïve expectations of its political behaviour. Instead of veering towards the left, it preferred the populism of the right – the DP and its successor parties. It seemed that there were two complementary dimensions to this preference. First, the improvement in living standards through migration had been considerable, notwithstanding the patronising deprecations of the shanty town and the romanticisation of the villages by most of the bureaucratic-intellectual establishment. Secondly, despite economic integration, the cultural life of the city – although under siege – appeared to the hordes at the gate closed and inviolable. This never attained formal dimensions as for example in the 1930s when peasants were not allowed to walk on the main streets of Ankara without western clothes; nevertheless, until the 1960s the city retained enough of its elite heritage to intimidate the newcomers. The shanty-towners reacted by staying apart and reproducing their village culture in the faubourgs. Such a separation meant that traces of the elite–mass confrontation which defined the 1950 movement would continue to play a role in social divisions, at least during the initial period. Political behaviour more consonant with the class model became prevalent with the second generation of immigrants, for whom relative improvements were no longer readily experienced. By this time also, the culture of the city was totally absorbed into that of the faubourgs. The resulting homogenisation was a strong factor in discounting the earlier dualistic problematic in favour of class-based perspectives.[34]

Between 1950 and 1960 the population of the four largest cities increased by 75 per cent, and the urban population (settlements of 10,000 or more inhabitants) from 19 per cent to 26 per cent of the total. This meant the arrival of 1.5 million immigrants into urban areas and 600,000 into the four largest cities (net of natural growth).[35] In other words, one out of every ten villagers migrated to an urban area during the 1950s. Such geographical mobility truly was the beginning of national integration, eradicating physical distances, and bringing into brutal confrontation the peripheral and central cultures. By the time this mass movement of population began to slow down in the late 1970s, Menderes's road network had pulverised cultural heterodoxy and eradicated most pretensions to traditional elite privilege.

At the level of entrepreneurial activity, the mobility experienced during the 1950s was of a totally novel dimension. Of the present 'captains of industry' in Turkey, most started their businesses or achieved their significant accumulation during the 1950s. There are very few important manufacturing concerns which can trace their history back to the pre-1950 period; and hardly any business dynasties. It was the accumulation of the 1950s which allowed the development of a domestic manufacturing bourgeoisie. Some of the routes leading to membership of the industrial bourgeoisie were the same as those taken by the rural migrants, in that their origins were found in the transformation of agriculture. One region of Turkey, Çukurova (Cilicia), stands out in providing most of the examples of this path. A fertile area of mostly nineteenth century settlement, Çukurova had experienced a cotton boom during the US Civil War, and had become important once again around the turn of the century, with rich Armenians purchasing land for purposes of commercial agriculture. The expulsion of Armenians led to a concentration in the hands of Moslem landlords, and by the time tractors arrived, sharecropping tenancy on cotton-growing land was prevalent. Mechanisation provided unprecedented opportunities to large landlords who had formalised their ownership titles during the early Republic, as well as to those who, through extra-economic coercion, could unilaterally enclose their holding by driving off sharecroppers.[36] In Turkey as a whole this was not a widely observed occurrence. According to one survey only 4 per cent of the village populations were thus driven off, and less than one-fifth of those actually left their villages. (Most of those remaining in the village found land to reclaim.) In the region including Çukurova, however, 12.4 per cent of the population were driven off; and in Çukurova proper the figure was probably much higher.[37] Enclosures were immediately remunerative in the case of cotton, where only seasonal wage labour was needed, and during the 1950s fortunes were made after a single harvest. The population of Adana, the capital city of the region, doubled during the decade, and its denizens behaved in typical boom-town fashion. In contemporary accounts comparisons with the Wild West are common, and it was probably true that the number of Cadillacs per capita was higher than in most American cities. Some of the more successful of these landlords made the jump from cotton to ginneries, yarn and textiles. During the 1970s, the heyday of Turkish industry, at least two of the main entrepreneurs vying for supremacy (out of five or six concentrations of 'holding companies', i.e. finance capital) had started in this way.

The case of Çukurova is unique. In no other region was agricultural surplus so great and so concentrated as to provide such dimensions of primitive accumulation and to open such opportunities for commercial activity. Other large companies and financial concerns were founded by urban capital, in large part accumulated through trade during the étatist period. Wartime shortages had increased the opportunity of accumulation by allowing merchants to reap unorthodox returns through black-market profiteering. The Wealth Levy discussed above became yet another factor aiding accumulation, as non-Moslems were forced to sell their businesses to Moslems. Most industrial investment projects of the period were supervised and funded by a bank (the Industrial Development Bank of Turkey) established for this purpose under the auspices of American aid agencies and the World Bank. It was through the overall perspective and management of this bank that the evolution of Turkish industry was supposed to be oriented towards its proper place in the world division of labour. There is hardly a large firm established in this decade which did not receive credit and precious dollar funds from the Industrial Development Bank: it was through this mechanism that the internationalisation of Turkish capital proceeded – through the internationalisation of bank credit to industry. While Istanbul's share in industrial investment was disproportionate, cities of earlier accumulation (such as Izmir) and of new-found wealth (Adana) also started emerging as poles of growth. Smaller towns in the western half of Anatolia participated in this atmosphere of economic development with the growth of trading networks and small manufactures.

Agricultural fortunes, greatly increased physical mobility, and opportunities for rapid accumulation were features of capitalist economies world-wide during the post-war boom. In Turkey, as in most peripheral countries, the scale of the change was devastating, especially since in terms of ideology, official and popular alike, stability and order had previously been considered the foundation stones of the society. Within a few years developmentalism and unbridled market freedom replaced such traditional values. As economic opportunity became the rule and self-enrichment an end, a frontier mentality began to assert itself over the freedoms sought by the citizenry. Not only was the state unable to devise new means of control over a society rapidly escaping the pre-capitalist mould, but the society had no tradition of autonomous regulation either. Public space had always been political space in the sense of being directly under the jurisdiction of the state. The withdrawal of the state from a part of its previous domain in the name of establishing economic freedoms created a vacuum which was filled with the excesses of individual expansionism rather than by any institution of the civil society. This situation was later remedied, not through the evolution of a civil society in any recognisable form, but because the state mechanism, using the excuse of safeguarding political stability, extended its control in new forms and frequently to an absurd degree. Public life became a running contest between individuals seeking to exercise economic freedoms where the state had not yet mined the ground. Before this contest developed its own rules it looked as if the state were receding from the public sphere (although not from the economy); an impression which prompted much of the restoration observed in the political order of the 1960s.

VII

The Political Economy of Import-Substituting Industrialisation

The 1960 coup was short-lived. In a year and a half the military had pushed through a new constitution by referendum and held elections to transfer power to civilians. In Turkish historiography, the evaluation of this first military intervention after the establishment of parliamentary democracy reflects the view which sees the struggle between populism and bureaucratic revanchism as the dominant axis of recent history – a theme carried on from the pre-1950 period. Thus either the reformism of the 1960 intervention and its paternalist constitution are extolled; or the coup is regarded as an attempt by the discredited state class to re-establish itself in the polity. After 1950 the dimensions of a society based on individual enterprise and market rewards had undermined the historical balances which had been created through the classical reproduction and evolution of Ottoman-Turkish entities. Naturally, the cataclysmic change of 1950 did invite an order of restorationism, which was evident in the discontent with the Menderes regime expressed by the bureaucracy and the military. The bureaucracy had always seen itself as heir to the reformist legacy, with reformism widely understood as the successful adoption of Western forms. It was therefore highly unlikely that any significant group within the bureaucracy – particularly in its civilian flank – would advocate a prolonged regime falling outside Western parliamentarism, especially since democracy was still the ideological export commodity of the world hegemonic power. More importantly, however, during the decade of the 1950s the economy had developed within the market paradigm, and interests had evolved to render difficult any reversal of its basic format. Physical and social mobility, and the economic development of both the bourgeoisie and the peasantry, constituted social forces which easily overcame the resentment of the civilian and the military bureaucracy, who had themselves lost their social status. Nonetheless it could be maintained that the evolution from a market society based on petty producers to a capitalist society with a dominant capital-labour relation had not yet advanced sufficiently to create a significant class differentiation along a capitalist axis. Class conflict proper to capitalism was still a subordinate current within the totality of social dynamics.

A faction of the bourgeoisie had however achieved a status from which they could forcefully express their wishes and preferences for a parliamentary regime at the political level. One reason for this preference was that in a competing party system attentive to electoral politics which were open to monetary influence, state agencies were much more accessible than in the case of a bureaucratic polity. The industrial fraction of the Istanbul bourgeoisie had already, during the second half of the 1950s, expressed its impatience and discontent with the increasingly populist bent of Menderes's economic policy. It had been instrumental in the formation of a third political party which presented an alternative to the statism of the opposition RPP and the petty bourgeois market ideology of the Democrat Party (DP). Having the support of liberal intellectuals and the progressive bourgeoisie, the platform of the urban coalition represented by the new party was far more influential than is suggested by its short life, which ended when the splinter group in the parliament joined forces with the RPP. This joining of forces injected new energy into the tired ranks of the RPP; a group of young, technocratic-minded and well-educated recruits changed the character of the opposition platform. During the latter half of the 1950s the RPP was associated with a vague notion of planned development while this new definition pushed the DP further into the populist camp. Rather than making any concessions in the face of urban-industrial-technocratic discontent, the DP was forced, because of its internal composition, to identify the new demands with the old bureaucratic character of the RPP. Through this erroneous identification the governing circle of the DP further alienated the urban industrialists and the intelligentsia with an even more militant populism.

At the electoral level the party in power had lost some of its support between the 1954 and 1957 elections. This decline in votes was due much more to short-term discontent springing from the downturn in agricultural fortunes than to alienated city dwellers. In addition parliamentary contest and ideological struggle had divided the country into opposing camps with hostility increasing between the partisans of the DP and of the RPP. As party politics became the dominant game in villages, all conflicts came to be expressed in the vocabulary of electoral struggle, and ancient animosities took on new colouring. Coffee houses were separated and politics gained an autonomy which temporarily served to suspend the more material underpinnings of voting behaviour. Nevertheless the DP continued to receive the larger portion of the rural vote, especially in the more commercialised coastal regions.[1]

With the hindsight of the 1960s transformation, we can argue that the crucial cleavage obtained between the petty bourgeoisie in the towns and the countryside, small capital, and the trading bourgeoisie on the one hand, and the manufacturing bourgeoisie on the other. The reflection of this division at the ideological level was the conflict between a petty bourgeois market ideology of seventeenth century vintage, and a bourgeois ideology more appropriate to the period of industrial development in the post-war world. In other words, the post-war evolution of a nationally based manufacturing bourgeoisie and its international links now necessitated regulation by the state of the process of accumulation – a task which the DP administration, severely politicised in its last years, was not capable of fulfilling. From this perspective the 1960 coup and its attendant consequences emerge as transformatory rather than restorationist. Akin to transitions in the state–economy relationship in other national contexts – the prototypical case is the inception of the New Deal in the US – the 1960 coup also led to the institution of a new administrative mechanism which served to formulate and implement economic policy. The two groups most immediately targeted as clients of this policy were the industrialists and organised labour. What distinguished the case of Turkey, a peripheral country, from similar transformations in the advanced nations were, first, the close dependence of the policy alternative on the particular context of inter-state relations and, secondly, the relatively small weight in the society of the two principal client groups.

The bureaucracy was not particularly privileged with the

inception of the new model of accumulation. It certainly registered a relative gain in its level of remuneration, and the more technocratic stratum within the state managers gained some new status through the emerging autonomy of the state within the domination of industrial capitalism. Neither of these developments, however, implied the reattainment of a class status for the bureaucracy reminiscent of pre-war years. The state remained, in its most general dimensions, a peripheral capitalist state, and the involvement of the state managers in the economy, as well as their social status, may best be understood within a model which ascribes the relative autonomy of the bureaucracy *vis-à-vis* the bourgeois class to the particular requirements of the prevalent model of accumulation.

What was achieved unwittingly by the authors of the 1960 coup and their advisers within the intelligentsia and the bureaucracy was in fact no less than laying the foundations for a new model of accumulation, with its social policy, political balances and administrative mechanisms. In the following two decades this model of accumulation functioned without radical transformation and with considerable success. Elements were added to the basic strategy as formulae for adaptation to new circumstances; and at one point (in 1971) another military coup intervened, resulting in a slight deviation from the trajectory. This is not to argue that the fraction of manufacturing bourgeoisie could implement its own project without opposition or support from other social forces. The emerging nexus of social and economic regulation, and the general orientation of policy, were certainly the result of a process of negotiation, in particular with the dominant powers in the world economy. At the time of its inception the model of accumulation in question was also supported and actively advocated by the hegemonic power (and its funding organisations). The model also accorded with the aspirations of the intelligentsia to a considerable degree; and, more importantly, with the as yet unformulated demands of the industrial working class. In other words the project of the manufacturing bourgeoisie, as it was underwritten by Turkey's international patrons, conformed well with the short- and medium-term interests of the working class and a certain stratum of the bureaucracy. This intersection allowed the installation of a fairly stable state form, the continuation of the parliamentary regime, and a concomitant regulation of the economy. Before exploring the political and economic dimensions of this period, I will try to account for the historical context in which the 1960 transformation (from the point of view of the model of accumulation) occurred.

It was argued above that the liberal trade regime into which the Turkish economy had been incorporated following its post-war transformation, was short lived owing to difficulties in balancing external payments. Exclusive dependence on agricultural exports proved to be an insufficient base on which to finance an increasing demand for imported goods, for both consumption and production. In fact, after the mid-1950s, there had been a *de facto* protection of domestic manufacturing, spurring local entrepreneurs to invest in industry. With the urging of the country's creditors, a stabilisation plan was agreed upon whereby new debts were granted to Turkey.[2] Since 1954, through complicated systems of quotas and tariffs, the political authority had been in a position to control the nature and quality of imports, and thereby decide on the extension of market privileges to chosen manufacturers. It was this enormously increased prerogative of the political authority which had led the burgeoning manufacturers of Istanbul to join the chorus of discontent directed at the increasingly haphazard and autocratic conduct of state affairs in the late 1950s. In what seemed at the time to be a marriage between bureaucratic hopes and the manufacturing bourgeoisie's demands, the 1960 coup promised a rational and planned allocation of scarce resources, especially of foreign exchange, in the service of rapid development. In practice, foreign pressure as expressed through the OECD-organised consortium of Turkey's creditors aimed at a similar orientation. By pressuring the Menderes government to centralise economic decision making and sanctioning the move away from trade liberalisation, they formally permitted the introduction of a new policy of planning, coordination, and import substitution. From this point of view, the coup responded to foreign pressure, as well as to discontent among various strata of urban public opinion, all of which served to promote the project of the industrial bourgeoisie. Within this implicit coalition, bureaucratic restorationist hopes were crushed early on, notably with the forced resignation of a team of statist-minded planners from the newly constituted planning authority.[3] The field was then open to accommodate demands for industrial regulation within an unchallenged bourgeois domination.

A significant dimension of the transformation effected by the 1960 coup was the precocious success of the industrial bourgeoisie in carrying out its project. What facilitated this transformation despite the obviously non-hegemonic nature of the industrial bourgeoisie was in fact bureaucratic discontent, articulated by the intelligentsia with its counterparts within the military.[4] By 1960 the entire bureaucratic class, and the intelligentsia, had become vocal partisans of a developmentalist ideology. Within a clearly articulated anti-populist dimension, this ideology extolled the role to be played by a technocratic elite in the industrialisation of the country. The working class had not yet been discovered; the dominant intellectual current was a Baran-inspired dependency analysis with 'non-capitalist' path overtones, which required the transfer of state power from self-serving and corrupt politicians to nationalist planners whose aim it was to serve the people.[5] Industrialisation, economic autonomy and social justice were to be the foundation stones of the desired order. The proponents of this view legitimated this ideological current through a peculiar reading of the 1930s Kemalist experience. According to this reading, étatism had conformed to what its left wing had advocated during the few brief years before its purge in 1933.[6] In other words, étatism had been developmentalist and nationalist (or anti-imperialist according to this version) and had not given free rein to capitalism. The authoritarianism of the Kemalist years was elevated to a virtue since it had become apparent in the 1950s that democracy for the uneducated masses, ignorant of their true interests, could only lead to a rule by demagoguery. For this reason the 1960 coup was precipitated and welcomed by the entire intelligentsia as signalling the inception of a new period of statist industrialisation.

It was clear in the aftermath of the coup that bureaucratic restorationism did not stand a chance, and that the new ideological battle would be waged between the supporters of a pure market ideology, referring to a 'simple market' society, and the proponents of industrial regulation. Because this had been a transformation by coup, the latter party gained the upper hand; under any other political process the proponents of market ideology would have carried the day. The coup, then, not only implemented the transformation, but by deflecting the argument towards the old axis of bureaucratic control versus the market, allowed for an obfuscation which obviously benefited the industrial bourgeoisie. The coup was basically benign, despite occasional excesses and the ridiculous trials of DP politicians charged with the intention of 'subverting the constitution'. After the interlude, the parliamentary regime was reinstated with new institutions and a new constitution providing the blueprint for the emerging model of accumulation.

As far as the bourgeoisie was concerned there were two differentiating elements of the new model of accumulation: first, the political allocation of scarce economic resources – especially foreign exchange and credit – and second, the assurance of a redistribution of income with the multiple aims of purchasing social and industrial *détente* and creating and sustaining an internal market. Each one of these elements was anathema to small capital and the petty bourgeoisie: state control subverted the market by introducing extra-economic factors into the profit-seeking game, while any institutionalisation of distributive schemes detracted from the pursuit of maximum gain and accumulation. Thus small capital was prone to the kind of reaction which characterised its counterparts in other historical examples in the throes of the transition to monopoly capitalism. The petty bourgeoisie pursued its divergent goals by means of electoral politics, and it frequently found the means to express its demands through the parliamentary system. Since the new dimensions of the regulation of the economy did not conform to the requirements of the petty bourgeoisie and small capital, and since contestation on the political platform was possible, the new period witnessed constant tension between the political and administrative spheres and concomitantly between the legislative and the executive branches of the state. Because of structural determinants, as well as the institutionalisation introduced by the 1960 coup, the governments in power found themselves constrained to act within the paradigm of monopolist regulation even though their electoral support clearly derived from a much broader base, partaking of a more strict market ideology. As we shall see below, this tension, originating in the inability of the manufacturing bourgeoisie to establish ideological domination, underlay every ideological and political struggle of the 1960–1980 period. For the industrial bourgeoisie, the administrative allocation of scarce resources and the distribution of income aimed at creating and sustaining an internal market amounted to a full economic strategy. We shall describe the forces determining the adoption of this strategy, and its functioning. First, however, a brief discussion of the institutional innovations harboured by the 1960 coup is in order.

The establishment of a State Planning Office (SPO) of chosen technocrats appeared to be the original purpose of the military coup, considering the tone of the debate around this new institution. The SPO was to exist alongside the various ministries concerned with the economy but because of its privileged constitutional position, it would have *de facto* ascendancy over them. In practice the SPO director functioned as a deputy prime minister in charge of the industrial sector. The much awaited and long pondered five-year plans, however, were no more than historical documents compiling statistics, and crude calculations relating to desired levels of investment. They were supposed to be binding for the public sector and indicative to private industry.[7] The plans constituted attempts to coordinate investment decisions centrally; yet the crucial aspect in the operation of the SPO was the fact that the allocation of subsidised credits and scarce foreign exchange (also subsidised because of the overvaluation of the Turkish lira, as will be discussed below) required its stamp of approval. In other words, a situation was created which privileged political allocation processes and, consequently, bargaining at the very top administrative level rather than in the market.[8] Scarce resources and the rent accruing to their users were thus secured for the manufacturing bourgeoisie with access to the top.

The second dimension of the new institutionalisation of the mode of accumulation derived largely from the status (unprecedented in Turkey) granted to workers' and other associations through the new constitution. The new constitution and subsequent laws which specified the mode of unionisation and collective bargaining allowed workers to negotiate their wages through channels which had been established in Western democracies after centuries of struggle. The precocious success of the Turkish labour movement may only be understood through the world-historical development of social democracy on the one hand, and through the legacy of bureaucratic reformism from above on the other. This conjunction accounted for a precocity which would have been unthinkable if the bourgeoisie had historically exercised full control over the state mechanism. Our argument emphasises precisely the 'fit' between bureaucratic reformism and the ascendancy of the industrial bourgeoisie, which allowed for the successful launching of the new phase of capitalist development. In effect, worldwide social democracy and bureaucratic reformism determined the early success of the industrial capitalist model, which emerged as a uniquely opportune response to diverse social demands.

We may add that this presentation of the interests behind the new model of economic regulation has relegated the working class to a passive status without any contribution to the designation of policy. Neither through increasing wage demands nor as a political force was organised labour active during the 1960 transformation. In other words it is the historical underdevelopment of the working class – both as an economic and as a political force – which invites an interpretation privileging the interaction between the bourgeoisie and the bureaucracy. Class struggle specific to the capitalist mode of production was not as yet the mobilising element in social transformation. The right to unionisation, collective bargaining and strikes, obtained by the workers, as well as the widened domain of social security, emerged as entitlements handed out to workers in accordance with the requirements of the new model of accumulation. Inasmuch as these institutional innovations strengthened their potential status, state managers acted as the spokesmen of social reform. The bourgeoisie might have disputed certain specific points in the agenda, but on the whole, it was a not reluctant participant.

From the bourgeoisie's point of view there were nevertheless excesses associated with the institutionalisation that followed the coup. For example, it was not only the organised working class which had obtained the privilege of bargaining through the new constitution. Because it emerged as a reaction to the usurpation of all administrative powers by the parliament during the 1950s, the 1961 constitution had instituted checks and balances through which social groups, even with rudimentary organisation, were capable of contestation at the level of the political authority. Government employees had recourse to enormously powerful state courts: the constitutional court frequently reversed parliamentary legislation and even the smallest political parties could block the functioning of various state processes through court action. As a result, a system of bargaining and vetoes was installed at the expense of administrative efficiency. In fact political procedure quickly came to reflect this system, with a large number of parties in the bicameral legislature, each containing several factions of quite divergent constituencies. Thus the petty bourgeoisie, the peasantry, and the ever-growing corps of state functionaries also had recourse to social bargaining to prevent them from blocking – with action akin to industrial strikes – the administrative mechanism.

The implications of such a system from the point of view of the politicisation of the society are obvious: by leaving administrative functions open to societal parcellisation, the state mechanism becomes prone to excessive growth and increasing weakness through privatisation. While a developed state mechanism may be desirable for purposes of efficient management, the associated politicisation is anathema to technocratic instrumentality. The new structure, therefore, contained from the outset an implicit dysfunctionality which would manifest itself as soon as difficulties were encountered in the reproduction of the economic system. On the other hand, from the perspective of the constitution of an internal market, just as the industrial working class obtained the right to bargain, so did various other social groups, albeit in a more mediated fashion and with less immediate success. The implication was the institutionalisation of a particular pattern of income distribution with the consequent constitution of an extensive internal market.

The two dimensions we have briefly outlined, namely the politicisation of certain economic allocation mechanisms and the constitution of a domestic market, provide the defining features of the political economy of Turkey during the 1960–1980 period. It has already been mentioned that both of these dimensions involve, separately and in their intersection, a regulation by the state of the mode of accumulation. This mode of accumulation served the needs of the industrial bourgeoisie while also responding to the demands of the state functionaries and the intelligentsia who had been eclipsed during the previous decade. At this level of generality, the resemblance between post-war Keynesianism and the regulation we have described will be evident. Keynesianism also involved management of the economy by the state, the ascendancy of state managers, and the redistribution of income in order to constitute and reproduce a domestic market as characteristic features of the mode of accumulation. What distinguished this peripheral cognate of Keynesian regulation (in addition to the much smaller weight of the regulated sector in the economy) was the external relations of the economy. The boosting of the market in the periphery is undertaken primarily for the benefit of the domestic manufacturing bourgeoisie. In other words, at the level of economic management, the peripheral industrial sector is characterised by a policy of total protection from international competition. The formula of Import Substituting Industrialisation (ISI) is an appropriate label for this economic regulation aimed at altering the location of the economy in the world division of labour. The defining feature of ISI is precisely the protection of domestic industry, which develops to produce the very manufactures hitherto imported.[9]

It must be mentioned that as a prescriptive formula, ISI does not include the aspirations for insular industrialisation contained in the 'national economy' model of Listian vintage. As a policy, it implies protection for the sake of building an industrial sector *in situ* rather than necessarily earmarking all the available slots for a 'national' bourgeoisie. Its internal bourgeoisie is relatively much weaker than the bourgeoisies of the previous century. This difference and the understanding that there is no question of competition in the world market but accumulation confined to the domestic market, allows for the absence of rivalry with international capital. In other words, neither in theory nor in practice does ISI exclude foreign direct investment in manufactures or prevent such direct investment from enjoying the same protection as domestic capital. Nor does the policy of ISI imply an attempt to reduce absolutely the degree of integration of the domestic economy into world markets. Since industrialisation proceeds according to established patterns, and is a 'tightly staged' process;[10] it necessitates the importing of technology, producers' goods, and frequently primary and intermediary inputs. In fact, once industrialisation along ISI lines begins, the potential volume of manufacturing output comes to be closely determined by the available volume of imports serving as inputs to the industrial sector. Alternatively, a stronger claim would be that the demand for imports is increasingly a function of domestic manufacturing output inasmuch as imports come to constitute inputs necessary to industrial production. In practice then, neither from the point of view of openness to foreign capital, nor in terms of its impact on the volume of trade, does ISI decrease or hinder world economic integration. Given the post-war structural transformation of advanced industrial countries, it may be argued that the relocation of certain standard-technology industries to countries pursuing an ISI strategy was desirable from the point of view of international capital pursuing a world-wide strategy.

In particular, since the domestic markets of countries following the ISI strategy were not closed to foreign capital, which could be invested in order to exploit this protected market, such a relocation of production might have corresponded to a globally rational strategy from the point of view of international capital. The presence of certain countries open to foreign capital, whose imports had shifted from consumer goods to manufactured goods, and whose markets were therefore ready for increasingly sophisticated commodities, did not constitute an obstacle to the functioning and evolution of the world economy – a view which was widely shared by international capital. The ISI strategy was not considered a rebellion against the world economic order except by the more gullible proponents of 'planned' industrialisation whose sights were focused on the misconstrued implications of political control over the economy.

The import substituting strategy could be easily distinguished from the more traditional strategy advocated in other instances by international capital (and pursued in Turkey in the early 1950s), namely export-led growth. The essential difference lay in the importance of the domestic market, an accepted feature of the economies of countries where ISI policies were pursued. A certain degree of industrialisation had already taken place in ISI countries prior to World War II. During the 1930s Depression, all of these countries had engaged to various degrees in state centred industrialisation and infrastructural development, which allowed them both to quickly establish national economic integration during the post-war boom and to build on the existing base of manufacturing production. We have described above the 1930s development of the Turkish economy: étatist industry and private manufacturing which were then active provided both a technological and an entrepreneurial background for industrial production during the ISI period. The one steel mill, even if inefficient, still produced an essential input for consumer goods manufacturers; railroads, although slow and costly, expanded the domestic market to a considerable degree; engineers and managers who gained their initial experience in state enterprises provided a cadre of cheaply trained personnel for private entrepreneurs. Furthermore, the few years of export-led growth based on widespread agricultural expansion during the early 1950s had created in Turkey all the preconditions for the successful pursuit of an ISI strategy. There was an accumulation of capital in private hands, a sufficiently large internal market, largely resulting from transformation of the agricultural sector, an infrastructure, and a technological background on which new industrial investment could be based.

The functioning of this particular type of capitalist industrialisation is constrained by the same two sets of elements which were already discussed, namely internal class balances and the pattern of relations with the external world. We shall discuss these constraints first at the level of the economy – in other words, from the point of view of the continuity of the capitalist accumulation process. In the next chapter we will introduce the analysis of political and ideological elements.

The process of expanded reproduction of Turkish industry could be seen not only as the substitution of domestic production for previously imported commodities, but also as a substitution of the products of a modern capitalist sector for those of various degrees of petty production. From a small base in the late 1950s, the modern capitalist sector expanded at a rate well above the average for the whole of the manufacturing sector, which was around 10 per cent per annum. During this expansion modern industry not only came to employ most of the organised labour force, but it also created a non-basic population of petty producers and services around its domination. This was a process of continuing colonisation accompanied by the destruction of previously existing forms of production. Such an expanding process required primarily the securing of the means of production, and then the means of realisation of the product, i.e. markets. In Turkey, as in most non-European countries, the post-war period had witnessed a dramatic change in demographic patterns, culminating in an increase in the population from 20 million in 1950 to 48 million in 1980. Even without the agricultural transformation of the 1950s, a reserve army of labour would have been available to supply the demands of the urban industrial bourgeoisie. With the previously described liberation of a section of the peasantry from the countryside, the potential labour force available to modern industry attained even greater proportions. The population increased by around 3 per cent per annum during the beginning of the period, declining to 2.5 per cent around 1970, and 2.2 per cent by 1980. The urban population increased from 30 per cent of the total in 1960 to 37 per cent in 1970 and 45 per cent in 1980. Only a small proportion of the new urbanites were incorporated directly into the modern industrial sector. Most remained loosely employed in services, small manufactures and petty commerce. The majority of the non-industrial labour force in large urban areas belonged to the so-called marginal sector of unorganised and sporadically employed labour. There was therefore a sufficient labour force in reserve to allow the modern industrial sector easily to avoid the labour shortage problems faced, for example, by most Western European economies during the 1960s.

Nor was technology a problem. Since the evolution of the industrial sector responded to a well-established pattern of consumer demand imported in its entirety from advanced capitalist countries, articles which had to be produced domestically were of a standard nature, with tried designs and production processes propagated and exported by international capital. In the case of Turkey, for reasons we shall explain below, the 'transfer of technology' was mediated primarily through patent and trademark agreements rather than through the importing of foreign capital incorporating such technology. The result from the point of view of the production processes was, however, the same, with the same technologies used in the production of commodities as would be the case with a heavy presence of foreign capital. The implication of the adaptation of standard technologies and commodities is a pattern of production which requires the importing, not only of blueprints but also of producers' goods and sometimes raw materials. In the case of Turkey, the excessive dimensions of this imposed requirement became all too visible during the 1970s, with a consumption pattern privileging passenger cars, oil-burning power plants, plastic packaging and import-using gadgets. Even before the increase in oil prices, Turkey's imports consisted heavily (95 to 97 per cent) of production goods and raw materials – a figure denoting at once the degree of success of import substitution and the excessive dependence of the manufacturing sector on the procurement of foreign exchange.[11]

Given that a sufficient volume of foreign exchange could be obtained, the next requirement for the perpetuation of successful accumulation in manufacturing was the constitution of a market. Industrial production aimed exclusively at the internal market, a result of the policy of protection allowing high profit rates to enterprises which could not hope to compete in the world market. With inefficient scales of production, ineffective management, and the situation of being forced to utilise expensive inputs when these were produced domestically, the availability of a protected internal market was a precondition for the continuation of industrial investment. Since the internal market allowed for high profits, even if industrial scale, management, technology and quality had been comparable to prevailing world standards, it would have been difficult to persuade manufacturers to attempt to break into difficult international markets. If foreign capital and multinationals had been prevalent in the manufacturing sector, there might have been greater opportunities for expanding into export markets. In the case of Turkey, however, neither was foreign capital prevalent, nor did economic policy favour exports. On the whole in fact economic policy tended to penalise exports.

Once the choice of exclusive internal market orientation was made, what was expected of the market was not simply a broadening, but a certain degree of deepening as well. Given that the composition of industrial production was in constant flux, that is to say, as the dynamic sector of the economy shifted from textiles to consumer durables, to automotives, consumers had to be found or created with sufficient discretionary income to constitute a market for new industries. This aspect of the model of accumulation points to the principal dimension of economic regulation undertaken by the state. As is repeatedly stated, for any individual capitalist, the logic of the capitalist system requires maximisation of profits and correlatively minimisation of wages, among other costs. For the capitalist class as a whole, however, wages make up the market, and need therefore to be of a magnitude consonant with the volume of production. The role assumed by the state gains importance at this juncture: a political authority with a degree of autonomy from individual capitalist interests may fulfil the function of the distribution of income to a degree which would serve the logic of capitalist accumulation on a global scale while overriding the particular interests of individual capitalists. This is an instrumental autonomy which derives from the requirements of the model of accumulation chosen by the dominant fraction of the bourgeoisie.[12] In other words, the structure is clearly delineated, together with the domination pattern within it; the state managers do not enjoy any possibility of challenging this structure or the model of accumulation indicated by the dominant class fraction. Consequently their relative autonomy will end, when world or internal conditions require the abandonment of that particular model of accumulation in favour of one where the state does not enjoy a similar economic role.

In Turkey during the 1960s and most of the 1970s, the state functioned as a guarantor of the mechanisms of income distribution we have already described. The margin for man-oeuvre left to contestation by social groups directly benefiting from this distributionary logic allowed the market to adjust itself to the requirements of production with astonishing rapidity. Labour incomes and agricultural incomes increased with industrial production. On the other hand, the flexibility with which state autonomy was transformed into state instru-mentality was notable whenever the model of accumulation encountered problems. On the two occasions in 1971 and after 1977, for example, when production and accumulation were blocked owing to problems in the external articulation of the economy, salaries, wages, and agricultural prices registered a downturn almost without a time lag. On these occasions, it was state policy which changed drastically towards relinquishment of the distributional logic. Concomitantly, the bureaucracy abandoned any pretension of autonomous reformism. Such rapid adjustment points to several distinguishing features in the model of accumulation; the integral relationship between industrial accumulation and the market; the effectiveness of the state's mechanisms of regulation; and the domination of the industrial bourgeoisie in the policy-making process.

Out of the social groups which remained outside the industrial sector, it was the peasantry which emerged with the strongest structural position for bargaining. The 1960 constitution had reformed the electoral system, building in greater sensitivity to voting patterns, based on a strictly proportional, large constitu-ency electoral system. Parties became successful at provincial level according to the degree of their vote attraction. Since with rural out-migration urban populations had concentrated in a few centres, most provinces had peasant populations far exceeding the national average of more than two-thirds in 1960. Each deputy had to take responsibility for his party's perform-ance in the government, which was judged by the peasantry strictly along economic lines.

Agrarian commercialisation and the beginnings of dispersed accumulation during the 1950s were factors which determined the nature of domestic market expansion during subsequent decades. The impact was both direct and indirect. On a direct level, successive governments refrained from imposing any direct taxes on agriculture, on either property or income. Had the agrarian structure been characterised by the dominance of a small number of large landlords, an industrial bourgeoisie might have felt the urge to extract and transfer this wealth in order to satisfy the needs of urban accumulation. Such a tactic was impossible in Turkey because of the exigencies of electoral politics and of market expansion. The traditional tithe on agricultural output had been abolished in 1925, thereby repudiating the inherited legitimacy of the Ottoman state. Attempts to replace the regressive tithe with various property taxes had not been seriously pursued when the nominal levies declined in relation to rising prices. During the Depression the real value of these taxes had in fact become burdensome to the peasantry, but during the period of wartime inflation and subsequently, these taxes had been allowed to lapse into oblivion. During the late 1950s and the 1960s, taxation of agriculture was one of the battle cries of the intelligentsia. Identifying themselves with a Saint-Simonian project of industrialisation, and armed with a distorted analysis of the agrarian structure, they felt that agricultural taxation would respond to the problems of development that beset Turkey. The urban-industrial bias in this diagnosis was evident, and derived in large part from a technocratic reading of the Soviet experience. Land was assumed to be controlled by large landlords even after the transformations of the 1950s. The intelligentsia could combine their industrialism with populism through the device of discovering a polarised agrarian structure. Thus the expropriation of the landlords would serve both to transfer the surplus to industry and to free the small peasantry from the yoke.

Politicians and industrialists were never attracted to this prescription however: electoral exigencies as well as a recognition of the petty-producer-dominated structure in the countryside prevented the dominant powers in the society from subscribing to a simplistic prescription aimed at providing industrial accumulation. There was one unusual region in terms of the agrarian structure and its exceptionality was related to the existence of an ethnic minority in Anatolia. It has already been mentioned that in the south-east tribal nomadism had given way to a settled ownership pattern which perpetuated the earlier social structure in the form of the political and religious impositions of former chiefs who had been transformed into rent-collecting landlords. Since this pattern existed preponderantly in Kurdish areas (but not all Kurdish areas were characterised by such landlordism) the existing social relations provided the central state with a ready-made social control mechanism. Various political parties made alliances with tribal chiefs by which allegiance to the centre was exchanged for the contribution of the coercive arm of the state apparatus to local domination mechanisms.[13] In other words, for these areas, non-intervention in the agrarian structure amounted to an endorsement of landlordism – an outcome quite contrary to the centre's reluctance to impose taxes on small peasants.

That agrarian property relations were characterised over-whelmingly by independent peasant proprietorship meant that any economic reward destined for the countryside would be shared by a large number of production/consumption units. This situation led to the continuation of the price support system which had been initiated by the Menderes government following the downturn in world agricultural markets after the Korean War. Governments of varying political inclinations in the period between 1961 and 1980 responded similarly to this most powerful lobby by subsidising agricultural inputs and artificially increasing support prices for most crops.[14] This subsidy pattern became all the more obvious immediately preceding elections, and served, on the whole, to prop up the peasantry's income. In certain years, its relative weight reached high proportions: for instance the value of the 'support' extended to the farmers in 1977 was equivalent to 22 per cent of that year's total agricultural output.[15] Since not all crops were subject to support, this proportion was even higher in relation to the marketised portion of supported crops. At the same time, the principal inputs purchased by farmers (including insecticides, fertilisers, improved seed, tractors and fuel) were heavily subsidised. As a result the terms-of-trade for agriculture improved continuously during the 1960s and the 1970s, except for the year of the military takeover in 1971. Depending on the indicators used, this improvement was between 20 per cent and 45 per cent between 1960 and 1977.[16]

What this argument amounts to is an assertion that the peasantry came to constitute for the capitalist sector an important segment of the domestic market. During the 1950s villages had started opening up to manufactures, thus losing more of their relative autarky. In the following decade this incorporation at the level of consumer goods accelerated as villages became important markets for the textile, clothing and food industries. Agricultural mechanisation gradually started to provide the impetus for the market. Tractors were produced by

Turkish capitalists before they ventured into automobiles, while various types of machinery were manufactured in small town centres by small capital using artisanal methods. In 1970, there were 100,000 tractors in agriculture and the annual rate of production was 15,000. In 1975 annual production had climbed to 30,000, and the tractor park numbered close to 250,000. By this time villages had also become significant markets for consumer durables, in particular radios, tape recorders and TV sets: a development which was due in large part to migrant workers and their remittances. Despite the industrial bias of planners and bureaucrats, the agrarian structure asserted itself in inducing a pattern of industrialisation reminiscent of the agriculture-led models of liberal parentage.

The indirect impact of the agrarian structure is more difficult to illustrate, but may be summarised as follows: peasants migrating to urban areas were not pushed out of the countryside because of landlessness and poverty. They did not arrive in the cities destitute and without any belongings. The average migrant had a claim to some land in his village which he had rented out or left to a family member in exchange for some compensation. More often than not he came to the city with sufficient capital to start building a house in the shanty town area already colonised by his co-villagers.[17] After this initial transfer, the migrant almost never lost contact with the village; he returned during annual leave, left his children with their grandparents, and he regularly received supplies in kind. If he remained a landowner he also received rent, or his share of the produce. All this meant that the migrant became part of the consumer market the moment he set foot in the city. Starting with the construction of his dwelling, and as a result of the additional income available to him, he served to expand the internal market to a much greater extent than would have been possible in the case of an urbanisation characterised by the migration of the landless poor.

At a more general level, and employing a comparative perspective, we may also claim that the agrarian structure exerted an upward pressure on urban wages. The argument concerning the US during the nineteenth century is well known. In a similar manner, Anatolia had had a high land/labour ratio and a predominance of family property. The marginal product of the rural migrant was certainly not high, but he always had the option of remaining in the countryside with a guaranteed average product, and sharing the household's income. Wages in the city therefore had to be high enough to induce the peasant – who was not being pushed out – to accept urban employment.

The last point concerning migration leads to a discussion of state policy towards the constitution of an internal market in urban areas. We may repeat that the Turkish working class obtained certain privileges and rights far in advance of its counterparts in other equally less developed societies. Most of these privileges were legislated from above and served to integrate part of the working class into the new societal equation. Thus the most important of these legislative measures – that of collective bargaining and the right to strike – was introduced in 1963; between then and 1971, the year of the military *pronunciamento*, real wages in the organised sector increased by 5 to 7 per cent each year. Real wages declined by around 10 per cent during the two years of military presence when strikes were outlawed and union leaders gaoled, but increased again after 1974. They leapt up by 21 per cent in 1975; by 5 per cent in 1976; and by 22 per cent between 1976 and 1978, to then stagnate until the military takeover in 1980.[18] Between 1964 and 1978 average wages had more than doubled. These averages, however, conceal an important duality, in that much greater wage increases were the rule in the 'modern' sector of import substitution. Large-scale manufacturing concerns, such as those producing consumer durables and cars, which used modern technology and in which there was generally some foreign investment, as well as state-owned sectors producing capital and intermediary goods such as steel, oil refineries and paper, became privileged foci of organised labour known for their high wages. In other words these sectors captured the logic of the new accumulation process: the working class was allowed a degree of organisation and contestation because it thus became integrated into the system, both politically and as constituting an essential element of the internal market. That section of the manufacturing bourgeoisie which captured the rent of import-substituting industrialisation was willing to go along with this scheme, as long as it did not threaten its profits.

It must be mentioned that (corresponding to the division within the bourgeoisie) a labour aristocracy had been created within the working class whose levels of remuneration and participation in the manufactured goods market were far superior to those of the majority of labourers. In small industry workers did not usually enjoy the rights gained through union organisation: there was no collective bargaining, no right to strike, and at times the owners managed to avoid social security regulations. In provincial towns and the shanty towns the legally sanctioned apprentice system prevailed which concealed the exploitation of child labour. We shall discuss below the social and political consequences of this division, but it is important to recognise now that the organised stratum we are discussing made up perhaps one-third of the working class; and the higher wage rates refer to this one-third. Of course such segmented labour markets are the rule world-wide, rather than the exception. Assuming that the labour aristocracy in Turkey was not exceptionally favoured (relative to other countries' labour aristocracies), we may note that the resulting wage levels in Turkish manufacturing reflect the argument above in that they were considerably higher than warranted by the relative level of GNP per capita. For example, in 1977 the average daily wage in Turkey was \$11.14; this compared with \$11.72 in Greece, \$20.48 in France and \$23.56 in Britain.[19] Per capita incomes in these countries were two and a half, six and four times the Turkish levels respectively. The comparison with South Korea is more interesting in that it reveals the radically different (export versus internal market oriented) development strategies of two countries of comparable levels of income: in 1974 Turkish manufacturing wages were three times the level of Korean wages. In 1977 they were double, and in 1979, despite very rapid increases in Korea, still 50 per cent higher.[20] There are some problems with these figures because they represent pre-tax wage rates, converted at an overvalued exchange rate in the case of Turkey. Nevertheless, the arguments we have advanced hold, in that both the agrarian structure and state policy were factors pushing up wage rates and preparing for an industrial development strategy based on mass consumption.

In addition to the private wage, we may mention that the social wage, that is, state expenditure designed to supplement the collective consumption of the working class and the petty bourgeoisie, was higher in Turkey than in comparable 'middle income' countries. Especially in the fields of health and schooling which, although grossly insufficient, are offered almost free at all levels, the Turkish performance was probably superior to other 'middle income' countries, while the institutionalisation of social security in the form of retirement benefits was also more advanced. There was, however, no unemployment benefit.

It must be remembered that the economy which is being described was undergoing rapid social transformation during this period and, as such, diverged from the more readily recognised social democratic mould, even if there are important similarities at the level of social policy and demand creation. There is one element which clearly reveals this dimension of transformation and stems from the not-too-distant past of the society. The migration mentioned above resulted in the urbanisation of large numbers of people who could not obtain housing within existing residential areas. The solution immediately hit upon was the construction of shanty towns on state-owned land surrounding inhabited areas. That there was still state-owned land so close to urban centres was due to the specificity of the Ottoman social formation; that contemporary governments accepted the *fait accompli* of land occupation and frequently ratified the situation through the distribution of legal titles on the eve of elections was due to the policy of inclusion which was an integral component of the industrialisation strategy. By the end of the 1960s around one half of the dwellings in larger cities were officially classified as shanty town or *gecekondu*. The typical *gecekondu* was built in stages, but looked permanent and sturdy when completed. It was owner-occupied, consisted of between two and four rooms, and followed in design the urban norm in Turkey which prioritises size over luxury. It was usually constructed with the help of neighbours and one or two builders, but principally using the family's own labour. The neighbourhood consisted typically of families originating in the same province or even the same village, although other affiliations, notably ethnic background and religious sect, also played a role. *Gecekondus* were normally built on fair-sized plots which left the owners some garden space for growing vegetables and raising poultry, and sometimes even for keeping a cow. The older the *gecekondu* area, the more secure was its legal status. Politicians promised and usually delivered titles to the occupiers of state land; since some time had to pass before the inhabitants of a particular neighbourhood became a pressure group, new *gecekondus* were always under the threat of expropriation. The seizure of land by police or municipal authorities was a rare occurrence; nevertheless, legislation of status served as a claim to municipal services, although these were more or less permanently lacking. Roads were unpaved and utilities arrived with considerable delay. Water remained a problem even after electricity was connected. After a few elections it was likely that some of the services would arrive, but in the meantime small-scale private enterprise substituted for the state in providing a range of services ranging from transportation to bottled cooking gas. The lack of public goods was perhaps the distinguishing variable that defined the character of shanty towns; for after a few years in construction the neighbourhoods took on the appearance of working class suburbs with fairly sturdy housing and small gardens.[21] This was due in no small part to the transfer of initial savings from the village, and to a continuing relationship with the place of origin which facilitated day-to-day reproduction. As legal titles were ratified the *gecekondu* owner also came to possess valuable urban property. Shanty town areas were geographically not very distant from urban centres (on account of the historical heritage of state property) and the urban rent accruing to these properties was considerable. Even if shanty town dwellers did not regularly sell their houses, the 'wealth effect' through which they were able to devote a larger part of their current income to consumption played a role. In short the shanty town was not only a major innovation responding to the problems of urbanisation and housing, but it also proved to contribute to the formation of an internal market. Its existence allowed the urbanites to participate in the market, first for construction items and then for consumption goods once the housing problem was solved. The *gecekondu* was also important in terms of the ideological evolution of its inhabitants, and in providing a focused counterpoint to large capital and organised labour: these are topics we will broach in the coming chapters.

VIII
Crisis Dynamics

Import substituting industrialisation is based on selective protection of the domestic manufacturing sector. In those countries which successfully employed this strategy, industrial development necessitated the importing of technology, capital goods and intermediate goods as inputs to the manufacturing process. For this reason import substitution was also a strategy of selective protection: while capital goods and inputs were imported, outputs of industries that developed domestically faced no competition from foreign producers. In the direct relationship between the volume of imports and the volume of domestic industrial production, the ceiling on the rate of industrialisation was determined by not only the classical crisis tendencies of a capitalist economy, but also by the importing capacity. We shall argue below that classical crisis tendencies were held at bay during the history of import substitution in Turkey; hence the constraints that limited the pace of industrialisation were always determined by the availability of foreign exchange, i.e. the importing capacity.

Furthermore, it will be shown that the break-up of the social coalition which sustained the ISI strategy occurred because of the crises brought about by the same foreign exchange constraint. In other words, the dormant conflict implicit in the alliance was not triggered by an intensification of the internal antagonistic situation: social crisis followed upon the economic crisis of the system. We can say that it was problems in system integration which forced the split in the balances established at the level of social integration.

Classical crisis tendencies in a capitalist economy resolve into either of two basic outcomes: underconsumption – insufficiency of market demand – or declining rate of profit – insufficiency of productive investment. Policies of import substitution seek to avoid both of these outcomes: they aim at ensuring satisfactory profits for industrialists while also creating and sustaining an internal market. Protection of the domestic market is principally aimed at favouring those manufacturers who are fortunate enough to be able to import their inputs. Since they face no competition in selling their output on the domestic market, they may realise high monopoly profits. Given the magnitude of such profits, it is unlikely that they will respond to temporary reduction in protection rent by holding back investments or through a 'capital strike' as long as the material conditions of reproduction and accumulation are maintained. In other words, as long as they can secure the physical inputs of the production process and they are reasonably certain of labour discipline, they will tolerate temporary reductions in profitability. This is why state policy aimed at creating an internal market, which amounts to high wages in privileged sectors of manufacturing, will enjoy space for manoeuvre as long as workers' demands are confined to the level of wages. When unions become more political in their struggle and begin to question the labour process, the industrialists reach an impasse: for now it is the material conditions of reproduction that are challenged. The ISI industrialist must be even more rigid in his response to labour demands concerning the process of production, for unlike his counterpart in advanced countries, he has to work with a given blueprint and a received technology, and is unable to introduce alterations and modifications necessitated by increasing labour demands. Certainly, this adjustability of the production process is a matter of degree; but we may evoke Hirschman's description of ISI as a 'tightly staged' process to add that it is also a strategy which does not allow much choice or variation at the level of technology.[1] While temporary reductions in profitability may be tolerated, disruptions in labour discipline may cause capital to react by forcing state managers to abandon their apparent neutrality in favour of disciplining the labour force.

The post-war Keynesian experience has made it clear that the presence of a strong state which seeks to ensure an income distribution and a market may lead to a declining profit rate and consequent capitalist reaction. In other words, a too successful

demand-creation mechanism becomes unpopular when capitalists begin to feel that their profits are at stake. Therefore the
capitalist state, both in the core and the periphery, attempts to
insure capital against declining profit rates. I have already
described the market creation mechanism in import substitution, in the form of terms-of-trade favouring the agricultural
sector and increasing real wages; it is now necessary to discover
the flows in the social surplus which allowed for a satisfactory
level of capital accumulation in industry.

We may begin by pointing out the mechanisms which served
to transfer the social surplus to the account of the industrialists.
Rents procured through protection are obviously the primary
channel of transfer. Because of both the suppression of foreign
competition and the creation of monopoly or oligopoly structures in the internal market, profit margins were allowed to
remain at high levels. Again within this framework, various
forces conspired to keep foreign capital out of Turkish industry,
with the result that the local bourgeoisie did not have to
compete (where it did not want to) with potentially more
productive capital. I will elaborate the reasons for the relative
absence of foreign capital below; suffice it to say that this was
one of the issues where a silent entente between the bourgeoisie
and the bureaucracy remained in force until the end of the
period, when external pressure forced its seams. A second
major mechanism was an entire set of subsidy schemes whereby
the state allowed the industrial bourgeoisie, directly and
indirectly, to enjoy preferential prices for inputs (some produced in state enterprises), low-cost credits, and tax rebates.
Within this collection one subsidy was of qualitatively different
dimensions, and its functioning was masked by a bogus market
appearance. In order to underline its importance, I will treat it
as a third mechanism. This is the exchange-rate policy which
served to subsidise importers (industrialists who utilised imported inputs) and penalise exports. Finally, I will discuss the
duality in the manufacturing sector as a source of unequal
exchange between modern industry and low-wage paying small
enterprises.

The scheme of tax rebates, preferential foreign exchange
quotas and low-cost credits does not require much comment:
these were mostly allocated through the Planning Office and
other political mechanisms, and favoured the same industrialists who stood to gain from the general policy of protection and

tariffs. Since these schemes were coeval with the inception of the industrial bourgeoisie's hegemony, they had evolved within the limits set by manufacturers' demands. Their existence potentially strengthened the bureaucratic decision-making mechanisms but such strength could not be employed for ends conflicting with the accumulation capacity of the manufacturing sector as a whole. In other words, the bureaucracy may have favoured one group or an individual within the industrial bourgeoisie over others, but this did not threaten the overall transfer effected by the subsidy schemes.

State Economic Enterprises (SEEs), although serving to provide low-cost inputs to the private sector, were a presence of a quite different order. They were inherited from the étatist period of bureaucratic domination and they had remained quantitively important within the industrial sector, despite changes in the political system and despite the loss of status suffered by the bureaucracy. Potentially, they posed a threat to the bourgeoisie since the instrumental autonomy enjoyed by the bureaucracy could be put to an unintended and contradictory use through strengthening the control over the means of production and accumulation that state enterprise represented. It is significant, therefore, that SEEs served to transfer value to the industrial bourgeoisie, and in doing so exhibited another dimension of the pattern of domination.

During the late 1940s, when the Democrat Party's leadership campaigned on an anti-étatist platform, one of the salient issues had been the transfer of state enterprises to private ownership. These were considered to be privileged seats of accumulation whose very existence inhibited the development of private capitalism. Soon after they came to power, however, DP leaders discovered that what mattered was the use to which the state enterprises were put within the overall orientation of economic policy. Instead of being dismantled as promised, the SEEs expanded their presence in absolute terms, but at the same time were effectively subordinated to the requirements of private accumulation. During the early 1950s, the SEEs' share of total manufacturing had fluctuated around 25 per cent; after a decline in 1954, state enterprises stabilised their share at between one-sixth and one-fifth of total value added in manufacturing.[2] At various points after 1960, the SEEs were brought on to the political agenda, although the discussion mostly originated in ideological conflict. Only when the bourgeoisie wished to express discontent with bureaucratic

administration did it evoke the issue of state enterprises, and
then it was not their existence, dismantling or transfer to the
private sector which was at issue. Arguments centred rather on
their mismanagement, employment policies, pricing guidelines
and on the inflationary effects of state subsidies – in other words
on the best use to which they could be put.

State enterprises served a multiplicity of objectives, ranging
from employment creation through regional development to
national autarky.[3] From the point of view of the industrial
bourgeoisie most of these goals could be construed as function-
ally desirable. At a more direct level, in terms of safeguarding
the profit rate, two aspects of the SEEs stood out – the
provision of backward linkages which required high initial
outlays of capital, and the production of low price inputs. State
enterprises had been initiated in the heady days of nationalist
development projects, with investments in steel, iron, paper,
superphosphates and artificial fibres, as well as in mining and
textiles. These production units were large by the standards of
the day and certainly very large compared with the prevailing
scale in the private sector. In other words, SEEs mobilised
volumes of capital which could not be brought together by the
private sector at the time. Until the 1960s, in fact, state
enterprises remained unequalled from the point of view of
scale. Secondly, with the exception of the sugar and textile
industries state enterprises did not venture into the consumption end of the market. Most of their products were designed as
inputs to private manufactures.[4]

These intermediary industries, although they were of high
prestige value, were by the 1960s hardly at the forefront of
modern technology. In addition to requiring large outlays, they
were also low profit sectors. While their existence was necessary
for national economic development, these sectors had already
lost their attractiveness on the world scale. Consequently, they
were not attractive for the private sector either, not only
because of the large outlay necessary but also because under
any world market sanctioning they would not experience
anything but low profit rates. There was therefore a structural
necessity for the state sector to be characterised by low profit
rates while its externalities remained available to the private
sector. In addition to such externalities, the product prices of
state enterprise could also be fixed to favour the private sector.

The fact that the operation of state economic enterprises
benefited the private sector does not imply that the industrial-

ists would not have preferred to import their inputs instead. In having to purchase from state enterprises they had to live with uncertain deliveries and varying quality. On the other hand, as long as each industrialist knew that his competitors faced the same supply situation as himself, he would be less inclined to complain. Particularly since there was no world-market sanctioning of either quality or prices, what happened inside the protected economy took on the character of a classical situation of bounded rationality: a lot of the variables were simply accepted as part of the environmental set of constraints. Everyone lived with them; it was therefore not (locally) efficient for individual capitalists to attempt to change the constraints; rather, optimisation had to take the constraints as part of the fixed environment.

Hirschman has argued that the first wave of import substitutions would constitute a natural obstacle to the rise of industrialists who aim at exploiting backward linkages, or, in other words, producing the inputs required in the first stage. Since the first wave would specialise in light consumer goods using imported machinery, they would prefer to continue their import link with outside suppliers who could provide reliable quality, definite delivery schedules, and price guarantees, features of a competitive world market. By contrast, local manufacturers of the same inputs, themselves protected from foreign competition, would be in a position to impose their own privileges in the form of higher prices, and uncertain quality and delivery schedules.[5] In the case of Turkey, first wave manufacturers were nurtured in an environment where state enterprises already held protected monopoly positions in some of the 'backward linkage' industries. This situation was advantageous to an industrial bourgeoisie which had already established domination over the state mechanism, because the conflict between the first and the second wave of import substitutors, identified by Hirschman, could thus be avoided. State enterprise could be confined to those fields which were not atttractive to the industrial bourgeoisie, and technological deepening could be achieved more smoothly. On the other hand, it also meant that industrialists had to adjust their production and management to the inefficiencies implied by state industries, thereby delaying the stage of assimilation of world market norms of quality and efficiency. In other words, with a less complete import substitution schedule, the economic field in Turkey might have been less insular. State enterprises served to

extend the chain which remained outside world market calculations, from the final product to the backward linkages, and the
rationality of the industrial sector as a whole increasingly lacked
any intersection with global norms.[6]

There were some state enterprises, in addition to those
producing intermediary goods, which manufactured the light
consumer goods that would have been expected to be the
mainstays of the private sector during the first phase of import
substitution – notably textiles. Here, however, there were no
grounds for conflict with private industrialists because of a fairly
strict product differentation. In the 1930s, the textile operation
had started to produce cheap, coarse cotton cloth for basic
needs, and woollens for the bureaucratic uniform – in various
shades of grey and brown. During the 1950s smaller private
concerns began to manufacture artificial and mixed fabrics in
more attractive patterns and colours. As these captured the
upper echelons of consumer demand, state manufactured prints
and woollens were relegated to the lowest income brackets,
where low quality was tolerated because of exceptionally
reasonable prices. We may argue that the existence of cheap
state-manufactured textiles may have been a factor in increasing the real incomes of both the peasantry and the urban
popular classes, thus contributing to the accumulation potential
of industrialists. As long as bureaucratic autonomy based on the
control of means of production could be prevented, state
economic enterprises served as a barely concealed channel of
transfer to the private sector.

The other important factor which illuminates the role of policy
in achieving the desired allocation of the economic surplus was
the overvalued exchange rate. During the entire period, with
the possible exception of a few years after the 1970 devaluation,
the Turkish lira was overvalued, the black market rate at times
exceeding double the official. What this signifies is that
bureaucratic, i.e. political, allocation rather than the market,
was the mechanism by which scarce foreign exchange was made
available to importers. All imports were subject to official
approval and since the consumer goods' share of total imports
was less than 5 per cent during the entire period (around 2 per
cent towards the end) industrialists competed for virtually the
entire supply of foreign exchange at the level of the proper
bureaucratic offices. An overvalued exchange rate reinforced
the instrumental autonomy of the bureaucracy through a

politicisation of economic decision-making. Thus a mutually rewarding exchange by which the currency was converted from political power at one end to pecuniary reward at the other, became a central mechanism of the political economy of import substituting industrialisation.

Since the dollar was made available to lucky industrialists at the favoured official rate, these were assured of collecting enormous rents once they converted the imported inputs into final commodities to be realised in the internal market. In principle, they faced no competition except from other manufacturers who themselves were in the same rent-seeking situation. There was some illegal competition from smuggled consumption goods, but the prices in this black market had to account for not only the unofficial rate of foreign exchange, but also what may be called the 'smuggler's returns'.

While allowing for the creation and collection of high profits by domestic manufacturers, an overvalued exchange rate also indicates the direction of surplus transfers within the economy through which such rents are made possible. In fact this is the obverse of the question which was posed initially: 'If, ostensibly, there is a redistribution of income favouring certain sections of the working class and the peasantry, at whose expense are the industrialists able to reap high profit rates?' An overvalued exchange rate is only one factor determining the allocation of the social surplus; it does indicate, however, that export farmers lost through foreign trade. As importers paid less than the market rate for the dollars they were privileged to use, exporters received less local currency (than they would have under a market rate) for the dollars they earned through selling their products. Until the end of the 1970s exports consisted overwhelmingly of agricultural goods. In fact it was one of the characteristics of import substitution in Turkey that the manufacturing sector did not generate exports as long as the internal market prevailed. Exports consisted of traditional items: if we take the average of 1968–71, for example, agricultural products accounted for 77 per cent of export earnings. The principal commodities were the ones which had developed in response to European demand during the nineteenth century: tobacco, cotton, hazelnuts, figs and raisins. Only during the second half of the 1970s did manufactured exports gain any significance, but the proportions were still small; the food industry (or processed agricultural products) accounted for 9 per cent and textiles for another 9 per cent of exports in

1975.[7] In other words the overvalued exchange rate primarily penalised producers of crops directed towards export. The exchange-rate policy contributed to the maintenance of industrial profit rates but also, through necessitating an administrative allocation mechanism, increased the state managers' political control over the market. Therefore it was a policy which faithfully reflected the basis of ISI regulation: by strengthening the instrumental automony enjoyed by the state managers it effected a transfer which aided the industrialists. The obvious question that the previous section poses is which social group, if any, suffered as a result of the economic regulation of the 1960–77 period. Unlike some Latin American examples, the agricultural sector and in particular large export-oriented landlords were not clearly victimised through any transfer mechanism. The only transfer from agriculture was through the exchange-rate policy, and there the effects fell mostly upon farmers who were otherwise beneficiaries of the distribution schemes. The internal terms-of-trade, which in a planned economy might have provided the industrialisation process with a means of primary accumulation, worked in favour of agriculture, contributing to the creation of markets for manufactures, but not directly to manufacturers' profits. Nor was it the case that the period of rapid industrial accumulation had been made possible through a super-exploitation of the working class as, for example, in the successful industrialisation of certain South-east Asian countries.

As long as there was a satisfactory growth rate, for most identifiable social groups an absolute decline in fortunes was not on the agenda; their relative unfavoured status, however, translated into a rapid accumulation potential for others. We have already presented the industrial bourgeoisie and the organised working class as constituting the defining elements of the economic model. The vanguard of the industrialists, the owners and managers of the largest one hundred or so private corporations and the part of the working class employed by them were at the core of this model.

It had been the constitution of an industrial bourgeoisie and an organised working class which had determined the success of the original model. The top industrialists were the paradigmatic import substitutors. They were either monopolists or strong oligopolists; in the absence of competitive checks they could continue to reap their rents through protection, and could, therefore, afford to yield to union demands for high wages.

They generally employed more than one thousand workers who were strongly organised and represented by a strong national union. Such firms were concentrated geographically as well: a majority could be found in the Istanbul area, followed by the Adana-Mersin and Izmir areas – these were the three growth poles of modern industry. We are talking about a geographically delimited class of industrialists confronted by a labour aristocracy within the working class whose wages remained much higher than those of the lower reaches of the spectrum. It should be pointed out that workers in state manufacturing enterprises were also included in this labour aristocracy. Of the 173,626 workers in 1971 (total employment in manufacturing was 1.3 million) who were employed in manufacturing establishments of more than one thousand wage-earners, 67 per cent worked for state enterprises. State employment declined rapidly towards the smaller end of the concentration spectrum.[8]

There was also a second order of both capitalists and workers whose fortunes were tied to the first group: capitalists, because they set up manufacturing or service firms which shared in the success of the vanguard industrialists in producing inputs or complementary commodities in tandem; and workers, because through sharing geographical location and collective bargaining privileges they could benefit from the same gains enjoyed by the core of the industrial proletariat. This status, which provided benefits during the growth period, did not however protect them against crises or conjunctural downturns. Because these industrialists produced in more competitive markets, any cartel-like arrangements which safe-guarded profit rates during good times had to be relinquished when markets were contracting; and workers, even if they were unionised, did not have comparable shopfloor or market strength in a factory employing only one hundred people. Although supported by their respective unions, they could not hope to muster the same bargaining strength as the 'labour aristocracy' of the first group. It was also true that high profits were a precondition of high wages and the fact that these manufacturers could not protect their high profit rates implied that they had to oppose demands for wage increases. In 1971 there were 1,278 firms and 186,000 workers in manufacturing establishments employing between 50 and 500 workers (14 per cent of the total), forming a category corresponding to the core of the second order. The 130 firms and 93,000 workers in companies employing between 500 and 1,000 workers (7 per cent of the total) must be considered as an intermediate category between the labour aristocracy of the first group (13 per cent of the total) and the second order: specific factors would determine their position.[9]

Despite rapid growth in the modern manufacturing sector, vast numbers of small industries remained active and even prospered. In terms of their genesis, two distinct groups in small industry could be identified: the first group which owed its existence to the economic growth of the 1960s, was located on the perimeter of the above-mentioned industrial sectors. It featured new entrepreneurs, and the new urban dwellers as workers. The second group was traditional small industry catering to local demand in various Anatolian towns. Its origins could be traced to the early 1950s and frequently to the 1930s; it was founded by small capitalists in such towns in order to take advantage of easy opportunities for import substitution. Given its technology, markets, and the nature of commodities produced, such small industry was condemned to being driven out of the market with the growth of the modern sector. The first category, however, owed its existence to rapid transformation of the urban economy: it explored urban markets that were complementary to those addressed by large industrialists. Despite the differences in genesis, in terms of their location in the socio-economic structure, there were important similarities. First, in both groups the exploitation of labour was severe. Workers were not as a rule covered by social security or minimum wage regulations; child labour was frequent under diverse forms of traditional practices and apprenticeship institutions; working conditions were primitive and hours arbitrary; the employment and firing of workers depended entirely on the will of the owners; finally, wages were a fraction of the prevailing rates in the organised sector. It seems that the average wage in the smallest scale operations (private firms employing 10 workers or less) was around 40 per cent of the average wage in firms employing 100 or more workers; or, to compare the two adjacent catagories, the average wage in the 10–50 worker firm was 50 per cent higher than the wage in the 0–10 class. [10] Moreover, it is likely that these data do not include the lowest wage category of under-age and uninsured apprentices, whose inclusion would change the picture considerably for the worse.

Within the group comprising small shops, savage competition was the rule. In each small sub-sector scores of shops, frequently congregated in one section of the urban belt, undercut each other's prices. This competition translated into the ever-present threat of bankruptcy, but more significantly from the point of view of social distribution, into low profit rates. Finally, for both categories the development of the modern industrial sector posed a major threat. Either through direct competition, for instance in the case of metal works, or through centralised organisation, as in the automotive industry with its licensed service and repair shops, the modern sector could drive small capital out of business. There were individual entrepreneurs who were successful: the owner of a small machine shop in Bursa managed to start a factory producing parts for the automotive industry; another entrepreneur who began on a small scale established the first mass market furniture enterprise in Ankara. For every success story, however, there were many bankruptcies and many more cases of businesses barely able to survive. The point here is that small capital in manufacturing was one sector where labourers were definitely relative losers, and capitalists themselves, if they were lucky enough to survive, accepted lower profit rates than those which prevailed in the modern sector. In other words, small capital not only paid low wages, but also was forced to lose the value it extracted from the workers through the market process. It had to charge prices which only afforded normal-competitive profit rates despite prevailing low wages; the social value created was thus transferred to the more privileged sectors. The number of establishments in the small manufacturing sector increased, however. In 1963 there were 158,000 shops with less than ten workers; and in 1970 there were 170,000; new enterprises replaced old ones and augmented the total.[11] The pool out of which value was extracted and transferred continued to grow.

Within small industry, the weight shifted from small towns to large cities, and from traditional sectors to new activities designed to respond to the new structures of industry and population. This shift brought with it drastic social consequences, as will be discussed below. It is important to repeat that the success of the modern industrial sector was based in part on the over-exploitation of low-wage workers in small industry who were mostly new migrants from the countryside. The point about small industry is that either through direct exchange with modern industry, or through supplying workers with wage goods, its activity entered the process of reproducing the economic system. Small capitalists extracted high levels of surplus value from their workers, which they lost to big capitalists through the market system. There were of course other groups in the population who fared badly relative to the average income growth rate. The subsistence-oriented peasantry of the eastern highlands was such a group; but in its case we cannot talk about a transfer of value. Any transfer through trade was minuscule; eastern peasants contributed to the accumulation process only when they became western workers.

In investigating the sources of capital accumulation in Turkey, what immediately emerges as of paramount importance is the extent of foreign funding. Starting soon after the war, the Turkish state and the bourgeoisie were able to convince the US government, supranational organisations and various funding agencies that the development of capitalism was desirable and should be subsidised externally. Turkey's geographical position on the 'southern flank of NATO' and its shared border with the Soviet Union were undoubtedly important factors contributing to the success of this endeavour. It was also important, however, that Turkey was potentially in the European periphery, and its development path might be expected to fall under the influence of the emerging European core. In fact this appurtenance gained appreciable importance during the 1970s when Turkish workers obtained access to northern European labour markets and started funding imports through remittances. Until that time, however, official transfers in loans and grants were primary.

The measure of the extent of external funding is the amount made available to a country augmenting the domestically produced output available for consumption and investment. In Turkey's case imports exceeded exports every year between 1947 and 1980; in other words available resources exceeded domestic output thus allowing for higher levels of investment or consumption or both. Alternatively, the availability of this extra resource allowed for a lower rate of exploitation by adding to the accumulation potential despite higher wages. This situation became so endemic that, far from aiming at national self-sufficiency, state managers were quite explicit in planning for foreign funds which would flow in to finance the envisaged levels of investment. Consequently, the domestic savings rate did not constitute a macro-economic ceiling on the rate of capital accumulation. It may be argued that the high probability attached to the perennial inflow of external funds may have caused a degree of laxity in the process of policy-making, with the consequence that domestic savings were not forced or encouraged to a degree which would have been appropriate given the rapid rate of accumulation. Or we might suggest that since external finance contributed to the augmentation of investable funds, domestic policy could be oriented primarily to consumption and to the creation of an internal market. To the extent that such a separation could operate (in other words as long as external finances accounted for a good proportion of investable funds) policy-making was made considerably easier and the market creation–capital accumulation trade-off could be avoided. This is fundamentally a question of distribution: the more that external funds contribute to capital accumulation, the less pressure there is to deprive the non-capitalist classes. Thus increases in real income may be sustained for workers and the petty bourgeoisie despite rapid accumulation in the capitalist sector.

Total resources were augmented between 1 and 4 per cent every year during the 1950s; during the 1960s the percentage ranged from between 1.4 per cent and 4.3 per cent of the national income. Until the middle of the 1960s, the additions to Turkey's resources derived overwhelmingly from official transfers in the form of aid and loans from governmental agencies or international organisations. The largest component consisted of US government grants and loans. To give an example of a typical year in this period, in 1963 commodity imports exceeded exports by US $193 million; the deficit in services was $80 million, and loan repayments by the central government amounted to $47 million. These deficits were covered by $71 million in US and other government grants, $118 million in loans from the US government, and $48 million from other lenders, as well as $22 million in American military off-shore expenditures.[12] Workers' remittances, which were to play a most important role later in the decade, were of minor importance at this time. The argument may be made that these transfers were not without cost from the point of view of the Turkish economy, especially since the quid pro quo was the maintenance of a large army and military expenditures out of state revenue which might have been used more efficiently in contributing more directly to the accumulation of capital. Nevertheless, given the necessity of foreign exchange in financing import substituting industrialisation, it may seem that from the point of view of the Turkish bourgeoisie it was not a bad deal. The maintenance of the army required mostly local currency expenditure, with the armaments granted from abroad, and there was certainly no shortage of labour; thus the large numbers under conscription did not become an element raising wages.

From the point of view of the US government the continuation of the Marshall Aid programme was a transition from European recovery to aid for development. As explained above, during the late 1950s, it had emerged that bourgeois interests inside Turkey had opted for an industrialisation under protection, thus separating the country from the rest of Europe and in particular from the experience of southern Europe.[13] While Greece, Italy, Spain and Portugal increased the importance of their foreign trade, Turkey's trade stagnated as a proportion of GNP. Italy's imports doubled between 1950 and 1955, for example, and quadrupled between 1955 and 1969. That is to say that in current dollars Italy imported eight times as much in 1969 as in 1950. Starting from a lower base, Spanish imports doubled between 1950 and 1956, quadrupled between then and 1962 and were eight times their 1950 level in 1965. For both Greece and Portugal, the figures show a slower rate of growth, with imports reaching twice their initial volume during the 1950s and doubling again during the 1960s. Turkey's performance clearly distinguishes it from the rest of the European periphery: although starting from a lower base, the value of its imports did not double until 1963, and at the end of the 1960s stood at only 2.2 times the 1950 level. Exports increased slowly after the Korean boom with frequent reversals when adverse weather conditions affected agricultural output; unlike in the rest of the European periphery, tourism did not become an important source of foreign exchange and workers' remittances began to attain a significant magnitude only in the late 1960s. The differences among southern European countries in balance of payments performance are revealing. Official assistance was of varying importance in each country: in Italy, for example, these funds declined to zero by 1954; instead, tourism gained increasing importance. By 1960 tourism revenue in Italy amounted to one-fifth of export earnings. During the 1960s tourism revenue continued to increase, although slightly declining in proportion to trade, but an unforeseen item, workers' remittances, gained momentum and increased to a peak in 1973. In the case of Spain, US aid started in 1953, but dwindled to a small amount after 1962. During the 1960s, however, revenue from tourism increased from one-third of export earnings to 100 per cent in 1965, and then declined relatively to stabilise at around two-thirds at the end of the decade. Since workers' remittances supplied additional exchange (equivalent to around one-quarter of export earnings) between 1962 and 1973 imports could increase despite a growing commodity deficit. For Portugal, both tourism revenue and workers' remittances began to increase after the first half of the 1960s. In 1968 they amounted to 85 per cent of export earnings. In Greece, American grants continued to be paramount, although these had a tendency to fluctuate. Nevertheless, they reached a peak in 1961 when they were equivalent to 35 per cent of Greek exports and covered one-quarter of the trade deficit. From then on they declined in importance. During the 1960s remittances and tourism revenue increased steadily, although a third item, deriving from the large shipping sector, contributed to foreign earnings.

In the case of Turkey, US economic and military aid provided the single most important credit item (after exports) each year until 1969. After 1969 workers' remittances rose to the top of the list, but American funds remained important, covering about one-half of the trade deficit until 1974. Turkey did not attract an important amount of tourism, and its earnings from workers' remittances began to grow several years later than was the case with the four other countries in question. We may add parenthetically that such a dependence on American funds significantly coloured the country's political environment. A persuasive argument is that the strategy of closed industrialisation adopted by the industrial bourgeoisie was possible only because Turkey was, and continued to be, largely self-sufficient in food production. Had this not been the case export orientation would certainly have come on the agenda in the face of the alimentary needs of a growing population. The positive counterpart to a low level of trade integration in world markets was the development of native industry under textbook conditions of infant protection. Even with the fortunate circumstances which exempted Turkey from having to import food, industrialisation at the aspired pace required foreign exchange in excess of what could be earned. Here the contribution of the world hegemonic power in reallocating international purchasing power came into play. With the dollar as the international currency, the US government was in a position politically to decide on subsidising the capital accumulation of certain national bourgeoisies for strategic purposes. It did so in the case of Turkey, and until 1970 such aid constituted the principal mode of covering the trade deficit as well as providing the funds to add to domestic savings.

The Turkish government hoped for larger aid and loan packages, as documented in the three five-year plans covering the period 1963–1978. According to these plans, foreign funds were supposed to provide between one and four per cent of the national income every year, and thus augment the savings rate from an average of 14.8 per cent to 18.3 per cent during the first five-year period; from 19.4 per cent to 21.3 per cent in the second five years; and from 23.3 per cent to 24.2 per cent between 1973 and 1978.[14] What actually transpired was somewhat disappointing: only after the emergence of workers' remittances as a significant item in the late 1960s were these aspirations realised.

The curious datum in this context was the relative absence of direct foreign investment. Despite the political connection, which in most cases aimed at cultivating the willingness of local authorities to accommodate foreign and, in particular, US capital, the Turkish economy remained relatively inviolate in its dealings with external investors. It was mentioned above that foreign capital constituted an important presence in the reconstruction period preceding the Great Depression. Yet during the 1930s most of these investments were liquidated, and some (such as railroads) were nationalised. After World War II American capital was busy in Europe, and despite a liberal 'foreign investment law' in 1954, whose adoption was strongly supported by the US, only $17 million of direct investment entered the country during the 1950s.[15] Flows were somewhat higher in the subsequent decade, with annual amounts in the range of $15–50 million. The figures in the yearly balance-of-payments accounts refer to all direct investment, including trading concerns and distribution agencies. In these accounts which include investment in commercial and other services, the peak year during the 1960s was 1966 with $30 million. It was after 1970 that foreign investment seemed prepared to take off, with $58 million in 1970, $45 million in 1971 and $42 million in 1972; dwindling to $27 million by 1976.[16] With the onset of the payments crisis in 1977, profit transfers became uncertain, causing direct investment flows virtually to stop until 1980. According to the State Planning Organisation and the OECD, with a few exceptions, all foreign capital in manufacturing entered the country under the 1954 legislation. The value of foreign capital under the 1954 law had reached $205 million in 1975 and, based on a later survey, 76 per cent of the capital in this category was actually invested in manufactures. This sum of $156 million represented 42 per cent of the capital of 129 firms. More than one-third of this capital was found in the chemical and food sectors, more specifically, in pharmaceuticals and beverages. One-third of the capital was owned by Swiss multinationals, 18 per cent by Germans and 12 per cent by US firms.

The principal impact of foreign capital was its role as the channel of technology, licences, and patents. The follower status of import substituting industrialisation requires imitation of already standardised technologies; and in some cases, 'joint ventures', or partnerships with foreign firms is local capital's only channel of access to technology transfer. We may attempt a calculation of the part played by foreign investment in capital accumulation in the manufacturing sector. If we suppose that the manufacturing capital which entered the country unprotected by the 1954 law was one-third of the $156 million mentioned above, we get a figure of approximately $200 million for the 1961–1975 period. During this decade and a half, total gross fixed investment in manufacturing was just under $9 thousand million.[17] In other words, the share of foreign investment in capital formation in the manufacturing sector was around 2.2 per cent. The figure of $9 thousand million includes public sector investments as well; a calculation based only on private investment would yield 3.8 per cent as the contribution of direct foreign capital. It must be repeated that these are crude figures especially hampered by the use of official exchange rates; an ideal calculation based on realistic values of the dollar would lower the figure for total investment somewhat, thus raising the contribution of foreign capital. The orders of magnitude however are clear: whatever its qualitative importance, foreign capital accounted for less than 5 per cent of private capital and less than 3 per cent of the total capital formation in the manufacturing sector. Manufacturing provided between 15 and 18 per cent of the national income during this period; in agriculture, still the largest sector, there was no foreign investment.

A comparative perspective also suggests that the flow of foreign capital into Turkey was far behind the levels to which

Latin American countries were accustomed. If $200 million represented the order of magnitude for the stock of direct foreign investment in the Turkish manufacturing sector, the corresponding figure was $1,480 million in Argentina (1973), $6,900 million in Brazil (1976), and $3,670 million in Mexico (1975).[18] During this period Turkey's total product was comparable to Argentina's, and per capita income on a par with Brazil's.

Turkey's relative deprivation in terms of foreign capital has traditionally been ascribed to the antipathy of the bureaucracy. In fact the finance ministry could appeal to one or more of the laws controlling dealings in foreign exchange to delay or reject investment permits and profit transfers. The US government and aid-giving agencies frequently complained about bureaucratic intervention and reluctance. Nevertheless, during the entire period between 1954 and 1980, project applications and approvals far exceeded actual flows of investment; in other words, foreign capital seems to have been discouraged after the initial steps were taken and bureaucratic approval obtained. This circumstance might suggest that rather than specific obstacles to foreign capital, the general atmosphere of government controls over foreign exchange and investment, and the sheer amount of paperwork, may have played a discouraging role. It is also true that during this entire period, Turkey's politics remained volatile, with a brief military intervention in 1971, which did not succeed in changing the rules of the game. Since the country appeared to be on the edge of political crisis, despite satisfactory economic performance, foreign capital might not have felt sufficiently confident to proceed, especially as alternatives were always available.

We might add the argument that Turkish capitalists were not especially keen on inviting foreign capital either. As long as it was possible to form joint ventures or to purchase licences and technology, actual investment by a multinational, whose size and network would overshadow protected local capitalists, was not necessarily desirable. During a period of rapid growth and expansion into new fields, Turkish industrialists may have used the 'bureaucratic reluctance' excuse to conceal their own negative reaction to a heavier presence of foreign capital. If such were the case, it must be admitted that the tactic was successful, for Turkish capitalism was the most 'national' in terms of the presence of multinationals, of all cases (except India) of successful import substituting industrialisation.

We can briefly suggest two more reasons for the relative paucity of foreign investment. Turkey was not in the US's back garden geographically, and despite unchallenged hegemony in the 1950s, US capital could not be overly interested in such distant prospects. Economically, Turkey gradually entered the European sphere of influence during the 1960s, as reflected in trade patterns and in the dominance of Swiss and German investments over American. Nevertheless, this was an ambiguous connection which might have kept US firms out, while not necessarily attracting European ones. Turkey's status within the European Economic Community (EEC) was not clear, its associate membership open to interpretation and revision. For purposes of free trade within the customs union, investment in the member countries was a more certain proposition: while if cheap labour were the issue, investment outside the European Community was more lucrative than investment in Turkey with its relatively high wages. In fact during the late 1960s, Turkey's role *vis-à-vis* the European north was to succeed other southern countries in exporting workers. Although exporting workers and importing capital are not mutually exclusive, the agenda of the late 1960s and early 1970s was filled with concerns over labour mobility within the EEC, and there was not much pressure on the Turkish government to adopt a more inviting attitude towards foreign investment. Secondly, as already suggested, export-oriented capital did not find Turkey particularly attractive owing to prevailing high wages in the modern sector, while the internal market was larger in other non-EEC countries, such as Spain. Nor did Turkey offer any advantages as a possible export platform – for example, toward Arab countries, mostly because of its pro-American foreign policy which clashed with Arab sentiments of the day.

An unexpected channel for Turkey's integration into the European economy developed during the 1960s in the form of workers' emigration. From only 13,000 in 1962, the number of Turkish workers in Europe increased to 480,000 in 1970, and to more than 800,000 in 1974, with the highest annual levels of emigration during the period 1969-73. At its peak, the ratio of these workers to the total labour force in Turkey had climbed to 5 per cent; in other words, in an economy with a less flexible employment structure severe labour shortages might have resulted. In Turkey, however, despite the fact that earlier migrants had originated from among the ranks of skilled labour in towns, shortage of labour did not appear to be a problem.[19] Rather, emigration quickened the pace of urbanisation, with more peasants finding employment in cities owing to the numbers who had left for Europe.

More important from the point of view of capital accumulation was the contribution that migrant workers brought to foreign exchange earnings through remittances they sent back, which allowed industrialisation based on imported technology and inputs to continue. Bureaucrats, politicians and, indirectly, industrialists, were delighted with this new source of foreign exchange which did not require difficult negotiations or political concessions. From the late 1960s on, planners concentrated on attempts to maintain and raise the level of remittances through concessionary exchange rates, import permits, and attractive investment schemes. They were successful to a large extent, especially with the devaluation of 1969, which served to redirect workers' remittances from unofficial to official channels. Remittances per worker rose to more than one thousand dollars by 1972, and to almost two thousand dollars in 1973–74.[20] Total flows surpassed the largest positive item after exports – net official transfers – in 1970, and were sufficiently large to cover the entire trade deficit in the 1971–73 period, before the oil price increase. In fact, during this brief span, Turkey's balance of payments troubles seemed to be over, resulting entirely from the contribution of workers' remittances. There was a current account surplus in 1973 which was added to the reserves, and for the first time in recent history, Turks could freely travel abroad, the government allowing the purchase by every national of up to $1,000 per year. Remittances began to decline after 1974: from $1.4 thousand million down to $980 million in 1976–78, and with the added weight of imports they fell far short of covering the trade deficit. Without them, however, imports would have had to be restricted to a much greater extent (the ratio of imports paid for by foreign exchange earnings through remittances was 38 per cent in 1974, 28 per cent in 1975, 19 per cent in 1976, and 17 per cent in 1977) and the ensuing crisis would have hit the economy sooner.

A less tangible but equally important element in the great westward migration of Turkish workers was the unimaginably accelerated pace with which they were integrated into a mass consumption ethos. Especially since the more developed regions in Western Anatolia had played a greater role in sending out workers to Europe, this demonstration effect found fertile ground. Workers' remittances and the commodities they brought back from Germany served to diffuse the new consumption pattern to even small towns and villages, and a large segment of the population was introduced to new consumption habits, particularly in durable consumer goods.[21]

The rhythm of the new and popularised consumption patterns followed the waves of emigration and of remittances, reaching a peak during the early 1970s. It coincided with the take-off in the production of consumer durables in local industry. Production of refrigerators, for example, increased from 137,000 per annum in 1969 to 306,000 in 1973 and 415,000 in 1975. Annual production of television sets reached 570,000 in 1976, starting from less than 5,000 in 1970.[22] The mid-1970s was truly a period of prosperity in terms of the purchasing ability of the masses, when every household in shanty towns of the large urban areas and in smaller Anatolian towns acquired a television set, often a refrigerator and a washing machine, and most middle-class families in the large cities could purchase a car. In addition to what domestic industry supplied, workers abroad frequently chose to transfer their savings in the form of commodities, which they resold in the market. On top of the visible remittances then, workers' savings also took the form of commodities purchased in Europe and realised in Turkey, which amounted to between 5 and 10 per cent of remittances officially, but more in terms of the price fetched in the market.

The first wave of emigration during the 1960s had originated from the skilled strata of urban craftsmen and workers. In the latter part of the 1960s German private and public agencies began actively to recruit the *gastarbeitern* and soon the vast labour reserve of Anatolia appeared on the scene with applications for employment abroad far exceeding German and other European demands. The Turkish government intervened rather belatedly in an attempt to impose official controls over the flow, but this attempt was only effective at the level of privileging certain regions, villages, or individuals. In the early 1970s the waiting period between application to the Turkish employment agency and final consideration by the German authorities had climbed to four years.[23] In other words, the demand by European capital had been exhausted after the euphoria of the 1968–74 period. Turkish labour had gained favour because of its low price and docility in adapting to difficult working conditions. By the same token, the workers of Italy, Spain, Yugoslavia and Greece had priced themselves out of the German labour market, as a result of the rapid relative exhaustion of low-wage labour surpluses in these countries. Given this exhaustion, Turkish labour remained competitive on the European market. Although privileges through associate membership in the EEC never materialised, geographical proximity, bilateral agreements (particularly with Germany), and the momentum already gained through the massive movement of labour in the early 1970s, were factors which contributed to maintaining the level of migration. Nevertheless, official migration declined after the so-called oil shock, from an average of more than one hundred thousand in 1969–73 to less than fifteen thousand per annum in 1974–77.[24] Illegal migration, where aspiring workers first left ostensibly to visit relatives or friends and then found employment abroad, became prominent during this time, although campaigns to crack down on it were frequent. This unofficial flow did not, however, compensate for the decline in legal migration.

From the point of view of the Turkish economy, the decline in migration implied a reversal in the trend by which foreign exchange earnings through workers' remittances had increased steadily since the mid-1960s. Not only were workers abroad more wary of losing their jobs and therefore were reluctant to transfer as high a proportion of their savings to Turkey, but also the economic policy pursued in Turkey had, by 1974, reached an impasse, manifested in the growing gap between the official and black-market rate of exchange for the dollar. Thus a smaller amount of savings were legally transferred, and there was a greater tendency to effect the transfer through illegal channels. The 1974 peak of $1,425 million declined to $983 million in 1976, and remained stagnant over the following two years. Remittances per official worker also declined from almost two thousand dollars per annum in 1974 to $1,300 in 1978. These reversals foreshadowed the crisis conjuncture which caused further problems in Turkey's balance of payments. Remittances had amply covered the trade deficit in 1972 and 1973, but they declined (as a percentage of the trade deficit) from 154 in this latter year to 39 in 1975 and 24 in 1977. In other words, the period when workers abroad were seen as the panacea of all economic ills came to an abrupt end, testing the limits of the political-economic model after another reprieve.

The mid-1970s was a period of intense political rivalry and unstable coalitions. Re-establishment of the unrestricted parliamentary model after the military intervention of 1971 had ushered in the government of the Republican People's Party (RPP) now under Ecevit and espousing social democracy. This was, however, a shaky rule based on a parliamentary minority which required a coalition with the religious party. After a brief tenure, the unwieldy alliance yielded to a different coalition, which remained in power until 1977, this time consisting of all the right-wing parties including the religious party. The result of political competition and unsteady rule during the period 1973–1977 was the reluctance and inability of governments to impose any radical measures on the economy, directing their efforts instead to perpetuating the existing situation through whatever means available. Since only ample foreign exchange could secure such a continuation, the governments led by Demirel (1974–77 and 1978–80) and Ecevit (1977–78) made their primary purpose the obtaining of hard currency.

There were two intervening developments which rendered this task of foreign-exchange seeking more difficult than in the preceding period: the Cyprus affair and the oil price increase. In the summer of 1974 the Ecevit government decided to occupy the northern part of Cyprus when confronted with a right-wing coup engineered by the Greek junta. This occupation brought with it an imbroglio at the diplomatic level forcing Western governments, and in particular the US, to cut back on the official funds they transferred to Turkey under the categories of grants, aid, long-term loans and military assistance. At the same time, the ability of the US government to continue its unilateral transfers had been severely hampered as a result of the so-called world monetary crisis. Thus soft loans of long-term gestation were not forthcoming, while the import requirement of the industrialisation programme was increasing steeply because of the rise in oil prices. Annual imports rose by 80 per cent from 1973 to 1974 and another 39 per cent between 1974 and 1975. With constant prices, the import requirements of the industrial sector would have increased by about 15 per cent annually. The elevated figures were therefore due principally to movements in oil prices.[25]

An industrialisation project which closely followed the pattern demonstrated by already advanced countries necessarily employed technologies dependent on cheap oil imports. In the case of Turkey, petroleum-intensive production and consumption habits had been especially prominent in the choice of techniques used in thermic electricity plants for example.

Improvements in coal mining had been neglected, as had the development of hydro-electric potential. Industrial production was dependent either directly on diesel and fuel oil or indirectly on oil-produced electricity. In transportation, railroads had been neglected since the 1930s, and the service allowed to deteriorate at the behest of US experts. A report drafted in 1948 had urged a road network which depended entirely on trucks and motor cars, with railways playing no role.[26] In fact, the 1950s boom had heavily mortgaged the future in its unilateral commitment to the US model to the degree that urban street cars, notably in Istanbul, were declared too traditional and pre-modern, and their tracks were dislodged in much the same way as their US counterparts had been during the pre-war boom. The consumption pattern is the final test of the possibility of a development that is relatively independent of the world economy's impositions. In the case of Turkey, the consumption pattern followed the American model very closely, to the extent that public consumption in the European mode remained undeveloped and insufficient. For these reasons, oil prices had more of an impact on the economy than was warranted by the average level of technological development.

The sudden jump in the import bill was initially met through foreign exchange reserves accumulated between 1971 and 1973, when workers' remittances had allowed some hoarding of hard currency. In 1974, 1975 and again in 1977, around 10 per cent of imports were paid for through depletion of reserves; in this last year, however, the Central Bank's gold and foreign currency ran out. What transpired in 1975 and 1976 was of even greater consequence because the right-wing coalition then in power chose to postpone the international insolvency by borrowing funds on the Eurodollar market with high interest rates and short-term maturity. Between 1975 and 1978, these expensive loans rose to $3.6 thousand million or about one-fifth of the total import bill of those four years.[27] The procedure was for Turkish industrialists to find creditors among European banks offering interest rates considerably above the prevailing levels in a fund-rich world economy. The Turkish government would then guarantee the repayment of these funds in dollars, while it was to be reimbursed in local currency by indebted firms. Needless to say (and parallel to what went on in many other countries), difficulties experienced in the repayment of such loans soon became a major factor in the foreign exchange crisis and, in 1978, precipitated the standard agreement with the

IMF, which the Turkish government had no choice but to sign.

An indirect consequence of this episode was the increasing distortion it introduced into capitalist calculation. A protected industrialisation certainly functions along axes of rationality that are peculiar to it. Notably, political allocation of foreign exchange brings with it a rent creation mechanism which renders meaningless the concept of 'normal' profit obtained through competition. The pursuit of foreign exchange loans by individual capitalists extended such rent-seeking outside the national boundaries. Especially since Turkish workers abroad were now in a position to supply a substantial proportion of the foreign exchange, they emerged as potential partners in the scheme. During the 1975–1980 period, industrialists and merchants purchased Turkish workers' savings abroad and other foreign currency belonging to nationals (smugglers and drug traffickers) by paying a price higher than the official rate. In the early period, some of these funds were brought back to Turkey in the guise of sellers' credit from European firms, and thus formed part of Turkey's short-term debt. After 1976, however, with the imposition of greater restrictions on imports, outright contraband trade gained prevalence. Industrialists could smuggle into the country any or all of the essential inputs they required for the continuation of their production activity.[28] The manufactured output which resulted from such smuggling naturally commanded higher prices and earned larger rents. In the 1977–79 period, not only was the foreign exchange scarcity at its worst, but also governments were reluctant to abandon any of the subsidy schemes which had been successful in promoting industrial accumulation. Such a combination had dire consequences in that for extended periods certain basic manufactures were taken off the market. Scarcity led to a second kind of extraordinary profit in the form of black market returns. Especially during Ecevit's tenure in 1977, the government clumsily insisted on circumventing the market mechanism through direct allocation of some state-produced and imported inputs, thus unleashing to its fullest extent the rent economy that was already implicit in import substitution. Such a distortion of the goals of industrialisation led to a transfer of the surplus away from industrialists who usually remained at the receiving end of the transaction, and concentrated fortunes in the hands of intermediating rentiers. The greater the scarcity of imported goods relative to what the economy had been accustomed to and expected, the larger was the magnitude of the rent economy and the greater the importance of the redistribution away from industrial profit. This was a principal element of the profit squeeze characterising capital–labour relations and the industrial sector's political response in the late 1970s. It was also a mechanism which redistributed incomes to a significant extent and thus contributed to the reversal of the fairly egalitarian distribution of the import-substituting years.

What transformed the systemic crisis into the crisis of capital – eventually leading the bourgeoisie to seek an appropriate solution through political means – was the apparent difficulty experienced in perpetuating the material means of production, and the growing dimensions of the profit squeeze. The physical shortages prevalent in procuring various inputs to industry have already been mentioned. Such shortages did not simply imply a rise in prices where black-market profits had to be yielded to intermediaries: there were also situations of absolute unavailability, particularly in commodities produced or distributed by the state. Petroleum, petroleum-derived intermediary goods, and electricity, were examples of this latter category. With the unavailability of any of these inputs, production stopped, although capitalists had to continue paying the fixed costs of production and notably the workers' wages. Legislation protected workers from firings at will and imposed heavy costs on capitalists in the form of severance payments awarded to workers' in proportion to seniority. As shortages became more the rule than the exception during the 1977–79 period, production stoppages became frequent and the import substituting industrial bourgeoisie came to constitute a permanent lobby protesting at the political authority's inability to procure the necessary foreign exchange.

Two elements of the profit squeeze have already been mentioned: an increasing share of the total surplus being yielded to intermediaries of all colours, but especially to smugglers, and the inability to economise on fixed costs in the face of difficulties in procuring necessary material inputs. These elements both derived from the systemic constraint manifested in the form of a foreign currency shortgage and the attendant difficulty in importing essential inputs for a dependent industrial structure. The third element was more distinctly political and derived from the inertia of the political-economic regulation characterising import substituting industrialisation. Labour legislation protecting the organised working class had created a

situation where collective bargaining every two years functioned in the manner of a built-in mechanism to ensure
increasing money wages. All the unions in all the sectors acted
upon the signals from a few pilot agreements; and regardless of
sectoral differentials in profitability, industrialists were called
upon to pay the average increase in wages. Growing union
strength after the 1974 elections had been prepared by the
success of economic regulation under import substituting
industrialisation. This same strength became dysfunctional
when the material conditions of production could no longer be
reproduced and when accumulation was no longer readily
feasible. The previous syncretism yielded to first simmering,
then galloping, conflict. The number of strikes and days lost to
strikes increased rapidly, from an average of 65 strikes and just
under one million days between 1973 and 1976 to 190 strikes
and 3.7 million days between 1977 and 1980.[29] At the same
time, investment in industry slowed down, its level decreasing
from 40.4 thousand million Turkish lira (TL) in 1977 to 38.7
thousand million in 1978, and 36.4 thousand million in 1979 (all
in 1976 prices).[30] Output levels in the manufacturing sector
exhibited a similar trend: the increase was only 3.6 per cent
between 1977 and 1978, while there was a decline of 6 per cent
in 1979. The 1980 output in manufacturing was 10 per cent
lower than the 1978 level.[31] Together with declining output,
wages as a percentage of industrial value added increased or
maintained their share. Between 1974 and 1976 the share of
wages in value added in the industrial sector had increased from
27 per cent to 31.7 per cent; in 1979 this figure reached 37.3 per
cent.[32] In other words, industrial workers as a group were
successful in avoiding the burden of the crisis, although within
this group, existing dualities were probably exacerbated because of growing insecurity of employment.

The systemic crisis in Turkey had been postponed until long
after the period when similar countries had had to submit to
radical restructuring of their political economies. Workers'
remittances fortuitously, and short-term borrowing deliberately, provided the bourgeoisie with the wherewithal to pursue
an industrial strategy which, by any criterion of world-wide
capitalist rationality, should have been long abandoned. In 1977
the government's misconception as to economic management
finally precipitated the crisis by translating the contradiction
between world economic integration and national capitalism
into local terms. No longer was it possible to shield the

industrial bourgeoisie from the effects of a world-wide economic transformation by means of palliative measures; nor was it feasible, in a shrinking economy, to postpone the difficult problems of distribution with all their political and social ramifications.

The discussion concerning the political economy of import substituting industrialisation already situated this model of peripheral accumulation within a particular international context. Without external subsidy in the form of an inflow of foreign capital (governmental assistance or private investment) and without an acceptance by the hegemonic power of the ramifications of such an accumulation pattern on the world division of labour, this path of internally oriented industrialisation would have been difficult to pursue. This accommodation, however, also signalled the limits of the model in that the cycles of the world economy and, in particular, the fortunes of the hegemonic power, left it vulnerable to external dynamics. The success of the model had depended on expansion of the world economy, and not on its retrenchment. The availability of easy loans, growing world markets, increasing opportunities for employment abroad, and cheap oil had constituted the conditions of Turkey's secular boom. With the global crisis these conditions were reversed, signalling an end to the economic success story.

The first casualty in the configuration was the hegemonic power's ability to redistribute the world purchasing power, in other words, to make available grants and almost-free loans to its clients. The flooding of the world economy with newly printed dollars during the Vietnam war had undermined the confidence necessary for the continuation of the policy, robbing the patron of an important component of its patronage. The declining power of the US implied a period of indeterminacy and rivalry at the world level rather than a new hegemony. In fact, had the latter been the case, Turkey's geographical location and growing ties during the 1960s would have allotted its economy to the charge of German capital. In this period, it was not only the Turkish politicians and intelligentsia, but also German and EEC circles, who discussed the likelihood of resuscitating the 'special ties' that had earlier bound Turkey to German expansionism. US hegemony, however, was not declining uniformly in all fields, and particularly not in the military sphere; nor was the German state in a position to assume the political responsibility which accompanied the envisaged suzerainty. Even at the economic level, the threat of free mobility for Turkish labour, which had been stipulated as part of the association agreement with the EEC, played the role of a damper on grander designs. Thus the increasing volume of trade with the EEC – and with Germany in particular – which relegated the US to a secondary role in economic relations, did not bring in its wake a shift to a European-dominated development pattern. Such a shift seemed to be on the agenda for other southern European countries, notably Greece and Spain, which received funds from the north in the form of workers' remittances, tourism revenue, and private investment. Their economic relations came to be dominated by the new orientation towards the EEC, which was reflected in their models of accumulation becoming increasingly freer of a dependence on the national market.

The role played by the developed centres of European capital in providing the needed funds for the Turkish economy has already been discussed. Although mediated by the inter-state system, the employment of Turkish workers in Europe and their remittances were essentially market phenomena which responded rapidly to economic conditions. Thus the slowing down of labour migration coincided with the so-called oil shock of 1973-74 and the net outflow of Turkish workers soon declined to zero. At the same time unemployment and the uncertainty of employment led workers abroad to greater prudence in repatriating their earnings. The world crisis thus took its toll through the decrease in indirect German, and other European, contributions to the funding of Turkish industrial-isation.

Nonetheless, workers in Europe had played a crucial role in buying extra time for Turkey's industrial effort. Had it not been for workers' remittances, the crisis would have hit Turkey much sooner, and the first part of the decade of the 1970s would have been characterised by a painful adjustment of the economy to restricted imports and a compulsory export drive. On the other hand, it may be argued that the postponement of the crisis precluded a smoother adjustment which could have taken place under less adverse circumstances for world trade than prevailed in the post-1980 period. It might have been possible gradually to 'open' Turkey's protected economy and wean its industrial-ists with less of a shock – which in turn would have brought with it a milder dose of redistribution than was necessitated by the destruction of the internal market. As it was, not only did industrialists and other beneficiaries of an inflated internal market enjoy the postponement, they also were able to create the pressure under which successive governments tried hard to extend the reprieve. The policy of short-term and expensive borrowing in the mid-1970s made the eventual adjustment process much more difficult because it added to the external burden, and increased the pressure that creditors brought. The argument has been made that economic policy in Turkey was overly indulgent towards protected industrialisation and did not prepare in the least for the day of reckoning when the international market would emerge as the measure of capitalist viability. Yet it seems misleading to pose the question in policy terms when the model of accumulation pursued was supported by an extensive bloc of class fractions. There was no room for the policy-makers to exercise even a limited degree of structural autonomy as required by the substitution of long-term goals for short-term success – especially when it was difficult to speculate on the nature of the future world. Of course, as short-term regulation succeeded, structures became less flexible and more resistant to change, with the consequence that even small shifts would have encountered much opposition. This became clear in the period between 1977 and 1980, when governments chose the route of confronting external displeasure orchestrated by the IMF rather than risking internal dissent.

By the mid-1970s, it was already too late for Turkish industry to emerge from a long period of insular development. The balance of payments effects of adverse terms-of-trade, and the impact of a shrinking world market for exports were taking their toll, and making adjustments in policy more difficult. Petroleum accounted for more than a quarter of imports in the period between 1976 and 1979, reflecting the quadrupling of its price. The cost of external funds also increased, raising the proportion of foreign debt servicing relative to export earnings (the debt-service ratio) from 13 per cent in 1973 to 33 per cent in 1977. Growing difficulties in procuring foreign exchange, together with the inertia of policy-making, resulted in declining growth rates in the GNP after 1976.

At the beginning of this chapter I claimed that classical crisis tendencies had been avoided in Turkey with the creation of the internal market on the one hand, and with subsidies and protection rent to ensure the profit rate of the industrialists on the other. What this statement refers to is the success of the

import substitution 'regulation' in Turkey in accommodating
the world boom of the 1960s. In other words, while the world-
wide boom lasted (and then continued during a local extension)
a local crisis was successfully avoided through securing the
distribution of the social surplus in a manner adequate to the
needs of capital accumulation. The crisis was triggered by the
growing difficulty of balancing the external account, which in
itself was a reflection of the world-wide crisis. Chaotic money
markets and rising oil prices (both indirect results of declining
hegemonic power), a shrinking market for peripheral exports,
slackening demand for Turkish workers in Europe, and a
general atmosphere of retrograde mercantilism were the most
proximate elements of the world crisis that precipitated
Turkey's internal difficulties. The local crisis, like the boom
before it, was the refracted appearance of the world economic
cycle in the mirror of import substituting industrialisation. In
this mirror the effective constraint on the economy took the
shape of the availability of imports. Without imported inputs
and technology the economy could no longer be reproduced.
Problems in securing inputs translated into obstacles in maintaining the material conditions of production. Through a chain
of causation from reduced use of capacity to declining profits,
and declining investment in manufacturing, economic growth
stopped, unveiling various shades of social conflict. Without
growth, social pay-offs could not be continued, and tensions
which had been harboured within the rapid transformation of
the society gained new dimensions. To understand the particular manifestation of these conflicts and their ideological
specificities, it is necessary to draw a picture of Turkish history –
albeit sketchy – paralleling the above account at the level of
culture and ideology. The following chapter attempts this task.

IX

The Impossible Rise of Bourgeois Ideology

The ideological spectrum of the 1970s in Turkey appeared to be heavily weighted toward a developmentalist-populist middle ground. The span of political currents represented in the spectrum was much wider than any time before in the history of the Republic, but there had also been an unmistakable agglomoration in the middle. Compared to the pre-1950 situation when the two main platforms were appreciably distinct, the new distribution was surprising. In this chapter I will discuss both the central convergence and its centrifugal by-product of ideological extremism.

The ideological conflict during the period of bureaucratic ascendancy had bred an aloof reformism from above and also a populism which brought together traditionalist sentiments championing market liberalism. Given the external context and material conditions of economic development during the 1950s, the Democrat Party had found it difficult to realise the anti-statist promises of its evolution. While the reality of statism was never admitted into the party's discourse, the practice of policy-making clearly betrayed its inability to avoid the statist fold. Concurrently, the developmentalist imperative which now dominated the platform of the opposition party came to define the object of market liberalism as well. The DP became developmentalist and, accordingly, the principal division in the political debate changed its axis from state vs. market to focus on the best use of state power for purposes of economic growth. During the late 1950s, discourse on both sides was dominated by economic concerns, but with minimum reference to distribution. Industrialisation was the shared goal, with income distribution and economic justice receiving scant attention. After 1960, the convergence around the formula of development became all the more striking as both right and left politics came to be exclusively dominated by macro-economic concerns. While the left appeared to be worrying more about national strength, both sides found Turkey's performance inadequate, both desired a more autonomously motivated industrial sector, and both proposed as success criteria the number of smokestacks and the volume of steel production. Distribution was considered a secondary problem whose solution would await the development of the economy. Once import substitution was entrenched as economic policy, the role of the state would differ in the two scenarios only in details; the political economy of import substitution closely determined the functions expected from the state, raising that area beyond political discussion.

It was certainly this ideological convergence by major groupings that left the political spectrum wide open on either flank, and conditioned the nature of the political struggle during the late sixties and seventies. The vacuum on the left and on the right was soon filled. On one side developed labour unions and a socialist movement, and on the other, right-wing movements attempted to substitute an 'idealist' construct for what they saw as left-wing materialism. Substantively, it was the rapid development of capitalism which provided constituencies for both sides: the quantitative expansion of the working class as well as the dissolution of petty production and traditional social structures had created the material conditions for social movements organised around new ideologies. The historical legacy of Kemalism fashioned the ideologies in question into more recognisable forms, and facilitated their local consumption. Nonetheless, through their own presence and through their influence on more centrist thought which had to redefine itself, the new ideologies effected an undeniable 'modernisation' of the entire political terrain.

The principal factor defining Turkey's ideological universe has been the absence of a contesting bourgeoisie. I described above the beginnings of a *bürgerliche* society in pre-war Ottoman Turkey whose effects could not be translated from the economic and the cultural into the political realm. After the end of the multi-ethnic empire, and the war-time destruction of the nascent bourgeois society, the nationalists of Ankara closely determined the allocation of economic positions, guiding a capitalist development without a corresponding bourgeois transformation. The bourgeoisie, therefore, did not have the occasion, until much later, to give themselves a separate identity. The bureaucracy who directed the transformation, on the other hand, were predominantly state oriented as epitomised in the concern of 'saving the state'. 'Saving the state' summarised an entire range of evaluations which, for example, sacrificed civil rights for *raisons d'état*, economic for fiscal strength, participation and democracy for solidarity behind leaders. This was a self-evident choice for the bureaucracy; in the absence of any challenge it became institutionalised as the dominant concern of the population as a whole. Kemalist education reproduced this concern in churning out graduates who thought in exactly the same fashion, feeling themselves to be natural candidates for 'saving the state'. This educational priority was so well-entrenched that, until the late 1960s, the educated considered their prerogatives to be self-evident. Even the anti-authoritarian wave of 1950 and after did not make much of a dent in the norms of the educated elite. They defended the republican model and worked to extend it further toward state-controlled industrialisation, while labelling the newly prospering businessmen as provincial upstarts.[1] In addition to the impoverishment of the institutions which might have provided the basis for a civil society, the dominant tendency in economic policy also worked toward inducing the bourgeoisie to passivity. The authoritarian character of the 1930s had been reinforced through the relative closure of the economy which persisted until the end of our period, with the exception of a few years in the 1950s. As a result the developing bourgeoisie was an exceptionally 'national' one in its practical orientation. Deprived of a strong international connection and able to restrict the extent of foreign investment, it became a full supporter of the centrality of the state. In fact, the international connection which existed boosted this centrality by moving the level of economic commerce to the inter-state plaform.[2] Thus, there was no desire on the part of the bourgeoisie to challenge the normative concerns of the bureaucracy; they were robbed of their imputed revolutionary will despite their economic success.

The same conclusion may be reached from the perspective of the continuity that characterised the Turkish state. Republican

Turkey, notwithstanding all the phoenix imagery, represented more of a transformation by coup under war conditions than a revolutionary break with the ancien regime. Since the Republic, most aspects of social life which have undergone change have done so through gradual evolution, without clear breaks with the past. Institutional reforms have remained punctuations that did not signal conquests by contesters. No anti-clerical movement preceded the abolishment of the caliphate, for instance; there was no women's movement before equal rights were won, no workers' movement brought about the right to organise and strike. In fact, by pre-empting such movements, reforms from above exercised a suffocating effect on societal dynamics, and a civil society lost its chance of learning-by-doing in the ways of participation. The rapid multiplication of urban dwellers after 1950 also diluted the potential *bürgerlichkeit* of this population. Their recent entry into urban society rendered migrants at least temporarily conformist. Also, their incorporation through populist policies was an instance of the state acting as global patron – not a situation conducive to the autonomisation of the society. Participation, therefore, remained a distant ideal, with only the more formal cloak of parliamentary democracy in current utilisation. Paradoxically, party competition assumed an all-important aspect which, rather than expanding the public space, made it subservient to the state. Equally on the left and right, politics was seen as exclusively leading to state power and democracy was interpreted in the narrow terms of electioneering.

Material conditions such as the absence of a landowning oligarchy and the insignificant presence of foreign capital had prepared for a smooth transition out of single-party authoritarianism in 1950. In addition, the inability of any one fraction of capital to establish unchallenged domination (thus, the continuation of intra-bourgeois competition), and more importantly, the perpetuation of bureaucratic autonomy, implied that state power could not be easily usurped. Political contestants were required to harness the weight of numbers as demonstrated in electoral behaviour. Furthermore, the orientation of the economy towards the internal market required a given income distribution which received its guarantee from the existence of certain participatory rights. Yet these factors only established the conditions for a restricted and formal democracy; the prevailing ideology was effective in its interdictions when it was forced to confront demands towards extending the space open

to public discussion. Various agencies of the state jealously
guarded prerogatives they were accustomed to enjoy. The
military, for instance, who had emerged as the custodians of the
statist tradition were beyond criticism. Foreign policy, and
especially its constants in terms of alliances and long-term
hostilities, also constituted a taboo, usually justified through
sensitive exigencies of national sovereignty. Freedom of speech
and civil rights could be exercised only when allowed by the
state. There were no 'self-evident' rights deposited in the
individuals, rather individuals gained privileges as suited the
reasons of the state. In fact, the 1971 military intervention
served precisely to set back the meagre gains in the extension of
the public space.

The military intervention also demonstrated that the formal
foundations of the civil society in the legal system were
retractable. By bringing to court and convicting members of the
socialist party and left labour unions as well as other associations (established legally under the 1961 constitution), the
military regime underlined the limits to the liberties citizens
were allowed to enjoy. The trial of Democrat Party politicians
by the 1960 Committee of National Solidarity had spelled out a
similar message, although the 1971 junta cast its net wider and
disregarded former taboos by mistreating respected intellectuals.[3] Once it became apparent that military intervention
could retrospectively redefine the legal framework, the material
construction of a civil society became even more tenuous than
before. Without a legal framework that could be assumed to
retain validity, indulgence in autonomous institutions of civil
society would be a luxury always carrying with it the risk of
retroactive sanctions.

Hence, it was not only populist trappings, introduced due to
an industrialisation directed to the internal market, that had
prevented the emergence of a politically liberal ideology. The
bourgeoisie had matured under conditions of an induced
capitalism, occupying their economic space in the wake of a
military victory. Their accession to the status of a class-in-itself
had occurred under state tutelage without the necessity of a
political struggle against pre-capitalist forces. The absence of a
feudal-commercial landowning class and the fact that they were
filling positions already carved out by the non-Moslem bourgeoisie had made the task of the Republican bourgeoisie
exceedingly easy. Only after the World War II did the
bourgeoisie feel the need to wage a struggle against a

cumbersome bureaucratic tradition, but this struggle too took
the form of demands for market freedoms more than political
democracy. Shortly thereafter, the requirements of import
substituting industrialisation once again permitted them to hide
behind a cosy statism and its populist integument. Thus the
Turkish bourgeoisie never developed an ideology designed to
conceal the intimate state-economy relations of capitalism from
the public eye. Instead they openly avowed the indispensibility
of a statist economy and a restrictive political system.

Populism, as the counterpart to an absent liberalism, was a
major factor fashioning the ideological history of the 1950–1980
period. After its anti-elitist victory in the 1950 election, the
victorious Democrat Party successfully appropriated the principal populist themes in defence of a platform of economic
incorporation of the peasantry. The 1960 coup against the
Democrat Party was therefore identified in the public mind with
the bureaucratic tradition and its personification in the leader of
the Republican People's Party, the former president, İnönü.
Although policies during the coalition governments headed by
İnönü (1963–1965) were increasingly social-minded (the union
law and the right to strike are legacies of this period), the RPP
could not escape its image until it declared a centre-left position
during the late 1960s. This centre-left image propounded by the
new leader, Ecevit, was an attempt to steal the populist
platform from the right, and met with relative success. Its
success, however, revealed a growing differentiation inside the
presumed solidarity of 'the people' that the earlier rhetoric had
attempted to create. For the new RPP received most of its
support from established shanty town dwellers in the cities and
from peasants of the least successfully commercialised regions
in the countryside. Its votes were invariably higher in large
cities and in the rural areas of backward regions. In other
words, the RPP started attracting both the modern working
class vote and the vote of those groups that the development of
capitalism had left behind. Yet this new identification which
implicitly signalled the end of any undifferentiated solidarity
was not sufficiently strong to create a social-democratic base.
This weakness was reflected in the difficulty encountered in
creating the institutional ties characteristic of European social
democracy: the RPP was not able to build a wide working class
base, nor could it establish organic ties with labour unions.
Within a social arithmetic where wage and salary earners

remained around one-fourth of the labour force, such a strategy may have proven less than optimal anyway. Against this background the almost charismatic personality of Ecevit, who dominated the centre-left platform until 1980, fitted the bill by reinforcing the tendency toward a less class-based and more populist strategy.

The Justice Party which emerged as the true successor to the Democrat Party tradition inherited another strand from the populism of the 1950s and sought to recreate the anti-bureaucratic coalition which had proven successful. For electoral strength its main appeal was to the peasantry and the aspiring petty bourgeoisie, especially the self-employed new urbanites. This constituency was sufficiently large in the population to warrant exclusive representation, but the structural constraints of state power in capitalism determined that they would yield increasingly more ground to the interests of big business under the mantle of the Justice Party. Nonetheless, the populist rhetoric of the Justice Party was vindicated through economic growth which permitted a broad coalition to be sustained on the right, including business circles as well as the marketised peasantry and the petty bourgeoisie. Party leaders persisted in their rhetoric of anti-elitism and anti-statist market liberalism while they obeyed capitalist imperatives and granted privileges to the bourgeoisie. Their populist appeal began to wane only with the slackening of economic growth in the 1970s.

The drift towards populist rhetoric was materially reinforced by a social structure dominated by small producers, which did not allow either a liberal-bourgeois or a social democratic ideology to develop in a pure form. In historical perspective, the official populism of the single-party state had been opposed by the genuine mass appeal of the Democrat Party, which in turn gave birth to both the right and the left-wing versions of a populism riding on the social mobility of an era of rapid development. The development of capitalism certainly introduced identifiable interpellations into populist platforms which clearly borrowed from class-based discourse, but the populist tenor remained dominant; and despite their attempts, the two major parties commonly referred to as the right and the left remained unable to present clearly differentiated images to the public. This duopolistic assimilation at the centre eventually revealed the lack of correspondence between social reality and its available political representation. As capitalism began to dismantle the economic and social world of small producers, what emerged was political extremism of the left and right, competing primarily outside the conventional political arena.

The principal problem with affirmative populism is that its credibility depends on the continuation of the conditions permitting the extension of rights and privileges to previously excluded groups in the population. When Turkish peasants arrived in the city, located some land on which to build their *gecekondus* and found jobs remunerative enough to sustain their aspirations, populism was in its heyday. When the state budget could subsidise both the urban petty bourgeoisie and the rural small producers, and the transportation network with accompanying services was extended to remote towns and villages, the state could in fact be legitimated through its munificence. As long as growth was sustained, social mobility continued: even the most exploited groups found themselves in improved standing relative to their immediate past. In other words, populism had perforce been developmentalist as well. It was perhaps this dimension of developmentalism which exhibited the similarity in political outlooks of the institutional left and right most clearly. Economic growth was seen as the sufficient condition for establishing desired social balances, and the formula of development served to replace all thought about distribution. When growth slackened in the 1970s, centrifugal forces ushered in by social differentiation asserted themselves. It became increasingly more difficult to sustain the populist pipedream of an ever-extending national market, and impossible to ignore the conflicts concerning the distribution of costs accruing from the inevitable rise of industrial capital. At the level of policy making, domination of large scale industrial capital led to an increasing split between the populist rhetoric and government practice. Policy increasingly responded to demands of modern industry while constituencies were necessarily drawn from wider bases.[4] This disjunction became a factor contributing to the disenchantment with populism of the centre: as the two parties lost credibility, their constituencies moved away to search for more loyal representation.

The temporal modulation of economic growth and stagnation was clearly the underlying mechanism determining the nature of the damage caused by monopoly capital. Rapid industrial growth between 1960 and 1973 (10.2% p.a.) was the weak cement which had held the political spectrum within manageable limits. The cohesion through the market, however, exhibited its fragility in crucially depending on the performance of the economy. After 1960, industrial capital defined the economic dynamic both through its pace of accumulation and through its manner of articulation with more traditional forms of activity. During the period of its rapid growth it drew labour and created new areas of valorisation for small capital. When its domination was being consolidated through a slower rate of growth (8.3% between 1973 and 1976), its hold on small capital implied a displacement. This displacement and its consequent social dislocation signalled that the market was no longer remunerative to the same degree for all social groups. The economy could not continue in the role of the guarantor of social cohesion, and instead revealed itself as the fount of conflict. The difference was that the intervening decades had witnessed a dismantling of traditional structures and the entire population had literally been mobilised not only into the labour market, but also to participate in political competition. Rapid growth always implied an availability of alternative economic opportunity potentially open to the very strata who initially lost their status due to the encroachment of monopoly capital. Slower growth until 1976 and then the crisis (industrial growth was only 2.1% p.a. until 1979) closed such options as well as ending the expansion of the labour market. The economic cycle took its toll by destroying the possibility of evolving a workable bourgeois ideology out of the veneer of a market society.

The effects of monopoly capital on traditional social orders were in the direction of differentiation and polarisation at several levels. It might be easiest to start with the most visible mechanism – that causing geographical differentiation – for uneven regional development became a defining factor in the expression of the ideological crisis. Geographical differentiation had been an important feature of the Ottoman era, and agronomic differences among regions were probably always important, but there is justification to think that the nineteenth-century expansion of export trade added to the advantage enjoyed by more fertile areas. During the late century, commercial development seems to have spread to previously less fortunate regions in eastern Anatolia, whose cities evolved as secondary centres under the enrichment of especially the Armenian population. One gets the impression of a declining regional inequality in the decades preceding the Great War. Given the economic consequences of the radical population upheaval during the wars, however, it is likely that there was

substantially greater regional inequality (roughly along east–
west lines) in the early Republic than in the late Empire. The
1930s depression probably exacerbated this inequality. While
the agricultural transformations of the 1950s may have been
geographically dispersed to some measure, industrial development after 1960 certainly was not: it was under the domination
of industrial capital that regional inequality and its popular
perception increased greatly.⁵ Following a familiar polar topo-
graphy, accumulation of industrial capital greatly favoured the
Istanbul region and then the Izmir and Adana-Mersin sites. As
these areas developed, concentration of capital, skilled labour
and technology evolved on a similar basis: large scale modern
units with unionised and well paid work forces were located in
these growth poles, exacerbating geographical inequalities.
Regional income inequality was probably at its most extreme
during the 1970s. We might mention in parentheses that income
inequality in Turkey seemed extreme by international standards
(although the statistics are minimally reliable) due in large part
to such regional unevenness.⁶ Within each region, incomes
were much more evenly distributed, as any observer comparing
visible differences in standards of living in Turkey with other
Third World countries could tell.

Regionalism, as an expression of geographical uneven development, came to stand in for a defensive identity under
conditions of a too rapid nationalisation – and internationalisation – of the economic space. A hitherto non-existent affiliation
typically evolved when an integration whose parameters were
beyond control forced everyone out of traditional isolation. In
Turkish quarters of German cities as well as shanty towns
within Turkey, social lines came to be drawn along geographical
differences, such groups constituting imaginary, and supposedly
traditional, communities. Chain migration, resulting in certain
neighbourhoods being inhabited by migrants from a single
locality, reinforced solidarities in the labour market and
political rivalries were inevitably superimposed on such divisions.

As the penumbra of monopoly capital expanded from the
concentration poles of modern industry, smaller Anatolian
towns experienced social cleavages at their own scale. It has
already been stated that the accelerated disruption of the
economic order, especially in small town Anatolia, was the
principal element of the social crisis in the 1970s. The relative
closure of the country during the depression and the subsequent
world war had created isolated and stagnating environments in

Anatolian cities which subsisted through limited interchange with their hinterlands. Post-war conditions allowed for an evolution of these town economies within basically unchanged parameters: accumulation proceeded on the basis of an already differentiated social structure and growth was autonomous and comprehensible, without undue disruption. When the internal dynamic was superseded by external impetus, and as modern industrial transformation began to dominate small towns, social change became less predictable and more disruptive of established balances. The most important facet of this new articulation was the effect of centralisation of industry on small town merchants and businessmen. The formation of large production and distribution networks centred on Istanbul or Izmir directly targeted the domain of local capital. As a result newcomers who obtained agencies and representation tended to displace local business of older origin, effecting a parallel circulation of small town notables. Remittances and savings of migrants originating either in Europe or in Turkish industrial centres played a similar role in introducing 'new money' and status associated with it.[7] In general, the extension of the labour market to the national space battered down the defences of provincial exclusionism and created exit options to destabilise the existing order.

The third axis of social mobility and disruption of traditional order could most visibly be observed in the shanty town experience which became the urban norm in the 1970s. Despite conflicts among immigrants to the city, shanty town dwellers shared a background which distinguished them from older urbanites: they saw their new standing as constituting territory gained from an exclusionary elite. However much there was a change in the ideology propagated from the centre, Kemalist culture had perpetuated privileges associated with linguistic competence and the ability to emulate European lifestyles. Thus, shanty-towners reproduced in urban context the anti–elite resentment they had carried with them. The strength of this consciousness militated against the apperception of class formation as the new axis of the society and alienated the newly urbanised population from class-based politics. Besides, a great majority of the shanty town population were former petty producers who wanted to see their new status as a temporary measure to earn money while the village, and the unrelinquished position of 'self-employed farmer' remained more permanent. Only in the second generation did proletarianisation become an acceptable datum. It was such ambivalence regarding class position as much as the more concrete conditions of marginality precluding the attainment of class consciousness which led most shanty town inhabitants to options at the extremes of the political spectrum.

Partly due to the closure of more attractive opportunities in large city shanty towns and in part through connections established with the new model economy, a second order of smaller towns began to receive migrants from their own hinterlands during the 1970s. The gastarbeiters' remittances contributed to the economic revival of such towns. During the 1970s in particular, a construction boom fuelled by German workers' investments in housing implied a rising demand for relatively cheap, unskilled labour.[8] It was workers from the surrounding countryside, itself relatively undeveloped compared to the hinterland of more advanced large cities, who now arrived in such small towns and unleashed the social confrontation that was in store. In larger cities, even when ethnic and religious affiliation constituted the basis for settlement patterns, the absolute size of the urban population and the non-proximity to many shanty towns had prevented the development of hostility which characterised the small town experience. Immigrants in small towns frequently retained stronger economic and social links to their villages and thus set out to reproduce a mosaic characterized by traditional ties. Their earlier xenophobia translated to an aggressive posture when employment in the town turned out to be a patronage phenomenon closely correlated with community affiliation. The accumulation of conflicts slowly triggered an explosion unleashing regional, ethnic and religious animosity whose reverberations were soon registered in villages. Thus, villages also underwent a social retrenchment, parallel to the decline of economic opportunities in nearby town centres. The transformation of the rural scene, an accelerating dynamic since the late 1940s, threatened a slowdown three decades later when one of its fuelling mechanisms involuted.

Economic differentiation in the geographic space, upheaval in small town social balances, and universalisation of the shanty town experience supply the three axes within which the dégâts of monopoly capital should be located. The secular trend in the economy had provided an ever-expanding realm dominated by monopoly capital, and its momentum could overcome cyclical modulations of short duration as long as the trend reasserted itself. The crisis of the late 1970s, however, unleashed the passions until then contained. The constituency of radical ideology during the stage of violence reached by Turkey in the late 1970s broadly derived from the corresponding social layers of the three axes identified above. Political extremism found its clientele primarily among youth of small town origin, from regions most recently introduced to the new economic model dominated by Istanbul, Izmir and Adana industrialists; the preferred locale of activity was the shanty town, with most of the militancy found in the newest shanty towns of recent migration.[9] In the rest of this chapter, I will analyse the three movements of political radicalism which occupied the stage in the 1970s: the left, the fascist right, and the religious right.

In terms of the articulation of their ideologies with Kemalist orthodoxy, the left and the fascist right faced much less difficulty than the religious movement. The developmentalist, nationalist current in Kemalism found expression in the anti-imperialism of the left. The left was more anti-imperialist than socialist and the mostly Latin American inspired groups justified their anti-capitalism through the presentation of import-substituting Turkish bourgeoisie in a 'comprador' garb. According to this interpretation, the society and the state were dominated by an oligarchic-comprador alliance, sustained through the support they received from the imperialist centre. For this reason, the severing of imperialist ties took on an urgency, since the internal domination patterns would then collapse. As we argued, however, the agrarian structure was not characterised by the existence of a landed oligarchy, and the internal market-oriented, state-supported bourgeoisie was hardly comprador. Given these drastically mistaken diagnoses, the political strategy of the left was also misdirected: it seemed that the working class was appealed to more in theoretical necessity than as tactical exigency and that the true historical agents of revolution were the intelligentsia and the students. The left's analysis of underdevelopment legitimated its departure from more customary socialist aims and shifted the emphasis toward national development within statist anti-imperialism. The continuity of this incarnation of the left with its sources in Kemalist radicalism could be easily seen even if its theoreticians preferred to trace their heritage to more venerable sources.

The more traditional left parties with their legacy in the Comintern remain outside of our discussion. Although they stood for radical solutions outside what the traditional centre had to offer, their appeal remained limited. They were largely unsuccessful in attracting the newly mobilised strata in shanty towns and smaller cities of Anatolia. Both their tired pro-Soviet rhetoric and their exclusive championing of the industrial working class were handicaps. Besides, they could not compete with the millenarian politics of the extreme left since they were greatly sensitive to international balances and given to seeking internal alliances following an openly reformist programme. Among the traditional left groups only the outlawed Turkish Communist Party, with its offices in East Berlin, had a measure of success among the sections of the population alienated by the politics of the centre. Nonetheless, compared to the many groups of the 'new left', its appeal was limited and derived in some degree from the mystery attached to an ostensibly underground organisation which attained a protean adjustability due to its insulating distance.

The 'new left' was characterised foremost by its fecund parthenogenesis and the resulting sectarianism.[10] Despite the militant defence of arcane differences, similarities among the various factions were paramount. First, was the youthful constituency and a consequent chiliastic style with its self-sacrificing devotion to the cause. Yet, more importantly, an attitude which made left radicalism into something akin to gnosticism became a feature of the movement. Each faction defended what it argued to be the correct line soon to be revealed through the inexorable unfolding of history. Left radicalism arrived at this platform through a largely unconscious internalisation of the main Kemalist precepts of a positivist belief in progress and science, leading to social engineering and an absolutisation of the definition of the 'national good' from above. Again, similar to the Kemalist platform, the left was not particularly populist: whatever populist rhetoric there was lacked romantic dimension. In fact, except in the Maoist case where it was coupled with a blatantly erroneous diagnosis of the agrarian question (arguing for the dominance of feudal relations in the Turkish countryside), populism directed toward the peasantry was notably absent. Populist motifs of socialist colouring were left to be exploited by mainstream politicians, notably those belonging to the reconstituted RPP.

On the fascist right, the considerable corpus of writing elaborating the themes of pan-Turkism, anti-communism, and anti-materialism was a synthesis of racist historiography of the

1930s, fascist social theory of the inter-war period and Cold War hysteria. Although the open avowal of Kemalism by the right was less frequent, its presence as interpreted in high-school curricula was easily visible. The fascist party also directly inherited an anti-socialist current whose organisation was abetted and funded by various state agencies under the period of American-dominated Cold War sensibility. The 'associations for the struggle against communism' articulated with pan-Turkism through the construct of 'Turks under the Russian yoke'.[11] All the themes of the right could thus be combined in the fascist platform. In addition, Kemalist appeals to classless solidarity found their direct echo in the condemnation of the left as fomenting class war, while constant references to the pre-Islamic Turkic tradition amounted to a xenophobic glorification of a legendary past.

It is not difficult to trace fascist ideology to its roots in the elite nationalism of the Republicans. As already mentioned, the exigencies of discovering a strong cohesive principle to define the new population of the new state had directed Ankara bureaucrats to the only ideology available to nineteenth century state-builders. Like all nationalists in power they first had to define a Turkish nation, the evidence for which was culled from a reconstituted historiography. Thus the claim that Anatolia had always been a Turkish land because Anatolian civilisations had been built by successive migrations of Turks from the Asian homeland was maintained in all seriousness. To bolster this hypothesis, a theory of language was appended to argue that Turkish constituted the root language of all other languages which spread to the world through migrations from inner Asia.[12] Nonetheless, Republicans had been careful to confine their claims to the domestic realm, castigating any remnants of the pan-Turkic sentiment.

During the post-1945 period the vocabulary of underdevelopment made inroads on the local ideology. The political right had to defend itself and take a position against a growing influence of the left on public opinion. Parallel to the left version of imperialism there evolved a chauvinist explanation which defensively glorified the history of Turkic states but at the same time identified a culprit in western attempts to subjugate the Turkish race. According to this version not only was a single Turk as valuable as the entire world, an exhortation of the early Republic, but Turks had to take on the entire world in self defence. In addition to communism, Christianity and 'the West' also sought to defeat the Turkish potential, which if victorious, would propel Turkey to the ranks of great powers. Turkey's economic development was purposely undermined by the West. Although the fascist movement did not openly declare an expansionist project, it diagnosed the level of threat to national sovereignty as acute, which justified its call for disciplined militarism. A strong leader was required to expurgate the society from undesirables and to lead the state to domestic omnipotence as well as international strength.

Fascist arguments were put forward in predominantly symbolic terms, which allowed theoreticians at the top both a latitude in political alliances and an extreme manipulative ability *vis–à–vis* the cadres. The most important features of fascist symbology derived from the absence of any radical break with the pre-capitalist past. Although the 1950 break was in the direction of widening the restricted limits of parliamentarism, it did not establish a full spectrum of democratic channels. When those aspects of social life that were not yet transformed were added to the wide range of issues that the political system declared taboo, a formidable array of traditionalisms was created for the fascist movement to rely on. For instance, the reluctance to challenge established authority, starting with an extremely rigid patriarchal order in the family and stretching to an integrated statism, was reproduced in every institution. The very notion of civil rights as being a natural counterpart to the political order is alien since civil rights were considered to be dependent on the nature of the political system, rather than constituting a basis for it. At a more quotidian level, freedom of speech, freedom of the press, freedom of association and even freedom of travel were considered in the popular mind to be granted by administrative measure, easily, and with impunity, revokable.

In the relatively traditional village society, and especially in its small town transposition with its self-imposed community ethic, the social rigidities we have mentioned were fully active. Fascism could readily build on these rigidities declaring them to be the foundation of the desired order and employing them to pragmatic advantage. Shame and honour, for example, keystones of village society, came to acquire new connotations referring both to the national community's place in the world, and to competitive militancy in political activity. The pragmatic manipulation of the inherited symbolic capital found a counterpart in its hungry consumption by mostly adolescent militants who attached their local significations to freely interpreted symbols. From this point of view, fascism represented an extremism of the conservative centre: none of the fascist themes was particularly original, but the dosage, the militancy and the radical tactics with which they were pursued exhibited a novelty.[13]

The religious right undoubtedly had the richest ideological tradition of which to boast, tracing their political heritage to Abdülhamit and to the opposition against westernising reformers. Its non-clerical wing shared a similar background with the fascist right, although its platform was more clearly specified in terms of a social model. Given the militant secularism of the legal system, the religious party concentrated its demands on a few points revealing the nature of its electoral support. Directly or indirectly, its proponents advocated measures to disperse capital accumulation geographically and to reverse the tendency toward economic concentration.[14] By identifying large industrial capital with a 'Western-Jewish-masonic' alliance against Islam, they defended a state-directed industrialisation whose benefits would accrue to the small businessmen of small towns. Yet its *undeclared* platform was certainly the more important component of the religious right's popular appeal. Similar to its previous incarnations, this platform consisted of an ill-defined yearning for a community life based on Koranic precepts. The religious right's opposition to the militantly secularist legal code and political tradition led parts of the left to envisage an alliance jointly contending for civil rights and democratisation. When the religious party felt itself more established, however, the issue of civil rights was quickly forgotten and a 'maximum' programme of fundamentalist Islam slowly began to emerge.

The economic crisis had signalled the bankruptcy of the secular nationalist promise of de-traditionalising and universalising development. According to this promise, economic development would eventually incorporate all citizens into the unitary fold organised around a single national market. The insulated communities targeted by this strategy employed the vocabulary of religion to provide for the concepts to deal with the everyday world. Economic growth had indeed introduced a new life-world (through commercialisation and through labour mobility) and had validated the claims of the new national ideology – without, however, eradicating the traditional vocabulary. In fact, the economic crisis and the crisis of the national ideology allowed for communal cohesion to re-assert itself in a defensive garb. Seeking to insulate themselves, recently urbanised groups found solace in the promise of a moral life conducted along Islamic precepts. It was for this reason that the religious right seemed unable to devise a platform appropriate for national politics, except to insist on the geographical dispersion of industrial investment. Given that the essential Islamic programme was based on community organisation and daily social life, its realisation at the national political level had always been problematic.

There was always a tension between the grassroots-level networks with their mutually beneficial survival strategies, and the level of national politics whose immediate impact could not be ignored or denied. The failure of the religious party to resolve this tension led the centre right and fascist parties to adapt their national political programmes in order to attract the more militant Islamic constituency. In the late 1970s, for instance, the fascist movement slightly shifted its emphasis from a purely ethnic reading of history to what they called the Turkish-Islamic synthesis. All that was needed for this attempt was to downplay the pre-Islamic past and to incorporate the Islamic right's imputation of crusaders' mentality to the West into the fascist analysis of Turkic revanchism. Since the fascist movement was more successful during this period of street militancy, the attempt at synthesis yielded the expected results and many young partisans were attracted away from the religious right.

The previous discussion of the ideologies of radicalism could be gleaned from the pronouncements of the leaders and the theoretical publications of the movements. At this level, there was scrupulous attention paid to completeness of the ideology – that it should present a totalistic overview dealing with all aspects of social reality – and to tracing its historical continuity from some unimpeachable source. At the level of cadres, however, separate heritages became less a historical genealogy and more a reference point justifying group affiliation. The profile of the average cadre did not vary greatly between the left and the right or within the right: usually male, he was a university graduate in a technical field or held a teaching degree. He attended university in Istanbul or Ankara, away from his birthplace – usually an Anatolian provincial capital – and was converted to the cause during his studies. He found a job within the state bureaucracy through the influence of an elder member of the movement. Both ideologically and socially he distrusted the new technostructure working for private industry and earning several times the government salary. There were, of course, exceptions to this prototype, notably within certain factions of the left. Maoist cadres, for example, reflecting the social backgrounds of their theoreticians, were more bourgeois. In general, cadres on the left attended better universities even if their social background did not vary greatly from the right's.

Except for a brief period in the 1970s, the networking potential of the right far exceeded that of the left due to immediate rewarding of the allegiance of the cadres. Right-wing coalition governments effectively parcellised the administrative apparatus and political fraternities were accommodated wholesale, as in the case of the Ministry of Education, colonised by the fascist party, or the Ministry of Industry overtaken by Islamic groups. It cannot be denied that such patronage was most effective in guaranteeing recruitment and continuing allegiance in an atmosphere of rival encampments when nobody wanted to, or had the courage to, stand alone. Patronage was an effective factor in the recruitment of the cadres.

The educational system which had grown increasingly dysfunctional over the years, contributed substantially to disenchantment leading to political militancy. More than 200,000 lycée graduates (220,000 in 1978–79) were turned out every year, most of whom completed a badly taught general curriculum based on memorising information, and gained very little of practical and professional use. The curriculum and the entire educational structure was geared to provide the requisites of elite training in the heady days of Kemalist nation-building. The sheer weight of numbers and the extension of the educational network to a geographically and socially more diverse group rendered education, especially secondary, increasingly anachronistic. University entrance required success in a test which allocated, according to their scores, only a sixth of the candidates to faculties. Thus, a vast majority of lycée graduates remained outside the university system, usually in a sort of limbo, hoping to succeed in a subsequent try. Of those who entered the university, again a majority ended up reading subjects which they had no desire to master, and more importantly, without any professional promise. In the less turbulent social structure of pre-1960s Turkey, a university degree and even a lycée diploma had been sufficient to insure status and a relatively desirable job within the bureaucratic corps. As we have seen, however, first the economic standing of the bureaucracy suffered in the 1950s, and subsequently, through the growth of modern industry, status ascriptions began to change. A traditional lycée education prepared students only minimally to work in modern industry or in any professional slot associated with the increasing complexity of economic life. Thus, Istanbul industrialists employed the graduates of English-language lycées and universities which were almost impossible to enter for students with provincial educational background. This is why state-employed university graduates played a large role in radical movements; for, even in the case of technical personnel, all universities were not equal and the public sector with its less exalted salary scale attracted graduates who could not find jobs in modern industry. In other words, those university students who found themselves enrolled in programmes which promised not even the relative security of a technical slot in public employment and lycée graduates who could not enrol in a university programme were potential participants in radical politics.

There was greater similarity in social background – as well as age – at the level of militants than cadres or leaders. The average militant was a lycée student or graduate, in or out of the university, whose background in terms of life experience or in terms of cultural preparation was not conducive to an appreciation of the subtleties in political theoretic argumentation behind current slogans. More than an abstract idolatry of the state, which was the common denominator within the cadres, it was frustration within an ill-understood transformation and the social rigidities that severely restricted the expression or sublimation of this frustration, that united the militants. The pretence that activities of a rival group were responsible for their problems became a useful fiction to legitimate mostly gratuitous violence, especially in the case of the fascist right. Such a conviction also created its own fractious inclination and graced all implicit rivalries with the gloss of political vocabulary. Street militancy started with writing slogans on walls, but quickly turned into gang-like behaviour with competitive 'protection' of merchants whose contributions were solicited. Neighbourhoods and city blocks were divided among rival factions that frequently resorted to arms in establishing territory. This form of evolution of political rivalry reinforced social divisions – geographical, ethnic or religious – which had originally led to the creation of existing urban settlement patterns. As a result of politicisation, divisions within recently settled urbanites became more pronounced and the rifts which usually separated shanty towns of diverse origin became insurmountable.

In terms of popular support, the right wing attracted by far the majority of the disenchanted: at their most successful, the two parties representing religious and fascist reactions jointly polled around fifteen per cent of the vote, while the left outside the RPP – had it found representation – might have reached a maximum of five per cent. The leftist Turkish Workers Party, which had polled three per cent in 1965, had received most of its votes from urban educated groups. Only a small proportion of these groups remained in radical politics in the 1970s and the radical left gradually turned to the same social stratum as the radical right for its constituency. The principal difference was that the right was organised in legal political parties with representation in the parliament and participation in the government, while the left, after the 1971 *pronunciamento*, was devoid of such institutionalisation. The relationship between legal parties and paramilitary organisations remained vague and exploitable, and the radical right-wing militia, of especially fascist tint, quite obviously received cooperation from coalition governments led by the Justice Party's Demirel. What permitted such collusion during a period of active belligerence were the constituencies enjoyed by the two flanks of the extreme right who returned a sizeable number of deputies to the parliament. The left, on the other hand, lacked any such legitimate representation and Ecevit's RPP attempted more to distance itself from any socialist politics than it endeavoured to attract a broad base – even against a self-styled 'national front' composed of the extreme right wing and the centre right. It was an unequal fight in terms of numbers as well: the militant left was perhaps more visible due to its concentration in university cities and a few other towns of significance, but on the whole, it was on the defensive against a widely spread fascist movement which slowly gained control of the interior.

In the latter half of the 1970s, political competition erupted into active belligerence: several *gecekondu* neighbourhoods and Anatolian towns witnessed prolonged battles, with the death toll reaching twenty to thirty countrywide every day. Cold-blooded assassinations as well as random multiple killings were commonplace and it became apparent that the right-wing militia was being utilised to create conditions of civil war which were intolerable to the largely passive majority of the populace, and from which the fascist party would emerge to deliver law and order.[15] The success of this scenario depended crucially on short-sighted and rigid attitudes of both the centre right and the centre left parties. Demirel appeared to steadfastly believe that fascists could be kept under control, that the RPP was in a league with the left, and that the mortgaging of the bureaucracy to the extreme right would have no impact on the functioning of the parliamentary system. Ecevit, for his part, refused either to consolidate the forces on the left through a call for anti-fascist unity or to admit to centrist homogeneity with the other mass party which might have led to a 'grand coalition' following the 1978 elections. As a result, the fascist movement rapidly metasticised, nurtured under benign governmental treatment and actively opposed only by the extreme left. The dominant discourse defined a universe where the existence of the left cancelled out that of the right, and no obvious sides had to be taken in the ongoing struggle which could be dismissed as 'anarchic terrorism'. By 1980, the fascist scenario had almost reached its climax with the Parliament deadlocked on the election of a new president; state forces, having lost their monopoly on violence, seemed unable to put an end to battles now erupting in several localities at once.

In their 'civil war' scenario which was supposed to lead to a take-over of the state, the fascist movement consciously utilised social divisions such as religious heterodoxy in the interior of the country and ethnic separation in the East and the Southeast. It was, of course, the existence of these divisions which ultimately permitted the fascists to entertain such a scenario. The ethnic conflict in the East had continued to brew after the 1925 rebellion. During the ideological blossoming of the 1960s, the Kurdish situation came to be openly discussed and became one of the issues which required a position from the left- and right-wing participants of the ideological debate. Some left factions openly wooed Kurdish separatists while at the other extreme, the fascist right avowed a Turkish suprematist position. In regions of ethnic cohabitation, this political split came to determine social commerce, especially since a separatist movement had also begun to threaten the established administrative and property structure. The traditional arrangement between Turkish government officials, Kurdish landlords and their peasant clients received a severe blow as left-wing militants and Kurdish nationalists agitated on a platform ranging from land reform through minority rights to separatism. The fascist right, however, was located on the side of the established order as defender of the status quo, and exploited this position to recruit in provinces where nascent ethnic conflict could be identified.

The religious division was more complicated and its political manifestation much less direct. The Shi'ite minority of Turkey are called *Alevis* and live scattered in the Anatolian interior, mostly in villages with relatively even distribution of land. The gradual diffusion of new economic forms towards the interior reached Alevi villages during the late 1960s and early 1970s. Labour migration served as the primary mechanism of capitalist integration, as these villages often did not produce much marketable surplus and the quality of the land did not warrant productive accumulation. Although external migration opportunities do not seem to have been readily exploited by Alevi villages, remittances from towns permitted migration-yielding households and villages to subsist at a higher level, and introduced new consumer goods into a stagnant social economy. Outside of the village, communal solidarity gained importance much like the regional identities discovered in shanty towns. The construction boom in Anatolian towns during the 1974–78 period and the ensuing shortage of labour was a boon for the Alevis who now established economic strongholds for themselves in towns of the interior, as well as in larger coastal cities. Once again, the economic crisis ushered in severe constraints in the labour market which translated solidary communities to hostile encampments. In the case of the Alevi minority, the antagonistic atmosphere led to closure and defensive strategies within their neighbourhoods, and the majority could be relatively easily mobilised against the imagined enemy.

Alevis in Turkey have traditionally been on the side of secular forces, since the gaining of state power by religious-minded groups would entail a curtailment of their liberties and possibly direct oppression. For this reason, the greater part of the Alevi population had sided with the Republican Party against the Democrat Party, which had liberally employed religious vocabulary during the 1950 elections and thereafter. The fact that their villages were relatively less developed and commercialised had also been a factor reinforcing Alevi estrangement from the centre right. During the 1960s, this estrangement evolved into a more consciously articulated preference for the centre left, and eventually for Ecevit's social democracy. Hence, when the fascist right attempted to exploit the simmering conflict between Sunnis and the Alevi minority, they found a willing audience among Anatolian small business-men whose allegiance to the right remained unshaken despite the growing economic threat posed by the dominant economic model. In this case, the religious right was also party to the conflict, as the issue resonated strongly in the fundamental articles of faith held sacred by the Sunnis. During the near civil war atmosphere of the late 1970s, such cohabitation readily exploded into fiery conflict and fascist strategy provided the necessary catalyst. In several Anatolian towns, but most notably in Maraş and Çorum, the scenario was acted out and pogroms conducted against Alevis.

While such attempts at catalysing mass involvement in the struggle were aimed at implementing a scenario to culminate with a 'march on Ankara', the daily activities of the fascist party were more in the line of terrorism directed to the left. The shooting of left-wing theoreticians, faculty and students, the bombing of union buildings, strike-breaking and violence toward workers in unionised factories, marches and demonstrations in urban centres, had become commonplace. It must be admitted that the fascist movement was successful in maintaining the level of tension it found necessary to implement the scenario delivering law and order. The public's call for law and order had indeed attained a high pitch by the time the military obliged with its intervention.

This discussion of political ideology may be concluded with a note on the authenticity and relative significance of Turkey's fascist movement. A genuine fascist movement in a peripheral country is a rare phenomenon, for the ideology is associated with the throes of rapid development in a latecomer rather than underdeveloped context.[16] Yet, as I have attempted to explain above, until the crisis had become irreversible, Turkey's economic and social transformation resembled a belated late-comer situation. Modern industry dissolved traditional forms, absorbing interior regions and local economies that until then had remained relatively insular. The social groups threatened by this absorption were integrated into a national labour market which exhibited a functional differentiation with a relatively privileged organised component, well-paid and espousing social democratic aspirations. Those remaining outside – unorganised urban labourers, the marginal sector of shanty towns, small town workers in and out of self-employment, and partly proletarianised villagers – were swayed by the promise – and disillusioned by the betrayal – of unified development. They provided a potentially wide social base for fascism. Without this promise, the fascist alternative would not have appeared on the agenda.

The success of the fascist movement depended on the failure of the political centre to cope with the crisis of the industrialisation project and the consequent crisis of its ideology. The grand industrialists were not sufficiently hegemonic to effect an ideological transformation and the political mechanisms were not adequate to such a task. The centrist parties on the right and the left could not repudiate their shared populist rhetoric since even with restricted democracy, universal suffrage imposes its own determinations on the political game. Small and medium capital and the petty bourgeoisie, therefore, could not be ignored or isolated. Had there been a lower level of politicisation, a party utilising the force of traditional legitimation might have succeeded in effecting a transformation from above.[17] But, precisely because of the degree of dissolution of traditional structures, this conservative path was no longer practicable. Again, for the same reason, traditionalist attempts were confined to the radical fringe. The balances within the bourgeoisie had changed irreversibly and a hegemonic bloc was not about to be constituted; the political centre, on the other hand, suffered from the inertia of success and the multiplicity of vested interests that had benefited from the populist policies of the boom. The fascist response to the dilemma was radically restorationist in attempting to employ the imagined glory of an ancient past toward the containment of social conflict. At the same time, though, it was ruefully naïve in its economics and perception of the outside world. A 'national' solution was simply not possible in the 1970s crisis, and given the international state system, fascism was too uncertain a solution. This uncertainty is probably the reason for the industrialists' reluctance to proffer any long-term support to the fascists, even when it looked as though civil war was impending.

When the exaggerated 'socialist threat' is considered, the grand bourgeoisie's distance from the fascist movement becomes more significant. For, during the entire crisis period, official rhetoric characterised the situation as one of imminent Marxist revolution against which strong measures had to be taken. This rhetoric and the much more modest reality of the socialist movement contributed to the success of fascism among small and medium capitalists. In their case, the anxiety of *déclassement* together with the actual fear of unionised workers rendered the 'extremism of the centre' understandable. On the other hand, although the socialist threat was palpable enough to be a factor in the success of fascism, it did not seem so real as to induce the grand bourgeoisie to rally to the ranks. In addition to the feebleness of the socialist threat, the unconvincing nature of the fascist solution, given the economic crisis and worldwide transformations experienced in the 1970s, contributed to the coolness with which the grand bourgeoisie received the fascists. More important, however, was the implicit faith that the military would intervene to establish the state's monopoly of violence. Whether this intervention would be successful in its economic and ideological strategies was a secondary concern: that the military had a domestic and international legitimacy made it preferable to the unknown quantity represented by the fascists.

It was the authenticity of its generation within a certain phase of capitalist development, the implications of this development on the traditional order, and the ideological heritage of nationalist statolatry, which combined to make the fascist movement in Turkey unique among peripheral countries during the post World War II period. Its affinity with the inter-war prototypes in Europe was genuine, and this affinity should cast a revealing light on Turkish social transformations.

X

Conclusion as Epilogue

For a brief period in the 1960s and the 1970s it looked as if Turkey would experience a transformation similar to those of Southern European countries, with a strong social democratic movement defending democracy and civil rights, maintaining a check against the renaissance of traditionalist and chauvinist reactions and able to secure a relatively even distribution of economic gains. The civilising impact of the dissolution of traditional social structures through economic growth, the integration of multitudes into the urban world and the gradual marketisation of agricultural petty producers seemed to augur a bright future within an expanding Europe. By contrast, the prognoses of the late 1970s were uniformly pessimistic: it became evident that whatever social contract had earlier emerged did not penetrate deep, and that economic growth was faltering. The state, which appeared to have completed its transformation into a capitalist one, was hindered by intense political competition whose rules were far from being settled or universally accepted. In giving way to privatisation and parcelling up of its agencies, the state rapidly lost its ability to fulfil its accumulation function *vis-à-vis* the bourgeoisie. Its legitimacy, already eroded in the eyes of the social groups excluded from the populist equation, declined parallel to its growing privatisation.

Given the extent of the crisis of legitimacy it was surprising how quickly after the military coup in September 1980 the state apparatus could be used with great effectiveness to fully dismantle the structures and institutions of the previous period. The military regime swiftly carried out its task of suppressing

223

radical politics with a heavy hand, and banning previous leaders of centrist parties from political life. At the same time new centre right groupings – but without any populist trappings – were delegated the responsibility of restructuring the state–economy relationship. During the two previous suspensions of parliamentary democracy through military intervention – in 1960 and 1971 – the military had had recourse to the services of a Republican elite, identified with the state due to having occupied high bureaucratic posts, but free from encumbering party affiliation. The 1980 coup came at a time when there was a widespread feeling that major restructuring was required at all levels of the state. The propaganda of the military party following the coup was directed primarily at instilling the view in the public that previous political, economic, and legal arrangements had been responsible for and had inevitably led to the crisis and made it incumbent on the military to intervene. Thus it was not restoration but radical innovation that was called for. Consequently the tenure of the Republican elite was brief while technocratic management and radical legal-institutional innovation became the order of the day. A frantic legislative activity succeeded in clearing the administrative system of a bureaucratic and populist heritage of sixty years.

Political matters were left to the military whose programme alluded broadly to the 'solidary nation' formula of Kemalist times, and set out to eradicate 'anarchy and terrorism'. The same formula served to retrospectively condemn democratic practices of the 1970s and justify the 'restricted democracy' framed in the new 1982 constitution. In its glorification of authority and hierarchy, of tradition and order, of stability and the national good, the framework of restricted democracy provided a most conducive medium for the recovery of the extreme right's ideas and cadres to the mainstream. The spectrum of political discourse contracted on the left flank, and the centre of gravity of acceptable politics shifted to accommodate ideologies previously considered extremist.

Despite their novelty in the Turkish context, there was nothing original in the political measures or the economic and social policies adopted by the military and right-wing groupings after the coup. As in many countries of similar evolution the military coup had happened in Turkey following a period of social and economic crisis. Both the bourgeoisie and the bureaucracy recognised that the period of an expanding national economy without world market sanctioning was over and a new type of regulation was necessary. The elaborate nexus of state controls and distribution policies were to be dismantled through a prescription of policies that IMF experts freely dispensed. What this blueprint of instant liberalism offered (in addition to the sanctity of the market) was increasing rates of profit through lower wages, reduced social expenditure, and declining agricultural incomes. At the same time the government would subsidise exports and devalue the currency to an acceptable rate. Imports would thus be reduced to essentials basically because domestic incomes would be lowered; and exports would increase due to low wages, a devalued currency, and an export promotion policy. The result of all these policies would be a shrinking of the national market. It is obvious that such a reorientation of manufacturing capacity would be difficult and would lead to the failure and bankruptcy of several firms which worked within the margins offered them through a protected internal market. Only those units with large capacity and credit availability had the wherewithal to set off an expensive restructuring with lower wages and new markets and come out ahead.

The new economic measures did lead to an upheaval within the manufacturing bourgeoisie. A rapid concentration and centralisation of capital took place; all but the upper ranks of the bourgeoisie were abruptly pushed into an uncertain economic environment. Yet critical or dissident voices were few and far between. There were certainly protests from smaller manufacturers and merchants, especially concerning the privileges accorded to large firms, but the bourgeoisie as a whole seemed to weigh political gains against economic losses and made the choice for restricted democracy, ideological hegemony, and a disciplined labour force.

Resistance against massive marginalisation on the other side of the social divide was also ineffective. Among workers, small commodity producers, the marginal population and the growing ranks of the unemployed, real incomes dropped precipitously – probably in the range of thirty to fifty per cent – but strikes and other protest activity were banned, political parties proscribed, and unions rendered impotent. The change in income distribution (the share of labour – wages and salaries – in national income dropped from around thirty-five per cent in 1976–78 to around twenty per cent in 1983–86)[1] reflects only part of the problem in that the social expenditures of the state also declined, with the visible deterioration of public education and public health sevices. Against a background defined by bureaucratic control and an assumption of administrative benevolence, these changes in the position of the political authority and the consequent repudiation of the paternalist image, were radical departures. Liberalism as a savage market credo had been anathema to the *raison d'être* of a bureaucracy; now it was preached from the pulpit as the necessary prescription.

It would be a mistake to underestimate the potential popular support for the dismantling of bureaucratic paternalism, even among some of the groups hurt most by the change. I have already touched upon the affinity between petty commodity production and the simple market mentality – a relation whose importance becomes apparent when the proportion of the self-employed in the labour force is considered. State-centred development and populist incorporation had not only provided a rudimentary safety net but also an obstacle to unfettered competition and accumulation. Thus, in addition to the grand bourgeoisie, who finally seized the chance to emancipate the dominant ideology from its bureaucratic encumbrance, self-employed petty producers also constituted a group that potentially supported the new orientation. Of course, for most of their ranks liberalism brought chagrin and disenchantment; for those, however, who could use the new era of opportunity to their advantage and 'turn the corner' as the Turkish colloquial expression had it, the market was vindicated.

In economic liberalism imposed from above, the bourgeoisie grasped the promise of ideological hegemony. During the entire import substitution stage the dominant ideology had remained within the confines of nationalist development and national solidarity. Economic growth was to proceed through anti-liberal tenets; it was to be a solidaristic engagement which, through its success, would prove the desirability of the nationalist model. From the point of view of a bourgeoisie come of age, this model was costly and contradicted the strict rules of capitalist rationality. It was not that the growth of large capital had been restricted but rather that various groups had been protected sufficiently to prevent the expedient destruction of traditional structures. In the same vein, the 'safety net' had extended to agricultural producers, to the newly urbanised, to the *gecekondu* population, and most significantly to industrial workers.

All this was in keeping with the expansion of the internal market – a necessary feature of import substitution – but it also precluded the internalisation of strict market rationality by the population. The ideology of national development borrowed freely from a certain strand of socialist discourse, especially in its statist developmentalism and populism. In that sense, the left had gained a certain legitimacy due to its being accepted as a significant interlocutor. But once national development, statism and populism were repudiated, and the political expression of the left banned, socialist ideology became entirely marginalised. Thus, the process of establishing the hegemony of bourgeois ideology did not encounter any resistance.

The military intervention of 1980 and its aftermath demonstrated the dissimilarity of Turkey's evolution from the Southern European trajectory; instead the pattern of populism–crisis–coup suggested a path more similar to Latin American experiences.˙ The industrialisation effort in its early stages had not required an extensive market. As the productive base of the economy became more complex through the industrialisation policy, however, its requirements in terms of labour and the market for its products changed. These requirements were met through the political and social incorporation of rural migrants as the new labour force, and through the state assuming the responsibility for regulating the growth of the national market. High wages for workers, easy conditions for immigrants to the city, and subsidised incomes for rural petty producers achieved rapid economic integration. Economic development fulfilled the universalising promises of Republican ideology through a populist expression.

The Republicans had exacted an exclusive affiliation from the population at the expense of traditional values and localist ties. A secular, anti-particularist society was designated as the aim, where community would coincide with the nation. During the 1930s, this formulation primarily served in a defensive capacity, and provided the justification for militant reformism. In the period of national economic integration through import-substituting industrialisation, it started to reflect a social reality. The masses were gradually being included in economic, political and cultural practices at the national level as they became urban workers, commercialised farmers, or shanty town marginals. There was, certainly, a considerable degree of unevenness in the process; the point, however, is that even the so-called marginal population and the least commercialised peasantry were drawn into the momentum of economic growth.

These groups found the promises of the populist discourse sufficiently concrete to allow themselves to be integrated into the national development programme and to subscribe to its universalist concerns. Nationalism, and its claim for a single integrating principle within political borders, seemed to work.

I have already discussed the contradictions of this successful period of development. Its denouement came in the form of a general and prolonged crisis whose political dimension provided the manifest reasons for interrupting the parliamentary regime. The programme of the military regime accordingly consisted of an effective dismantling of the constitutional framework and the redistributive institutions of the previous period. All this could only be achieved under the political and social conditions of a military regime and 'restricted democracy'. The similarity to the extensively studied 'bureaucratic-authoritarian' regimes is evident – a similarity that continued into the subsequent period of cautious and halting democratisation.

The picture of an apparent slide into the Latin American configuration has to be complemented in one important respect. This concerns Turkey's curious position, in terms of the concentration of its meaningful transactions, between Europe and America. In fact, the uncertainty of the democratisation process led parts of the bourgeoisie, the working class and the intelligentsia to seek a closer relationship with Europe, and, in particular, with the European Community. The bourgeoisie feel that such a connection provides safer anchoring for liberalism, while workers and the intelligentsia place their faith in the democratic institutions which will have to be adopted as the condition of Europeanisation. In this respect, Turkey's democratisation process bears a certain similarity to the Southern European countries emerging out of dictatorships a decade earlier. The existence of this option perhaps increases the likelihood of a successful structuring of the post-authoritarian stage, despite the relative weakness of the social groups mobilising behind the platform of democracy.

Notes

Chapter 1

1. For a short statement on Byzantine taxes see André M. Andréades, 'Public Finances: Currency, Public Expenditure, Budget, Public Revenue', in N.H. Baynes and H. St. L.B. Moss, *Byzantium, An Introduction to East Roman Civilization,* Oxford 1949.

2. The actual victory of the provincial magnates is usually dated in the eleventh century although the palace started struggling against the *donatoi* earlier. G. Ostrogorsky's chapter in the *Cambridge Economic History of Europe* is comprehensive: G. Ostrogorsky, 'Agrarian Conditions in the Byzantine Empire in the Middle Ages' in M.M. Postan (ed.), *Cambridge Economic History of Europe,* vol.1: *The Agrarian Life of the Middle Ages,* Cambridge 1971. Also G. Ostrogorsky, *History of the Byzantine State,* Rutgers 1969, pp. 272–76, 329–30.

3. On the Turkish side the most important text is by one of the founders of nationalist historiography: F. Köprülü, 'Bizans Müesseselerinin Osmanlı Muesseselerine Tesiri Hakkında Bazı Mulahazalar' (Some Considerations on the Influence of Byzantine Institutions on Ottoman Institutions) in *Türk Hukuk ve Iktisat Tarihi Mecmuası* vol. I, 1931. By far the majority of Turkish historians of all political persuasions see the Ottoman Empire as the reconstitution, on the basis of a new dynasty, of Seljuk state power. See *inter alia* T. Timur, *Osmanlı Toplumsal Duzeni* (The Ottoman Social Order), Ankara 1979, pp. 57 ff. H. Inalcık is an exception; his view on the continuity of the agrarian system is presented in his 'The Problem of the Relationship between Byzantine and Ottoman Taxation' in *Akten des XI Internationalen Byzantinisten-Kongresses 1958,* Munich 1960.

4. A Marxian version of this usually culturalist view argues that the Byzantine Empire had become feudalised after the eleventh century and thus asssimilated within the European entity. Before this period it was characterised by the dominance of the Asiatic Mode of Production, and the Turkish invasion reconstituted a despotism which was historically a backward step. See H. Antoniadis-Bibicou, 'Byzance et le Mode de Production Asiatique' in *Sur le Mode de Production Asiatique,* CERM, 1974.

5. The most impressive account of this syncretism is found in Speros Vryonis Jr., *The Decline of Medieval Hellenism in Asia Minor and the Process of*

Islamization from the Eleventh through the Fifteenth Century, California 1971. See especially chapters 3,5, and 7.

6. G. Ostrogorsky, *History of the Byzantine State,* pp. 90n, 134–7: 'The peasants whose legal relationships are regulated by the *Law* are free landowners. They have no obligations to any landlord but only to the state, as taxpayers . . . The [Law] pays particular attention to the maintenance of the individual's title to his personal property'(p.135).

7. H. Inalcık, 'Osmanlılar'da Raiyyet Rusumu' (Charges on the Peasantry in the Ottomans), *Belleten*, vol. 23, October 1959; Inalcık, 'Land Problems in Turkish History', *The Muslim World*, vol. 45, July 1955. Inalcık describes the sucession by 'a universal state' (p.221) of feudal practices where 'the formation of large estates . . . was prevented' and a 'definite control against any regime of landlords' was sought, (p.224).

8. H. Inalcık, 'Capital Formation in the Ottoman Empire', *Journal of Economic History* 1969, no.1, especially pp. 98, 106 ff. For the Ottoman guild system see G. Baer, 'The Administrative, Economic and Social Functions of Turkish Guilds', *International Journal of Middle East Studies*, January 1970.

9. For the effects of the price revolution on the Empire, see Ö.L. Barkan, 'The Price Revolution of the Sixteenth Century', *International Journal of Middle East Studies*, January 1975; for the impact on the peasantry and the disturbances in the agrarian society see William J. Griswold, *The Great Anatolian Rebellion 1000–1020/1591–1611*, Berlin 1983. Again, the most comprehensive treatment is in H. Inalcık, 'The Ottoman Decline and its Effects upon the *Reaya'*, in H. Birnbaum and S. Vryonis eds, *Aspects of the Balkans: Continuity and Change*, Mouton 1972.

10. One innovation was the *malikane* system, devised in the late seventeenth century, whereby tax-farms were granted on a lifetime basis, and the grantee acquired the right to manage his farm independently of state supervision. See Mehmet Genç, 'Osmanlı Maliyesinde Malikane Sistemi' (The *Malikane* system in Ottoman Finances), in *Türk Iktisat Tarihi Semineri*, Ankara 1975. The fiscal crisis argument is elaborated in H. Islamoğlu and Ç. Keyder, 'Agenda for Ottoman History', *Review*, vol. I, no. 1, summer 1977.

11. H. Inalcık, 'Centralization and Decentralization in Ottoman Administration', in T. Naff and R. Owen, eds, *Studies in Eighteenth Century Islamic History*, Southern Illinois University Press 1977; also the Introduction to Part I by Naff. See also Y. Özkaya, *Osmanli Imparatorluğunda Ayanlık* (Ayans in Ottoman Empire), Ankara 1977. A recent contribution to the vast literature on *ayan* is by N. Sakaoğlu, *Anadolu Derebeyi Ocaklarindan Köse Paşa Hanedanı* (Köse Paşa Dynasty: An Anatolian Family of Lords), Ankara 1984, where the rise of a family of *ayan* in a provincial centre in Sivas *vilayet* is documented.

12. The most extensive treatment of this period from the point of view of Great Power relations is in V.J. Puryear, *International Economics and Diplomacy in the Near East, 1834–1853*, Stanford 1935; see chapter 3 for Mohammad Ali.

13. See the excellent article by Andrew G. Gould, 'Lords or Bandits? The Derebeys of Cilicia', *International Journal of Middle East Studies*, October 1976.

14. In the sense of radically altering the land regime. B. McGowan's conclusion for the Balkans that 'Ottoman government did *not* erect a second serfdom . . . It had no interest in doing so, since the government was not simply the instrument of a landholding class and had nothing to gain, as a corporation, from the degradation of the peasantry' is echoed by G. Veinstein for Western

Anatolia. B. McGowan, *Economic Life in Ottoman Europe, Taxation, Trade and the Struggle for Land, 1600–1800*, Cambridge 1982; G. Veinstein, 'Ayan de la region d'Izmir et commerce du Levant (deuxième moitié du XVIIIe siècle)', *Études Balkaniques* 1976.

15. See Inalcık, 'Centralization and Decentralization' and Ö. L. Barkan, 'Turk Toprak Tahinde *Tarinzimat* ve 1274 (1858) Tarihli Arazi Kanunamesi' (*Tanzimat* in Turkish Agrarian History and the 1858 Land Law) in his *Turkiye'de Toprak Meselesi*, Istanbul 1980 (originally published in 1940).

16. Kemal H. Karpat, *An Inquiry into the Social Foundations of Nationalism in the Ottoman State: From Millets to Nations, from Estates to Social Classes*, Center of International Studies, Princeton 1973.

17. For the full argument, see Ç. Keyder, 'The Cycle of Sharecropping and the Consolidation of Small Peasant Ownership', *Journal of Peasant Studies*, January–April 1983.

18. O. Kurmus, *Emperyalizmin Turkiye'ye Girisi* (The Penetration of Imperialism into Turkey), Istanbul 1974, pp. 99–115.

19. C. Issawi, *The Economic History of Turkey 1800–1914* , Chicago 1980, p. 38; on this issue see also K. Boratav, G. Ökçün and Ş. Pamuk, 'Wages in Turkey', *Review*, Winter 1985.

20. Tax-farming practice was as old as the Empire but it had been confined to certain monetary prestations. With its extension to all government revenues and with the parallel weakening of the central authority, the implications of tax-farming as to the social structure became more consequential. See for example the discussion in R. Owen, *The Middle East in the World Economy, 1800–1914*, London 1981, pp. 10–21; also D. Quataert, 'Agricultural Trends and Government Policy in Ottoman Anatolia, 1800–1914', *Asian and African Studies*, vol. XV, no. 1, 1981.

21. Travellers to the Empire often remarked on this division. The classical statement is in A.J. Sussnitzki, 'The Ethnic Division of Labor', in C. Issawi, ed., *The Economic History of the Middle East*, Chicago 1966, pp. 115–24.

22. T. Naff, 'Ottoman Diplomatic Relations with Europe in the Eighteenth Century: Patterns and Trends', in T. Naff and R. Owen, eds, *Studies*.

23. Ibid., pp. 100–103. Nasim Sousa, *The Capitulatory Regime of Turkey*, Baltimore 1933, is still the most comprehensive treatment of the subject.

24. See Naff, 'Ottoman Diplomatic Relations'; also R. Davison, 'Nationalism as an Ottoman Problem and the Ottoman Response', in W.W. Haddad and W. Ochsenwald, eds, *Nationalism in a Non-National State: The Dissolution of the Ottoman Empire*, Ohio University Press 1977, p.42: 'A British consul, judge of the supreme consular court in Istanbul about the time of the Crimean War, later wrote his impression that there were "little short of a million" in the Levant who were "so-called British protected subjects"'. Although the Ottoman government sought to 'curb the abuse by issuing regulations concerning the protégés of foreign powers' it was not ultimately successful.

25. See the extremely interesting study by S.T. Rosenthal, *The Politics of Dependency: Urban Reform in Istanbul*, Westport 1980.

26. There are many studies of the reform movement: R. Davison, *Reform in the Ottoman Empire, 1856–1876*, Princeton 1963; F.E. Bailey, *British Policy and the Turkish Reform Movement*, Harvard 1942; and C. Findley, *Bureaucratic Reform in the Ottoman Empire*, Princeton 1980. S.J. Shaw and E.K. Shaw, *History of the Ottoman Empire and Modern Turkey*, vol. II: *Reform, Revolution, and Republic*, Cambridge 1977, is a useful review. Among Turkish historians the reform movement has been variously celebrated as the beginnings

of modernisation and derided as an imperialist ploy. For a revisionist view from the left see I. Ortaylı, *Imparatorluğun En Uzun Yuzyılı* (The Longest Century of the Empire), Istanbul 1983.

Chapter II

1. H. Inalcık describes the classical age in *The Ottoman Empire, The Classical Age*, New York 1973. Certainly the mediation of tax-collection by tax-farmers had introduced a new element into the social structure. During the nineteenth century, probably more than half of the surplus was appropriated by tax-farmers. See Issawi, *The Economic History of Turkey*, p. 356, for a description of how taxes were farmed in Erzurum and the 'profit' margins. Ş. Pamuk, *Osmanlı Ekonomisi ve Dunya Kapitalizmi, 1820–1913* (The Ottoman Economy and World Capitalism), Ankara 1984, p. 54n, cites an estimate that only a third of the taxes collected reached the treasury.
2. H. Inalcık, 'The Nature of Traditional Society' in R. Ward and D. Rustow, eds, *Political Modernization in Japan and Turkey*, Princeton 1964. Of course, this symbiotic relation is appealed to in the ideological reproduction of all agrarian societies.
3. See C. Findley, *Bureaucratic Reform*; and S.J. Shaw, *Between Old and New: The Ottoman Empire under Sultan Selim III, 1789–1807*, Harvard 1971.
4. For the background to the treaty see Puryear, *International Economics and Diplomacy in the Middle East,* chapter 4; the text of the treaty is printed in C. Issawi, *The Economic History of the Middle East*, pp. 39–40.
5. Şevket Pamuk, *The Ottoman Empire and the World Economy 1820–1913: Trade, Capital and Production*, Cambridge University Press forthcoming, chapter 2; Issawi, *Turkey*, pp. 74–82.
6. European merchants thought that the principal obstacles preventing the expansion of trade were Ottoman trade monopolies and internal customs. Merchant vessels always had difficulty in finding return cargo. Although the 1838 Convention abolished trade monoplies and reduced internal customs, the Empire never became an export-surplus area like most peripheral countries in the nineteenth century. See R., Owen, *The Middle East in the World Economy*, p.91; also Issawi, *Economic History of Turkey*, p. 76: 'Over the whole period, exports rose about 6 times and imports 7.6 times in money terms and about 8 and 10 times respectively in real terms. These figures are far below the 50-fold increase in real world trade from 1800 to 1914.'
7. This argument is insufficient insofar as it is based on the risk aversion of the individual peasant producer. What is necessary is a model deriving from the relations inside the village economy and articulating the obstacles to commercialisation that these relations engender. There is almost no social history of the Ottoman Empire, nor has a social history of the Anatolian countryside ever been written.
8. Pamuk, *The Ottoman Empire and the World Economy*. chapter 2, appendix 1.
9. Pamuk, chapter 2, appendix 1; see chapter 6 for the consequence to cotton manufacturing. Also Owen, *Middle East*, pp. 93 ff, for the decline in craft production.
10. For a criticism of this argument, see Ç. Keyder, 'Proto-industrialization and the Periphery', *Insurgent Sociologist,* winter 1981; cf. O. Köymen, 'The Advent and Consequences of Free Trade in the Ottoman Empire', *Études*

Balkaniques, vol. VII, no. 2, 1971; and O. Kurmuş, 'Some Aspects of Handicraft and Industrial Production in Anatolia', *Asian and African Studies*, vol. XV, 1981.

11. R. Kasaba, *Peripheralization of the Ottoman Empire*, Dissertation, SUNY Binghamton 1985, for Izmir; A. Vacalopoulos, *A History of Thessaloniki*, Salonica 1963; S.T. Rosenthal, *Politics of Dependency* for Istanbul may also be cited. Again, the paucity of material on the social history of port cities is deplorable.

12. See A.I. Bağış. *Osmanlı Ticaretinde Gayri Müslimler* (Non-Muslims in Ottoman Trade), Ankara 1983; also Kasaba, *Peripheralization*. For attempts to increase the share of Moslem merchants in trade with Europe, see M. Çadırcı, 'II Mahmud Döneminde (1808–1839) Avrupa ve Hayriye Tüccarlari' ('Ottoman Merchants in External Trade in the Time of Mahmut the Second' in O. Okyar and H. Inalcık, eds, *Social and Economic History of Turkey*, Ankara 1980.

13. See Ç. Keyder, 'The Dissolution of the Asiatic Mode of Production', *Economy and Society*, May 1976.

14. A. DuVelay, *Essai sur l'Histoire Financière de la Turquie*, Paris 1903, remains the most comprehensive treatment of the early period of Ottoman indebtedness.

15. The classical statement of this argument is in R. Luxemburg, *The Accumulation of Capital*.

16. J. Thobie, *Les intérêts economiques, financiers et politiques français dans la partie asiatique de l'Empire Ottoman de 1895 à 1914*, Dissertation, Paris 1973, estimates 4,950 million gold francs as the effective yield of the debt and 4,210 million as total payments until 1914 (p.560) and a total of 4,680 million repayment in 'Finances et politique extérieure: l'administration de la dette publique Ottomane, 1881–1914', in Okyar and Inalcık, eds, *Social and Economic History of Turkey*. Ş. Pamuk calculates differently to reach a negative balance of 15 million: *Osmanlı Ekonomisi*, p. 15.

17. 'Imports rose more rapidly than exports, and both Turkey and the whole Empire had a consistently adverse balance of trade,' Issawi, *Economic History of Turkey*, p. 76. See also Pamuk, *Ottoman Empire*, chapter 4.

18. There are several studies of the period: H. Feis, *Europe, the World's Banker*, Yale 1930; D.C. Blaisdell, *European Financial Control in the Ottoman Empire*, New York 1929; R.S. Suvla, 'Debts during the Tanzimat Period' in Issawi, ed., *Economic History of the Middle East*.

19. Blaisdell, *European Financial Control;* the subtitle of this book is 'A Study of the Establishment, Activities and Significance of the Administration of the Ottoman Public Debt'.

20. For tobacco, the activities of the Régie, and popular resistance see D. Quataert, 'The Régie, Smugglers, and the Government' in his *Social Disintegration and Popular Resistance in the Ottoman Empire, 1881–1908: Reactions to European Economic Penetration*, NYU Press 1983.

21. F.S. Rodkey, 'Ottoman Concerns about Western Economic Penetration in the Levant, 1849–1856', *Journal of Modern History*, December 1958.

22. Carpet-weaving as an export activity was one of the only fields in which there was considerable direct foreign investment. Outside of loans foreign capital invested in railroads, banking, commerce and municipal services. In 1914 only 5.3 per cent of foreign capital was found in 'industry'; see Pamuk, *Osmanlı Ekonomisi*, p.65. For a description of the organisation of carpet-weaving industry by British merchants see Kurmuş, *Emperyalizmin Türkiye'ye Girişi*, chapter 5.

234

23. Ö. L. Barkan, 'Türk Toprak Hukukunda Tanzimat'; also Kurmuş, *Emperyalizmin Türkiye'ye Girişi*, chapter 4.
24. E.M. Earle, *Turkey, the Great Powers, and the Bagdad Railway*, New York 1923, is an indispensible study of imperialist rivalry.
25. Thobie, *Les Intérêts Economiques*, pp. 1055–56.
26. Paul Dumont, 'A propos de la classe ouvrière Ottomane à la veille de la Révolution Jeune-Turque', *Turcica*, vol. IX; no. 1, 1977. For an Ottoman census of manufactures immediately prior to the war, see A.G. Ökçün, ed., *Osmanlı Sanayii: 1913, 1915 Yılları Sanayi Istatistiki* (Ottoman Industry: Industrial Statistics for 1913 and 1915), Ankara 1970. According to these statistics which covered Istanbul, Izmir, and Western Anatolia (the Empire lost Salonika in 1912) there were 214 privately owned establishments employing more than ten workers; 107 of these had been established between 1901 and 1915. See V.Eldem, *Osmanlı Imparatorluğunun Iktisadi Şartları Hakkında Bir Tetkik* (An Investigation Concerning the Economic Conditions of the Ottoman Empire), Istanbul 1970, p. 121.
27. G. Haupt and P. Dumont, *Osmanlı Imparatorluğunda Sosyalist Hareketler* (Socialist Movements in the Ottoman Empire), Istanbul 1977; P. Dumont, 'A propos de la classe ouvrière', pp. 245–46. D. Quataert's essays in *Social Disintegration and Popular Resistance* relate confrontations that attempt to straddle ethnic divisions.

Chapter III

1. C. Findley, *Bureaucratic Reform*, pp. 63–4.
2. S.J. Shaw, *History of the Ottoman Empire*, pp. 105–15.
3. 'The Tanzimat created a centralized government based on the new Ruling Class, the bureaucrats ... This class constituted a modern generation of Ottomans that sustained the tempo of modernization mainly oblivious to, or even in spite of, the waves of political and military crisis that hit the Empire ...', Shaw, *History*, p.71.
4. The promulgation of constitutional government and a parliament was the culmination of the political reforms of 1839–76. In 1876, in the aftermath of 'Bulgarian incidents' and a crisis in the Balkans, a Great Power conference convened in Istanbul. The Great Powers' demands for political reforms coincided with the progressive bureaucrats' long-standing constitutional aspirations. Since the military had deposed Sultan Abdulaziz (1876), and his successor was declared mentally unstable, the powerful bureaucrat Mithat Paşa had been able to convince Abdülhamit to accept the Constitution. Abdhülhamit, however, was able to outmanoeuvre Mithat Paşa; the parliament sat for three months in its first session and two months in the second session before it was dissolved by the Sultan in February 1878. For the period prior to the Constitution, see Davison, *Reform in the Ottoman Empire*; for the parliament and its dismissal, Shaw, *History*, pp. 172–87.
5. Şerif Mardin, *The Genesis of Young Ottoman Thought: A Study in the Modernization of Turkish Political Ideas*, Princeton 1962, is a masterly study of the intellectual currents of the period.
6. Ş. Mardin, *Jön Turklerin Siyasi Fikirleri, 1895–1908* (The Political Ideas of the Young Turks), Ankara 1964; E.E. Ramsaur, *The Young Turks: Prelude to the Revolution of 1908*, Princeton 1957.
7. This protection was an extension of Russia's territorial gains in Eastern

Anatolia. In fact the Berlin treaty could be considered as the beginning of the final period for the Empire: Britain no longer seemed in favour of the containment of the Russian threat, Slavic nationalism and Balkan separatism were in the ascendant, and Russian expansionary momentum was strong. For the Armenian community in the Empire as well, 1878 was a turning point, when the disappointment over Abdülhamit's abrogation of the Constitution and dissolving of the parliament was translated into support for Great Power intervention to secure reforms and measures leading to autonomy.

8. Rifat Önsoy, *Turk-Alman Iktisadi Münasebetleri (1871–1914)* (Turkish-German Economic Relations), Istanbul 1982, pp. 42–3. K. Helfferich, *Die Deutsche Türkenpolitik,* Berlin 1921, is the principal text arguing the 'naturalness' of the 'Drang nach Osten' politics.

9. J. Thobie, *Les Intérêts Economiques,* pp. 1057, 1146; Eldem Osmanlı Imparatorluğunun Iktisadi Şartları, pp. 181–3.

10. Önsoy, *Türk–Alman Iktisadi Münasebetleri,* pp. 55–8.

11. It might be argued that the Russian factor prevented such a solution. Otherwise, with France dominant in Syria and Alexandretta and Britain laying claim over Iraq, Germany would have been satisfied with Anatolia. It was Russia's intentions over most of Anatolia, and especially Istanbul, that complicated the territorial division from the point of view of the Great Powers.

12. Paul Fesch, *Constantinople aux derniers jours d'Abdul-Hamid,* Paris 1907, is a good example of this appreciation.

13. See Feroz Ahmad, 'Great Britain's Relations with the Young Turks, 1908–1914', *Middle Eastern Studies,* July 1966, pp. 302 ff.

14. On this counter-revolution, see Sina Akşin, *31 Mart Olayi* (The Incident of 31 March), Istanbul 1972.

15. Cemal Paşa, *Hatıralar, Ittihat-Terakki ve Birinci Dünya Harbi* (Memoirs – CUP and World War I), Istanbul 1959, pp. 36–153, relates the reluctant acceptance of the German alliance by one of the leaders of the CUP. It seems that revanchism did play a role in Enver's pro-German attitude although this was not shared by most members of the committee.

16. A. Ter Minassian, 'La permanence d'une revendication', *Temps Modernes,* Juillet–Août, 1984, p. 429.

17. See E. Llewellyn-Smith, *The Ionian Vision,* London 1975, on the background and consequences of Venizelism.

18. For this early period of nationalist ideas see D. Kushner, *The Rise of Turkish Nationalism, 1876–1908,* London 1977.

19. Note from the Ottoman minister of foreign affairs, Sait Halim Paşa, to Ambassadors in Istanbul, dated 9 September 1914: 'that consequence of the Capitulations which renders foreigners exempt and free from taxes in the Ottoman Empire renders the Sublime Porte powerless not only to procure the necessary means for providing for the carrying out of reforms, but even for satisfying current administrative needs, without having recourse to a loan . . . The fact that foreigners trading in the Ottoman Empire and enjoying there all sorts of immunities and privilege are less heavily taxed than Ottomans constitutes at the same time a manifest injustice and an infringement of the independence and dignity of the state'. Reprinted in Sousa, *Capitulatory Régime,* pp. 329–30. Capitulations were abrogated beginning 1 October 1914.

20. The most comprehensive work on the economic policy of this period is Zafer Toprak, *Türkiye'de 'Milli Iktisat'* ('National Economics' in Turkey), Ankara 1982. See pp. 26–7, 33 for the argument on a Moslem bourgeoisie.

21. A. Emin (Yalman), *Turkey in the World War,* Yale 1930, contains many

perceptive anecdotes on the economy of the war period.

22. Harry Stuermer, *Deux Ans de Guerre à Constantinople*, Paris 1914, p. 153. Stuermer was *ancien correspondant* of the *Gazette de Cologne*.

23. F. Ahmad, 'Vanguard of a Nascent Bourgeoisie: The Social and Economic Policy of the Young Turks 1908–1918', in Okyar and Inalcık, eds, *Social and Economic History*, pp. 341–5. See also Toprak, *Türkiye'de Milli Iktisat*, pp. 59–62, 150–165.

24. Toprak, pp. 264–6; Ç. Keyder, 'Ottoman Economy and Finances (1881–1918)', in Okyar and Inalcık, eds, *Social and Economic History*, p.326.

25. I. Tekeli and S. Ilkin, 'Ittihat ve Terakki Hareketinin Oluşumunda Selanik'in Toplumsal Yapısının Belirleyiciliği' ('The Impact of Salonikan Social Structure on the Formation of the CUP Movement ')' in Okyar and Inalcık, eds, *Social and Economic History*; Elie Kedourie, 'Young Turks, Freemasons and Jews', *Middle Eastern Studies*, January 1971.

26. S. Vryonis, *The Decline of Medieval Hellenism*, chapter 7; for the Hellenisation of a particular coastal area in Western Anatolia see T. Baykara, 'XIX. Yüzyılda Urla Yarımadasında Nüfus Hareketleri' (Population Movements in the Urla Peninsula during the Nineteenth Century), in Okyar and Inalcık, eds.

27. 'Armenian land-owners, already in possession of the richest areas of the Cilician plain, were rapidly increasing their holdings; and . . . the Armenian population prospered and multiplied while the Moslem population declined. The Moslems of Cilicia, indeed, were gloomily brooding over Armenian affronts to their patriotism, and economic Armenian encroachments on their position as the dominant and ruling race. These matters combined formed a mass of highly inflammable material . . . ' W.J. Childs, 'Armenia', *Encyclopaedia Brittanica*, new volumes added to the eleventh edition, vol. XXX, London 1922, p.197.

28. Richard G. Hovannisian, *Armenia on the Road to Independence*, 1918, California 1967, p. 42: 'Although most Armenians maintained a correct attitude vis-à-vis the Ottoman government, it can be asserted with some substantiation that the manifestations of loyalty were insincere, for the sympathy of most Armenians throughout the world was with the Entente, not with the Central Powers. By Autumn 1914, several prominent Ottoman Armenians, including a former member of Parliament, had slipped away to the Caucasus, to collaborate with Russian military officials.'

29. Llewellyn-Smith, *Ionian Vision;* Arnold Toynbee, *The Western Question in Greece and Turkey: A Study in the Contact of Civilizations (1922)*, New York 1970.

30. D. Pentzopoulos, *The Balkan Exchange of Minorities and its Impact upon Greece*, Mouton 1962, is the most complete account of this great population movement. There is no study of the exchange from the Turkish perspective.

Chapter IV

1. There are several diplomatic histories of the period. Noteworthy among these are Harry N. Howard, *The Partition of Turkey*, Norman, Oklahoma 1931; P.C. Helmrich, *From Paris to Sèvres, The Partition of the Ottoman Empire at the Peace Conference of 1919–1920*, Ohio University Press, 1974; Lawrence Evans, *United States Policy and the Partition of Turkey, 1914–1924*, Baltimore 1965.

2. This is the principal argument of Eric J. Zürcher's *The Unionist Factor, the*

Role of the Committee of Union and Progress in Turkish National Movement, 1905–1926, Brill 1984; especially chapter 3.

3. Sina Akşin, *Istanbul Hükümetleri ve Milli Mücadele* (Istanbul Governments and National Struggle), Istanbul 1983, is an excellent account of the intellectual and political atmosphere of the capital between 1918 and 1919.

4. Yves Lelannou, 'La fin de l'empire Ottoman vue par la presse française (1918–1923), *Turcica*, vol. IX/2 and X, 1978, p. 185.

5. Theda Skocpol and Ellen Kay Trimberger, 'Revolutions and the World Historical Development of Capitalism', in B.H. Kaplan, ed., *Social Change in the Capitalist World Economy*, Sage 1978.

6. Paul Dumont, 'A propos de la 'classe ouvrière' Ottomane à la veille de la revolution Jeune Turque', *Turcica*, vol. IX/I 1977, p. 240.

7. There is a great deal of literature on the issue of the relation between the agrarian structure and the nature of the state, Barrington Moore, Jr., *Social Origins of Dictatorship and Democracy*, Beacon 1966; and Robert Brenner, 'Agrarian Class Structure and Economic Development in Pre-Industrial Europe', *Past and Present*, February 1976, are the most directly relevant to the discussion.

8. Vital Cuinet, *La Turquie d'Asie,* four volumes, Paris 1890–95, contains information on most of the important cities in Anatolia. Recently, *Yurt Ansiklopedisi*, published in Istanbul in 1982–84, has compiled all the available historical data on provinces of present-day Turkey. It is an invaluable source. See also Mesrob K. Krikorian, *Armenians in the Service of the Ottoman Empire*, London 1978, in which the author discusses each province separately; and the sources in n.9.

9. This issue is discussed in two recent contributions to Ottoman population history: Kemal H. Karpat, *Ottoman Population 1830–1914, Demographic and Social Characteristics*, University of Wisconsin Press,. 1985, and Justin McCarthy, *Muslims and Minorities: The Population of Ottoman Empire and the End of the Empire*, New York University 1983.

10. Population census figures calculated from Karpat, *Ottoman Population*, pp.162–6; war losses estimated by McCarthy, *Muslims and Minorities*, p.133.

11. Pentzopoulos, *Balkan Exchange of Minorities*, p.99.

12. Istanbul's population figures are much disputed. The latter figures refer to the findings of the 1927 Population Census.

13. L. Erder, 'Tarihsel Bakiş Açısından Türkiye'nin Demografik ve Makensal Yapısı' (Turkey's Demographic and Spatial Structure in Historical Perspective), in I. Tekeli and L. Erder, *İç Göçler* (Internal migrations), Ankara 1978, pp. 175–6.

14. Karpat, *Ottoman Population*, p.69.

15. For the social and political impact of these immigrations see J. McCarthy, 'Foundations of the Turkish Republic: Social and Economic Change', *Middle Eastern Studies*, April 1983; G. Kazgan, 'Milli Türk Devletinin Kuruluşu ve Göçler' (The Foundation of the National Turkish State and Migrations), *I, Ü. Iktisat Fakültesi Mecmuası,* October 1970–September 1971.

16. This move to the interior was connected with military conscription. Until 1909 non-Moslems did not serve in the army, and many observers claimed that this was one reason why the Moslem suffered more than the Christian population: conscription left many families without their valuable male offspring. One of the demands for reform had been for universal conscription, and was instituted by the CUP in 1909. During the war, however, the Ottoman army was wary of mobilising the Greek population on to active duty. So it

formed the *amele taburları*, literally work gangs, and Christians between the age of 17 and 45 were drafted to work in these teams in the interior. Pentzopoulos, pp. 54–57, cites a figure of 480,000 Greeks who were thus sent to the interior. Again according to Pentzopoulos, p. 54, 150,000 Greeks escaped to Greece in order not to be conscripted.

17. The exchange agreement was underwritten by the League of Nations, see Pentzopoulos, *Balkan Exchange of Minorities*, and Stephen P. Ladas, *The Exchange of Minorities: Bulgaria, Greece and Turkey*, New York 1932, for the official agreements.

18. For greater detail on the period see Ç. Keyder, *The Definition of a Peripheral Economy: Turkey 1923–1929*, Cambridge 1981, especially chapters 4 and 5.

19. The best account of the politics of this period is in Mete Tunçay, *Türkiye Cumhuriyeti'nde Tek-Parti Yönetimi'nin Kurulması (1923–1931)* (The Establishment of Single-Party Administration in the Turkish Republic), Ankara 1981.

20. François Georgeon, 'Aperçu sur la presse de langue française en Turquie pendant la période kémaliste (1919–1938)', in *La Turquie et la France à l'époque d'Atatürk*, Collection Turcica, no.1, 1982, p.202.

21. Zürcher, *The Unionist Factor*, p. 146, Tunçay, pp. 149–161.

22. Zürcher, chapter 6.

23. Mustafa Kemal read his *Speech* to the parliament in October 1927: Atatürk, *A Speech Delivered by Mustafa Kemal Atatürk*, Istanbul 1963, where he defended his actions from the beginning of the nationalist struggle. This speech has provided the basis of official historiography since its delivery. Both Tunçay and Zürcher judge it to be a justification for the gradual elimination of rival factions and personalities, and Zürcher is more specific in claiming that 'Mustafa Kemal's famous speech . . . must be seen not simply as a historical survey of the years 1919–27 but as an attempt at justification for the purges of 1926', *The Unionist Factor*, p.172.

24. Çetin Yetkin, *Serbest Cumhuriyet Fırkası Olayı* (The Free Party Incident), Istanbul 1982, pp. 85–6.

25. Ilber Ortaylı, *Tanzimattan Sonra Mahalli Idareler (1840–1878)* (Local Administration after the Tanzimat), Ankara 1974; Shaw, *History of the Ottoman Empire*, pp. 221–254.

26. The parliament became all-powerful in 1909. Ahmad says: 'The question as to whom was the supreme authority in the Empire had already been decided in favour of the Chamber of Deputies', *The Young Turks, the Committee of Union and Progress in Turkish Politics, 1908–1914*, Oxford 1969, p.58. The various parliaments in 1908, 1912 and 1914 were ethnically diverse and representative, ibid., p. 155. The parliamentary debates of the period are astonishing in their seriousness and breadth, and the deputies emerge as extremely knowledgeable and intelligent.

27. D. Farhi, 'The *Şeriat* as a Political Slogan – or "Incident of the 31st Mart"', *Middle Eastern Studies*, October 1971.

28. This is the argument already referred to in Vryonis, *Decline of Medieval Hellenism*.

29. See Ş. Mardin, 'Religion and Secularism in Turkey', in A. Kazancigil and E. Ozbudun, eds., *Ataturk, Founder of a Modern State*, London 1981, p. 207; also Binnaz Toprak, *Islam and Political Development in Turkey*, Brill 1981.

30. Mardin, 'Religion and Securalism', p.191.

Chapter V

1. These areas were also crucially dependent on draught animals. Since wartime mobilisation led to a severe decline in the number of draught animals, economic losses would have been proportionately higher in subsistence agriculture.
2. A. Toynbee, *The Western Question in Greece and Turkey*.
3. W.J. Childs, 'Armenia', p. 202.
4. G. Kazgan, 'Milli Turk Devletinin Kuruluşu ve Göçler', p. 314; J. McCarthy, 'Foundations of the Turkish Republic', proposes an argument based on the demographic structure altered by immigrations.
5. S. Ladas, *The Exchange of Minorities*, p. 714.
6. Ç. Keyder, *Definition of a Peripheral Economy*, pp. 38–40.
7. A. Emmanuel, 'White Settler Colonialism and the Myth of Investment Imperialism', *New Left Review*, May–June 1972. R. Kasaba substantiates this argument in his description of the conflicts between Greek merchants and the British capital in Western Anatolia, *Peripheralisation of the Ottoman Empire*, chapters 5 and 6.
8. Ç Keyder, 'Credit and Peripheral Structuration', *Review*, spring 1980, for more detail.
9. Calculated in Keyder, *Definition*, pp. 59–62, from data supplied in G. Ökçün, *1920–1930 Yılları Arasında Kurulan Türk Anonim Şirketlerinde Yabancı Sermaye Sorunu* (The Issue of Foreign Capital in Turkish Corporations Established in the 1920–1930 period), Ankara 1971.
10. Y.S. Tezel, '1923–1938 Döneminde Türkiye'nin Dış Iktisadi Ilişkileri' (Turkey's External Economic Relations during the 1923–1938 Period) in *Atatürk Döneminin Ekonomik ve Toplumsal Tarihiyle Ilgili Sorunlar Sempozyumu* (Symposium on Problems Relating to the Economic and Social History of the Atatürk Period), IITIA, Istanbul 1977, pp. 218–22.
11. Keyder, *Definition*, chapter 5.
12. A.H. Başar, *Atatükle Üç Ay ve 1930'dan Sonra Türkiye* (Three Months with Atatürk and Turkey after 1930), Istanbul 1945, is a description of Mustafa Kemal's trip in Anatolia in 1930 when he sought to understand the reasons for the general discontent among the population. It is a graphic account of the intitial impact of the economic crisis.
13. O. Kurmuş, '1916 ve 1929 Gümruk Tarifeleri üzerine Bazı Gözlemler' (Some Observation on 1916 and 1929 Tariff Regimes), in S. Ilkin, ed., *Turkiye Iktisat Tarihi üzerine Araştırmalar* (Research on Turkish Economic History), *METU Studies in Development*, 1978 Special Issue, Ankara.
14. Ilhan Tekeli and Selim Ilkin, *Para ve Kredi Sisteminin Oluşumunda Bir Aşama: T.C. Merkez Bankası* (The Central Bank of Turkey, a Stage in the Formation of the Money and Credit System), Ankara 1981, contains the intricate background history of the establishment if the Central Bank.
15. Ilhan Tekeli and Selim Ilkin, *1929 Dünva Buhranında Türkiye'nin Iktisadi Politika Arayışları* (Search for Economic Policy during the 1929 Crisis), Ankara 1977, pp. 92–98.
16. Ibid., p. 212.
17. Çetin Yetkin, *Türkiye'de Tek Parti Yönetimi, 1930–1945* (Single-Party Government in Turkey), Istanbul 1983, p.98.
18. François Georgeon, 'Les Foyers Turcs à l'époque kémaliste (1923–1931)', *Turcica*, vol. XIV, 1982.

19. Yetkin, *Tek Parti Yönetimi*, pp. 70–76.

20. Georgeon, 'Foyers Turcs', pp. 212–14.

21. Korkut Boratav's 'Kemalist Economic Policies and Etatism' provides a good overview of the economic policies of the period, although it is somewhat partisan; in Kazancıgil and Özbudun , eds, *Atatürk*.

22. Y. Effimiadis, *Cihan Iktisadi Buhrani Önünde Türkiye,* vol.2 (Turkey in Front of the World Crisis), Istanbul 1936.

23. Ş.R. Hatiboğlu, *Türkiye'de Zirai Buhran* (Agricultural Crisis in Turkey), Ankara 1936, pp. 52 ff. This book is an excellent compilation of available information concerning the effects of the crisis on the peasantry.

24. Başar, *Atatürkle Üç Ay;* see Keyder, 'The Cycle of Sharecropping', for the full argument.

25. G. Kazgan's calculations using data in Hatiboğlu, *Turkiye'de Zirai Buhran;* Kazgan, 'Türk Ekonomisinde 1927–35 Depresyonu, Kapital Birikimi ve Örgütleşmeler' (The 1927–35 Depression in Turkish Economy, Capital Accumulation, and Organisation), in *Atatürk Döneminin Ekonomik ve Toplumsal Sorunları*, p. 247.

26. Tezel, '1923–1938 Döneminde', p. 201.

27. I. Tekeli and S. Ilkin, *Uygulamaya Geçerken Türkiye'de Devletçiliğin Oluşumu* (The Formation of Etatism in Turkey on the Eve of its Application), Ankara 1982, pp. 24–26.

28. T. Bulutay, Y. Tezel, and N. Yıldırım, *Türkiye Milli Geliri (1923–1948)* (Turkey's National Income), Ankara 1974, table 8.6.C. Although some of the assumptions are debatable, the statistics compiled in this study are the only macro data available for the period.

29. Kazgan, 'Türk Ekonomisinde 1927–35 Depresyonu', pp. 263–64.

30. Tekeli and Ilkin, *Uygulamaya Geçerken*, pp. 219–20.

31. S. Ilkin, 'Devletçilik Döneminin Ilk Yıllarında Işçi Sorununa Yaklaşim ve 1932 Iş Kanunu Tasarısı' (Approaches to the Problem of Workers during the Initial Years of Etatism and the 1932 Draft for Labour Legislation), in Ilkin, ed., *Türkiye Iktisat Tarihi* (1978), pp. 253, 277–8.

32. Ibid., pp. 285–7.

33. These are the words of the general secretary of the ruling party: Yetkin, *Tek Parti Yönetimi*, p.102; also see K. Sülker, *Türkiye'de Işçi Hareketleri* (Workers' Movements in Turkey), 3rd edn, Istanbul 1976, p. 54.

34. Kazgan, 'Türk Ekonomisinde 1927–35 Depresyonu', p. 270.

35. Sülker, *Işçi Hareketleri*, p. 57.

36. Kazgan, pp. 264–5.

37. Bulutay, Tezel, and Yıldırım, *Milli Gelir*, table 8.2.A, and Kazgan, p. 235.

38. Afetinan, *Devletçilik Ilkesi ve Türkiye Cumhuriyetinin Birinci Sanayi Planı* (The Etatist Principle and the First Industrialisation Plan of the Turkish Republic), Ankara 1972, is an edition of all the relevent documents.

39. T. Bayar, *La Türkiye Iş Bankası*, Montreux 1939, pp. 83, 162.

40. E. Soral, *Özel Kesimde Türk Müteşebbisleri ve Kapitalist Kalkınma Yolu* (Turkish Entrepreneurs in the Private Sector and the Path of Capitalist Development), dozent dissertation, Ankara 1971, p. 117.

41. S. Giner, 'Political Economy, Legitimation and the State in Southern Europe', *British Journal of Sociology*, June 1982, pp. 184–90.

42. Bulutay, Tezel, Yıldırım, *Milli Gelir*, table 8.2.C.

43. F. Birtek and Ç. Keyder, 'Agriculture and the State: An Inquiry into Agricultural Differentiation and Political Alliances, the Case of Turkey',

Journal of Peasant Studies, July 1975.

44. Yetkin, *Tek Parti Yönetimi*, pp. 186–90.

45. A. Fleury, 'La pénétration économique de l'Allemagne en Turquie et en Iran après la première guerre mondiale', *Relations Internationales*, 1, 1975.

46. Alan S. Milward, *War, Economy and Society 1939–1945*, California 1979, p. 322.

47. E.C. Clark, 'The Turkish Varlık Vergisi Reconsidered', *Middle Eastern Studies*, May 1972, p. 205; also Yetkin, *Tek Parti*, pp. 203–15.

48. Faik Ökte, *Varlık Vergisi Faciası* (The Tragedy of the Wealth Levy), Istanbul 1951. The author was the head of the tax office in Istanbul.

49. I. Tekeli, 'II. Dünya Svaşı Sırasında Hazırlanan Savaş Sonrası Kalkınma Plan ve Programları' (Post-war development plans and programmes prepared during World War II), in S. Ilkin, ed., *Research on Turkish Economic History II, METU Studies in Development*, 1979–1980 Special Issue.

Chapter VI

1. Yahya Tezel, *Cumhuriyet Döneminin Iktisadi Tarihi, 1923–1950* (Economic History of the Republican period), Ankara 1982, p.255.

2. The terminology is C.B. Mapherson's: *The Political Theory of Possessive Individualism,* Oxford 1962.

3. Tezel, *Cumhuriyet Döneminin*, p.99.

4. Ibid., pp. 173, 205.

5. M.W. Thornburg *et al.*, *Turkey, an Economic Appraisal*, New York 1949, p.91.

6. Ibid., pp. 141–2.

7. Mardin, 'Religion and Secularism in Turkey', is an argument to explain the clash between religion in its social function and the bureaucratic ideal of secularism.

8. B. Toprak, *Islam and Political Development*, pp. 46–53.

9. Ibid., p. 69.

10. E. Laclau, *Politics and Ideology in Marxist Theory*, New Left Books 1977; also see N. Mouzelis, *Politics in the Semi-Periphery*, Macmillan 1986, Part I, for some theoretical considerations on populism.

11. W.F. Weiker, *Political Tutelage and Democracy in Turkey, The Free Party and its Aftermath*, Brill 1973, pp. 71, 80. See also Yetkin, *Serbest Cumhuriyet Fırkası*.

12. A. Leder, 'Party Competition in Rural Turkey: Agent of Change or Defender of Traditional Rule', *Middle Eastern Studies,* January 1979.

13. Ö.L. Barkan, 'Çiftçiyi Topraklandırma Kanunu ve Turkiye'de Zirai Bir Reformun Ana Meseleleri' (The Law for the Distribution of Land to the Peasantry and the Principal Problems of Agricultural Reform in Turkey), in Barkan, *Turkiye'de Toprak Meselesi* (Land Problem in Turkey), Istanbul 1980; Ç. Keyder and Ş. Pamuk, '1945 Çiftçiyi Topraklandırma Kanunu üzerine Tezler' (Theses on the 1945 law for the distribution of land to the peasantry), *Yapıt*, December–January 1984–85, are the classical and revisionist statements on the reasons for the legislation.

14. D. Taraklı, *Çiftiyi Topraklandırma Kanunu ve Uygulama Sonuçları* (The Law for the Distribution of Land to the Peasantry and its Results), Ankara 1976, p. 112.

15. Compare the discussion in E. Özbudun, 'Established Revolution vs.

Unfinished Revolution: Contrasting Patterns of Democratization in Mexico and Turkey', in S. Huntington and R.M. Moore, eds, *Authoritarian Politics in Modern Society,* New York 1970, where the author argues that the absence of land reform in Turkey led to the downfall of the bureaucratic party.

16. For an extensive treatment of the subject and the implications of land abundance see Ç. Keyder, 'The Genesis and Structure of Small Peasant Ownership in Turkish Agriculture', *Review,* Fall 1983.

17. Turkey, State Institute of Statistics, *Statistical Yearbooks* for various years.

18. *Turkiye'de Zirai Makinalaşma* (Agricultural Mechanisation in Turkey), Ankara 1954, pp. 119–20. This is a survey conducted by the Faculty of Political Science, Ankara University.

19. Taraklı, *Çiftçiyi Topraklandırma Kanunu,* for the process involved. Through this scheme more than 400,000 families were granted more than 3 million hectares of land, State Institute of Statistics, *Zirai Istatistik Özetlerı, 1940–1960* (Summaries of Agricultural Statistics), Ankara 1965.

20. *1950 Ziraat Sayımı Neticeleri* (Results of the 1950 Agricultural Census), Ankara 1956; and *1963 Genel Tarim Sayımı Örnekleme Sonuçları* (Sample Results of the 1963 General Agricultural Census), Ankara 1965.

21. Calculated on the basis of an average household size of 5.7, which is the figure found in population censuses of the period.

22. Oktay Varlıer, *Türkiye'de Iç Ticaret Hadleri* (Internal Terms-of-Trade in Turkey), Ankara 1978.

23. United Nations, *Statistical Yearbook 1955,* p.81.

24. United Nations, *Statistical Yearbook 1960,* p. 337.

25. M. Singer *The Economic Advance of Turkey, 1938–1960,* Ankara 1977, pp. 193–5. This is a very useful book, especially for economic data relating to the 1950s.

26. Ibid, p. 392.

27. Compare similar experiences in Latin America, A.O. Hirschman in D. Collier, ed., *The New Authoritarianism in Latin America,* Princeton 1979.

28. A.O. Krueger, *Foreign Trade Regimes and Economic Development, Turkey,* New York 1974, chapter II.

29. Singer, *Economic Advance,* pp. 194–5.

30. Kreuger, *Foreign Trade Regimes,* chapter IV.

31. See E. Günçe, 'Early Planning Experiences in Turkey', in S. Ilkin and E. Inanç, eds, *Planning in Turkey,* Ankara 1967.

32. Singer, *Economic Advance,* p. 242A.

33. Ibid, p. 295.

34. There is a rich literature in the sociology of shanty towns. For the Turkish case, see Kemal H. Karpat, *Gecekondu: Rural Migration and Urbanization,* Cambridge 1976; and S.K. Kartal, *Ekonomik ve Sosyal Yönlerıyle Türkiye'de Kentlileşme* (Urbanisation in Turkey: Its Economic and Social Aspects), Ankara 1983. Kartal contains an excellent bibliography.

35. Calculated from population censuses. These censuses are taken every five years by the State Statistical Institute.

36. J. Hinderlinck and M. Kiray, *Social Stratification as an Obstacle to Development: A Study of Four Turkish Villages,* New York 1970. Although all four villages in the study are in Çukurova, there are structural differences between them.

37. *Zirai Makinalaşma,* p. 129.

38. E.C. Clark, 'Varlik Vergisi Re-considered'.

Chapter VII

1. C. Eroğul, *Demokrat Parti, Tarih ve Ideolojisi* (The Democrat Party, its History and Ideology), Ankara 1970.
2. A.O. Krueger, *Foreign Trade Regimes, Turkey*, pp. 21–2.
3. D. Avcioğlu, *Türkiye'nin Düzeni* (Turkey's Order), Ankara 1968, pp. 335–6, argues that there were three issues of contention: land reform, greater taxation, expecially on agriculture, and the degree of autonomy of state economic enterprises. The planners wanted to increase state revenue and grant non-political status to public enterprise by instituting a bureaucracy-controlled organisation.
4. See W.F. Weiker, *The Turkish Revolution 1960–1961*, Washington, DC 1963.
5. This view was argued in the journal *Forum* during the 1950s, and most significantly in *Yön* in the 1960s.
6. In Turkish political discourse this current is identified with a journal which appeared in the early 1930s until its publishers were banned from spreading their views. The movement around the journal *Kadro* was a forerunner of Third-Worldist ideologies and contained an astonishingly complete catalogue of all the arguments which again became current in the 1960s. Ş.S. Aydemir's *Inkilap ve Kadro* (Revolution and Cadres), Ankara 1968 (first published in 1932) is the principal theoretical text. For a recent critical perspective, see H. Gülalp, *Gelişme Stratejileri ve Gelişme Ideolojileri* (Strategies and Ideologies of Development), Ankara 1983, part 4.
7. A very useful collection of essays on the Turkish planning experience is O. Türel, ed., *Two Decades of Planned Development in Turkey, METU Studies in Development*, 1981 Special Issue, especially the essays by Küçük, Porokhovsky, Şaylan, Bulutay, and Eralp.
8. G. Şaylan, 'Planlama ve Bürokrasi' (Planning and the Bureaucracy), ibid.
9. The classic definitional article on import substitution is A.O. Hirshman, 'The Political Economy of Import-Substituting Industrialization in Latin America', *Quarterly Journal of Economics*, February 1968.
10. Ibid.
11. Unless otherwise indicated all the figures used in this chapter derive from Statistical Yearbooks for various years.
12. The terminology is borrowed from Nora Hamilton, although the usage is slightly different: 'State Autonomy and Dependent Capitalism in Latin America', *British Journal of Sociology*, September 1981.
13. See the extremely interesting article by N. Yalman where the author describes the various modes of dissolution of pre-capitalist landlordism, 'On Land Disputes in Eastern Turkey', in G.L. Tikku, ed., *Islam and its Cultural Divergence*, Ann Arbor 1977.
14. See I. Bulmuş, 'Türkiye'de Tarımsal Taban Fiyat Politikası ve Etkileri' (Agricultural Support Price Policies in Turkey and their Effects), in O. Türel, ed., *Two Decades of Planned Development*.
15. K. Boratav, 'Türkiye'de Populizm: 1962–76 Dönemi üzerine Bazil Notlar' (Populism in Turkey: Some Notes on the 1962–76 Period), *Yapt*, October–November 1983, p. 13. As Boratav says, the impact would be higher if only those crops where support prices apply were considered.
16. O. Varlier, *Türkiye'de Iç Ticaret Hadleri*, Ankara 1978.
17. Kartal, *Türkiye'de Kentleşme*, pp. 157–203.
18. Boratav, 'Türkiye'de Populizm', pp. 9, 17. These figures derive from

244

annual manufacturing census data rather than Social Security Administration figures, which are biased downwards because of institutional 'ceilings' on official pay. During the 1970s the take-home pay of an average worker was between 50 and 100% above what appeared in his pay-cheque because of bonuses and other benefits written into the contracts bargained for by unions.

19. IBRD, *Turkey, Policies and Prospects for Growth*, mimeograph, 1980, p. 184.

20. Ibid.

21. See T. Şenyapili, *Gecekondu: 'Çevre' Işçilerin Mekanı* (Gecekondu: Housing for Peripheral Workers), Ankara 1981. Of course there are exceptions to this observation; see, for example, L. Tekin's excellent novel, *Berci Kristin Çöp Masalları* (Garbage Stories), Istanbul 1985.

Chapter VIII

1. Hirschman, 'Political Economy of Import-Substituting Industrialization'.

2. B. Wålstedt, *State Manufacturing Enterprise in a Mixed Economy. The Turkish Case*, Johns Hopkins University Press 1980, p. 239.

3. See M.D. Rivkin, *Area Development for National Growth, the Turkish Precedent*, New York 1965, especially for its discussion concerning the impact of public enterprise on regional growth.

4. See the list of state enterprises envisaged in the 1934 Industrialisation Plan, Afetinan, *Türkiye Cumhuriyetinin Birinci Sanayi Planı*.

5. Hirshman, 'Political Economy'.

6. The question addresssed here is whether the demise of ISI was inevitable, or if there were alternative policies available which would have weaned the economy off protection dependence, while at the same time counteracting the crisis tendencies. For a discussion of these issues, see K. Boratav, 'Iktisat Politikasi Alternatifleri üzerine bir Deneme' (An Essay on Economic Policy Alternatives), in K. Boratav, Ç. Keyder, and Ş. Pamuk, *Krizin Gelişimi ve Türkiye'nin Alternatif Sorunu* (The Evolution of the Crisis and the Problem of Alternatives for Turkey), Istanbul 1984.

7. Unless otherwise indicated the figures derive from Turkey, State Institute of Statistics, Statistical Yearbooks.

8. State Institute of Statistics, *Yıllik Sanayi Anketi, 1971* (Annual Manufacturing Questionnaire), Ankara 1976, p. 117, table 3C.

9. Ibid.

10. A. Aksoy, 'Wages, Relative Shares, and Unionization in Turkish Manufacturing', in E. Özbudun and A. Ulusan, eds, *The Political Economy of Income Distribution in Turkey*, New York 1980, p. 436.

11. R. Margulies and E. Yıldızoğlu, 'Trade Unions and Turkey's Working Class', *MERIP Reports*, February 1984. Here the authors cite figures from a useful work on the small manufacturing sector: R. Bademli, *Distorted and Lower Forms of Capitalist Industrial Production in Underdeveloped Countries*, dissertation, MIT 1977.

12. For these and subsequent figures concerning external accounts IMF, *Balance of Payments Yearbooks* are readily accessible.

13. For the full argument see Ç. Keyder, 'The American Recovery of Europe: Aid and Hegemony', in G. Arrighi, ed., *Semiperipheral Development: The Politics of Southern Europe in the Twentieth Century*, Sage 1985.

14. The five year plans are published by the State Planning Office. These figures are from the *Third Five Year Plan*, p. 172.

15. OECD, *Investissment Etrangers en Turquie, Changement des Conditions dans le Cadre du Nouveau Programme Economique*, Paris 1983, is a good summary account and contains figures based on a 1982 survey. Figures for total flows, p. 8; figures for sectoral and country-of-origin distributions cited below, pp. 9–10.

16. Figures from OECD, *Economic Surveys: Turkey*, various years.

17. Calculated from data in five-year plans and official exchange rates.

18. UN *Statistical Abstract for Latin America*, 1980.

19. See S. Paine, *Exporting Workers: The Turkish Case*, Cambridge 1974.

20. A.Y. Gökdere, *Yabancı Ülkelere Işgücü Akımı ve Türk Ekonomisi Üzerine Etkileri* (Flow of Labour to Foreign Countries and its Impact on the Turkish Economy), Ankara 1978, p. 178.

21. N. Abadan-Unat *et al.*, *Migration and Development*, Ankara 1976, is a comprehensive study which covers all aspects of migration's impact on small-town structures. For an extreme case where new consumption habits have entirely taken over, see Ş. Alpay and H. Sarıarslan, *Effects of Emigration: The Effects on the Town of Kulu in Central Turkey of Emigration to Sweden*, Stockholm 1984.

22. *1977 Statistical Yearbook*, p. 225.

23. The first wave of emigration from relatively developed regions and sectors ended in the late 1960s; the second wave, mostly from Central Anatolian villages, ended with the German ban on labour migration in late 1973. The Turkish employment service was the only official channel of migration; although in the heyday of migration, workers in Europe could usually invite relatives or villagers by name; and after 1974, Germany allowed family reunion through which spouses and children were allowed to enter Germany.

24. By the end of 1973, close to 800,000 workers had migrated to Europe through official channels. Probably another 100,000 workers had migrated illegally. In 1980 the number of workers had not changed appreciably, although the number of dependants increased from around 400,000 to 1.1 million. There were around 1.9 million Turks living in Europe in 1980 in various degrees of permanence. See A.S. Gitmez, *Yurtdışına Işçi Göçü ve Geri Dönüşler* (Workers' Migration Abroad and Returns), Istanbul 1983, pp. 20–23.

25. Turkey's oil imports were US$221 million, $746 million, and $1,661 million in 1973, 1974, and 1979 respectively. These sums represented 11%, 20% and 34% of total imports in those years.

26. Thornburg *et al.*, *Turkey, an Economic Appraisal*; see also Rivkin, *Area Development*, part III.

27. K. Ebiri, 'Turkish Apertura (Part I)', *METU Studies in Development*, 1980, nos. 3–4, p. 241.

28. The information on most of this activity is anecdotal. On this period see Y. Doğan, *IMF Kıskacında Türkiye, 1946–1980* (Turkey in IMF's Stranglehold), Ankara 1980.

29. Y. Kepenek, *Türkiye Ekonomisi* (The Turkish Economy), Ankara 1983, p. 570. This is a useful work of synthesis.

30. Ibid., p. 572.

31. In constant 1969 prices. See *1981 Statistical Yearbook*, p. 401.

32. Boratav, 'Türkiye'de Popülizm', pp. 9, 17.

Chapter IX

1. Ş. Mardin, 'Center-periphery Relations: A Key to Turkish Politics?' *Daedalus*, winter 1973. This is by far the most sophisticated statement of this view. For a popular version see A. Gevgilili, *Yükseliş ve Düşüş* (Rise and Fall), Istanbul, 1981, especially parts II and III.

2. Ç. Keyder, 'The American Recovery of Europe'.

3. For these episodes see F. Ahmad, *The Turkish Experiment in Democracy, 1950–1975*, Boulder, Colorado 1977.

4. See A. Öncü, 'Chambers of Industry in Turkey: An Inquiry into State-Industry Relations as a Distributive Domain' in Özbudun and Ulusan, eds, *The Political Economy of Income Distribution in Turkey*. This is an excellent source. A much more extensive treatment now exists in R. Bianchi, *Interests Groups and Political Development in Turkey*, Princeton 1984.

5. During this period the State Planning Office evolved regional categories to encourage private sector investments in more backward areas, and a spate of articles and popular books appeared on the plight of the East. See M.N. Danielson and R. Keleş. 'Urbanization and Income Distribution in Turkey', in Özbudun and Ulusan, eds,; also R. Keleş, 'The Effects of External Migration on Regional Development in Turkey' in Hudson and Lewis, eds.

6. All such international comparisons rely on the results of an income distribution study carried out in 1973, whose method, assumptions, and results, especially as to rural incomes, are difficult to accept. On the other hand, it is possible to obtain a high degree of income inequality nationally together with a relatively low level of inequality inside both the developed and the backward regions. cf. Devlet Planlama Teşkilati, Soysal Planlama Dairesi, *Gelir Dağılımı Araştırması, 1973* (Income Distribution Study, 1973), Ankara 1976. The findings of this study do not support the claims advanced here.

7. For one case study see H. Toepfer, 'The Economic Impact of Returned Emigrants in Trabazon, Turkey', in R. Hudson and J. Lewis, eds, *Uneven Development in Southern Europe, Studies of Accumulation, Class, Migration and the State*, London 1985.

8. Unfortunately there is not much research conducted on small towns. L. Van Velzen's *Peripheral Production in Kayseri, Turkey*, Ankara 1977, is a good description of the productive sphere, although it contains very little on the social structure. Dissertation research by M. Uzbay at University of Hull on Çorum is promising; see also B. Akşit, 'Ortakent'te Toplumsal Farklılaşma ve Siyasal-Kültürel Çatışma' (Social Differentiation and Political-Cultural Conflict in Middletown), in his *Köy, Kasaba ve Kentlerde Toplumsal Değişme* (Social Change in Villages, Towns and Cities), Ankara 1985.

9. There have been several newspaper accounts of political extremism, the most informative one being E. Çölaşan, *Sağda ve Solda Çarpışanlar* (Those Who Fight on the Right and the Left), Istanbul 1983. See also D. Ergil, *Türkiye'de Terör ve Şiddet* (Terror and Violence in Turkey), Ankara 1980; at a different level of sophistication, Ş. Mardin, 'Youth and Violence in Turkey', *Archives Européennes de Sociologie,* vol. 19, no.2, 1978.

10. A. Samim, 'The Tragedy of the Turkish Left', *New Left Review,* March–April 1981, is the best short account of the left in the 1970s.

11. J.S. Szyliowics, 'Students and Politics in Turkey', *Middle Eastern Studies*, May 1970.

12. B. Lewis, 'History Writing and National Revival in Turkey', *Middle Eastern Affairs*, 1953, pp. 218–227, is informative. For an intelligent attempt to

justify nationalist historiography see H. Berktay, *Cumhuriyet Ideolojisi ve Fuat Köprülü* (Fuat Köprülü and Republican Ideology), Istanbul 1983.

13. The argument of ideological continuity does not intend to belittle the discontinuity in social transformations which gave rise to the fascist movement. I have used 'fascism' and the 'fascist movement' to refer to the specificity of the social composition of the political current; I am not making any argument as to the appurtenance of the discourse to a determinable 'fascist' ideology.

14. On the religious political movement see A.Y. Sarıbay, *Türkiye'de Modernleşme, Din ve Parti Politikasi; MSP Örnek Olayı* (Modernisation, Religion and Party Politics in Turkey: The Example of the National Salvation Party), Istanbul 1985; and I. Sunar and B. Toprak, 'Islam in Politics: The Case of Turkey', *Government and Opposition,* autumn 1983.

15. The best contemporary analysis of these events appeared in a monthly journal, *Birikim*, published in Istanbul.

16. The analysis here owes much to N. Poulantzas, *Fascisme et Dictature*, Paris, 1970, but is much more eclectic. See G. Eley, 'What Produces Fascism: Pre-Industrial Traditions or a Crisis of the Capitalist State?', *Politics and Society*, vol. 12, no.1, 1983.

17. For a review of the recent debate on these issues (transformation-from-above, bourgeois revolution, and fascism) see the article by Richard Evans, 'The Myth of Germany's Missing Revolution', *New Left Review* January–February 1985.

Chapter X

1. Süleyman Özmucur, *Milli Gelirin Üç Aylik Dönemler Itibariyle Tahmini* (Quarterly Estimates of National Income), Istanbul 1987, p. 79.

Index

249